LILLEE
MY LIFE IN CRICKET

LILLEE
MY LIFE IN CRICKET

METHUEN

First published in 1982 by
Methuen Australia Pty Ltd
44 Waterloo Road, North Ryde 2113
150 Burwood Road, Hawthorn 3122
Cnr Allenby and Leichhardt Streets, Spring Hill 4000
6 Sherwood Court, Perth 6000

Printed in Australia 1982 for
Methuen London Ltd
11 New Fetter Lane, London EC4P 4EE

National Library of Australia
Cataloguing-in-Publication data
    Lillee, Dennis, 1949-
    My life in cricket.
    Includes index.
    ISBN 0 454 00361 7
    1. Lillee, Dennis, 1949-   . 2. Cricket players—
    Biography. I. Title.
796.35'8'0924

British Library Cataloguing-in-Publication data
    Lillee, Dennis
    My life in cricket.
    1. Lillee, Dennis 2. Cricket players—
    Australia—Biography
    I. Title.
796.35'8'0924 GU915.L/
ISBN 0-413-51410-2

Printed at Griffin Press Limited, Netley, South Australia.

Contents

ACKNOWLEDGEMENTS

There are a whole host of people whom I wish to acknowledge as having helped me in the years of my cricket career and in the preparation and presentation of this book. Going right back to my original coaches, Geoff McPherson, Mick Basile, and to men like Ray Lindwall and Alan Davidson, all of whom have had a profound influence on my bowling. More recently I have been fortunate to have benefited from the knowledge I have gained in the art of running from Austin Robertson senior.

My thanks to my managers, Austin Robertson junior and John Cornell, and to Sam Chisholm, Lynton Taylor and Kerry Packer. And on the official side, from the Metropolitan Seniors in Perth through to the Australian Cricket Board, even though we've had some differences over the years. I also wish to recognise all the players I've stood alongside and battled against on the cricket field, culminating in the members of the Melville Cricket Club in Perth, chaired by David Hope-Johnston. Special thanks to the Melville club for their support right up to and including my testimonial year.

I am indebted to a band of medicos and related people, to Bill Gilmour, Rudi Webster and Frank Pyke (to mention a few), who have done a job akin to creating a bionic man in keeping me out in the middle over the years. To the umpires, who at times must have thought I had pushed them to the limit, my gratitude and the hope that we're still friends. Likewise to those employers who understood and helped me in my endeavours to combine cricket with a career.

My thanks go out to all my long-standing mates in cricket—they know whom I mean—and to a loyal and faithful public, whom at times I've probably let down but who never failed me. To the game of cricket, which has afforded me the opportunity to make all the contacts and friendships that have stood me in such good stead over all the years. I only hope I've been able to repay some of those favours.

Also my appreciation for their help in getting this book together, to statistician Jack Cameron, to Geoff Lawson and Martin Kent, Sir Garry Sobers, Bill Mitchell, Peter Taylor and Tom Prior. To Ian Brayshaw my heartfelt thanks, for without his tremendous cricket knowledge and understanding I'd have struggled.

And not forgetting all those I haven't mentioned . . .

Finally, those I'll never forget: my immediate family. My two Mums and Dads, 'Pop' Halifax, my brother Trevor and sister Carmen and, most important of all, my sons Dean and Adam and my wife Helen, for their unfailing support and love.

Foreword

When I arrived in Australia early in the summer of 1971-72 to captain the Rest of the World in a series against Australia I had learned about a new, young, fast bowler called Dennis Lillee. He had played in one or two Tests against Ray Illingworth's England team the summer before and apparently had raised a few eyebrows with his turn of speed. Never having seen him in action, I didn't know what to expect and so I went to Brisbane for the first international with some degree of anticipation. I must admit I was taken aback at his speed and I recall saying to Ray Lindwall, 'This chap has got a bit of pace!'

He was a little erratic, like most fast bowlers early in their career—and Freddie Trueman and Wes Hall were no exceptions in this regard. Wes even had to miss a whole series as a youngster because he was so erratic and because he had a bad habit of bowling too many no-balls. Noting that Dennis had bowled second on a slow track in Brisbane, and yet made a big impression on me, I cast my thoughts to the next game on the Perth wicket, which, traditionally, helped fast bowlers. Of course, I never expected the type of wicket we got when we faced Dennis on the second morning of the game. The wicket had sweated considerably under the covers and I soon found out what Lillee was going to be like on a wicket that helped him!

Dennis literally devastated a batting line-up that included several of the world's best players of the day. He took 8 for 29 in a great spell of express bowling. We were 5 down for 49 when I went in and 6 for the same score a few moments later. I had become one of the early victims of that great combination: caught Marsh, bowled Lillee for 0! That was 11 December 1971 and since that day Dennis has gone on from strength to strength to the point where one could say he is among the greats of all time—and how he deserves it, after all he has done.

It hasn't always been a smooth passage for Lillee. Like most fast bowlers who give everything to the cause, he has suffered his fair share of injuries. He has taken most of them more or less in his stride, but he was very nearly lost to cricket in 1973 when he suffered stress fractures of the spine. The way Dennis emerged from that setback showed just what sort of a man he is. He won through because of his sheer determination and will-power, plus the will and enthusiasm to play again—he came back stronger than ever.

Dennis Lillee deserves the highest praise as a bowler and a cricketer. He is a man I've always admired, who always gives a 100 per cent effort and any happenings on the field during his career have only occurred because of what he puts in. Some people hasten to brand Dennis, but those reactions are not a mirror of the man. I am very pleased to have been given the honour of writing these few words about Dennis and finally I'd like to offer him and his family every good wish for the future.

Garry Sobers

Prologue

The boys in the outer at the Melbourne Cricket Ground. Those with starch in their collars and a stiff upper lip would probably say they are nothing more than drunken louts, but I love 'em all! They have meant more to me than they could imagine. They've been a constant source of inspiration and strength throughout my long love-hate relationship with that strip of unyielding, unforgiving turf out in the middle of that great cricket arena. When they are behind you in full voice, as they have been so many times when I've bowled for Australia from the Southern Stand end, it's almost a physical phenomenon. As I push off from my mark some thirty metres away from them, their waves of sound seem to push me faster, harder and stronger until a great crescendo at the delivery stride.

It's as though they're trying to offer me a bit of their own strength and muscle power. And, when there's something there to be lifted, I'm lifted. Occasionally as I walk back to my mark I glance up at them and see them throwing their hands up and yelling, urging me on, willing me to do something special. The over finishes and I go down to them at fine leg and it continues, this marvellous 'thing' we have going. I respond to them with a bit of a wave, a nod of thanks and a smile, but I don't do too much talking and carrying on with them because I'm trying to catch my breath and gather myself for the next over. They understand. We've got a pretty good rapport.

For a brief period, almost a fleeting moment, on Boxing Day 1981, the boys in the outer at the MCG rose to their greatest heights—and took me with them. It was the first day of the first Test against the West Indies. Australia had been dismissed for just 198 some 45 minutes before stumps, leaving us a little over half an hour to have a crack at the kings of world cricket. A wicket or two before stumps and we'd be up on cloud nine.

As it turned out the West Indies limped from the field at six o'clock with 4 wickets down for 10 runs, with the master batsman Viv Richards being bowled by Lillee for 2. The cacophony of sound from the MCG outer had lifted me to my most devasting short spell of bowling in Test cricket: 3 wickets for 1 run in the space of 12 deliveries.

As we walked from the ground to a sustained roar from the crowd, I looked up at the scoreboard and it was almost unbelievable. (When I walked back onto the ground the following morning I had a quick look up at the board to make quite sure it was still there!) Somebody later told me that it was at least half an hour after the stumps had been pulled from the ground before the chanting mob in the outer finally broke up and went home. Deep down in the Australian dressing-room on the other side of the ground I was with them in spirit. It was a long, long while before I came down to earth after play that day.

Those three wickets had taken me into second place on the all-time wicket-takers' list and just one off equalling Lance Gibbs' world record. Two more victims and I'd be number one! Then all that pressure that had been gradually building up over the past twelve months or so would be gone. I had needed twenty wickets to break that record when the 1981-82 season began.

There were to be three Tests against Pakistan and then three more against the West Indies . . . and that would surely be enough, I had thought, for the record to be mine before the summer was out. Wouldn't it be just marvellous, I had wished privately before that summer's onslaught had even begun, if I could take wicket number 310 in front of my mates in the outer at the MCG? What a way to repay, in some small way, all that they had done for me.

A check of the programme for the 6 Tests had revealed that the third against Pakistan and the first against the West Indies, both in the heart of the summer, were to be played in Melbourne. What a stroke of luck! And when I'd put 15 wickets under my belt in the first 2 Pakistan Tests it looked to everybody a mere formality that I'd break the record during the first of those 2 games. In a master-piece of promotion Channel Nine, the commercial television net-work covering the series, flew Lance Gibbs himself from Florida, where he now lives, to Melbourne for that game to share the big moment. Internationally renowned cricket photographer Patrick Eagar flew to Melbourne from the England tour of India partly in the hope of capturing the event in his lens. Also, during the game I even received several congratulatory telegrams from people over-seas punting on the fact that I'd be breaking the record.

In the plane on the way to Melbourne for that game I felt as though the world was closing in on me, so great was the pressure on me to break the record. The newspapers were full of it, every time I turned on a television set or a radio there was somebody talking about it and everybody I saw mentioned the record and wished me luck. It got so that I wished I'd never heard of the world record for wicket-taking in Tests.

In the cold, hard light of day I knew there was a good chance that I'd struggle to take any wickets at all in that game if we bowled first. On the MCG track you just have to get wickets bowling late in the game—with the ball keeping very low all you've got to do is bowl straight—but bowling first it can be very hard work indeed.

As it turned out we did bowl first and it's in the record books that Pakistan made a huge score and that I failed to take a single wicket for the game. Looking back, I have no doubt whatsoever that had we bowled second I would have broken the record in that game. But we didn't. As the game progressed and I realised I'd have to wait for another day to have a new tilt at it, I felt a great mixture of emotions. Disappointment that Lance Gibbs had wasted a week of his time in the futile hope of being present when his record was broken and frustration that I would have to go through all the terrible build-up again. I also felt a bit worried that perhaps we'd get the same end of the MCG wicket in the Test to follow and that I'd fail again, to be left dangling hopelessly on a string.

So Lance Gibbs wasn't to be there to hand over his crown, but I did record a television segment with him and Richie Benaud before he left to return home. During the interview Lance said, 'I saw your first couple of overs and I said to myself, "He won't break the record in this Test!"'.

Those words were ringing in my ears on Boxing Day morning as Greg Chappell and Clive Lloyd walked out on to the MCG for the toss. I knew whoever won the toss would choose to bat first, there was no doubt about that. Would Greg stand up after the coin had hit the turf and indicate to the dressing-room that we were batting? My heart was in my mouth as the two heads went down with the falling coin—and it nearly burst when Greg rose with a smile and played a phantom stroke. We were batting . . . now the record must be mine . . . you little beauty!

A strange thing occurred when play resumed on that fateful second day with the West Indies score at 4 for 10. There was already a huge crowd at the ground, yet as I bowled my first spell, needing just 1 wicket to equal and 2 to beat the world record, there was an eerie silence around the ground. You could almost have heard a pin drop . . . amazing after the deafening roar of the night before. I can only think that the boys in the outer were just as nervous as I was about the closeness of the big moment.

Even when Greg Chappell dropped Larry Gomes at slip during that first spell they didn't find any voice. I thought I bowled pretty well in that stint, but nothing seemed to go right and when it finished I was no nearer to the record. Was that to be the end of the road for me in that Test? Would I be frustrated yet again?

Fortunately I was spared the agony. About halfway through the afternoon session I summoned up everything I had and gave it all in a short one to the Test newcomer Jeff Dujon. He slipped inside and hooked it high and wide out to deep backward square leg. Kim Hughes ran and ran and miraculously got both hands to the ball and threw it to the heavens. The record had been equalled. Not so long after (it was 2.54 p.m., to be precise) I managed to run one away from Larry Gomes. He sparred, the ball took the edge and this time Greg Chappell held the catch. The record had at last been broken.

I suppose the boys in the outer roared. I suppose the Melbourne Cricket Club members even stood and applauded spontaneously. I was oblivious to all of that. I just dropped my head in relief that it was all over, that finally I wouldn't have to worry about it any more. My head was bowed and my eyes closed in a moment of inner relaxation, of being with nobody but myself, when all of a sudden I felt as though a five-metre white pointer shark had grabbed me by the legs and was about to break me in two! I opened my eyes to find that Marshy was there. He'd grabbed me by the legs like a rugby full-back might tackle an on-coming opponent. He was trying to lift me high on those broad shoulders of his.

It was then that I heard the roar of the crowd for the first time. But through it all I saw the broadest grin from my mate Marshy, and heard the words I'll never forget, 'Well done mate . . . well deserved.' That was when I started to smile for the first time. In a flash the rest of the lads were there and I soon realised that they were so happy for me, too. It was a great moment to remember.

Seated in the members' area were my wife Helen and our youngest son Dean (I later learnt that Adam was out the back of the pavilion playing with some friends). Back home in Perth watching it all on television were Mum and Dad and my grandfather, Len Halifax, all of whom had meant so much to me through all the years. I thought of them and of all the sacrifices they'd made for me . . . that moment was a triumph for them as much as it was for me.

12

It was a happy coincidence that Helen and the boys were in Melbourne at the time. Before the season had even started we had decided that the family should all come across from Perth for a five-week period embracing the Christmas and New Year celebrations. And it was a pure coincidence that before we'd even left Perth for the trip we'd made arrangements for a night out on 27 December with some friends who were living in Melbourne. So, there could be no special celebration that night—just a pleasant Chinese meal, a few glasses of wine and back to bed at a reasonable hour because the game had to continue the following day. But before that I'd been through a half-hour press conference at the ground. It was about the last thing I wanted, but I felt I owed it to the public to share the moment with them. Hundreds of telegrams arrived over the next few days and I am deeply grateful to all those people who took the time to send them. They helped make the occasion even more memorable.

When I think about it now, it's a rather sad thing that after breaking the record my initial feeling was so strongly one of relief that it was all over. That reaction left little room for any feelings that I might have had of happiness and elation. However, I think as the years go by I'll appreciate it all so much more. Having said that however, I realise it's probably one of those records which won't stand for all that long. There's so much Test cricket played nowadays that somebody like Ian Botham or Kapil Dev is bound to go past my final mark before too long. But perhaps I'll have a couple of years after I've retired to sit back and enjoy it along with all the other memories.

1. Becoming a Cricketer

There are plenty of things for which I am truly thankful and not the least of them would be my childhood. I will always cherish it as a marvellous time in the happiest of surroundings. It's true we never had any great material wealth; in fact at times I could sense that there was a struggle to make ends meet. But what may have been lacking in that regard (which never bothered me a scrap), was made up for in terms of love, warmth and honesty—and I now know what was more important.

Mum was nineteen and Dad was twenty-two when I arrived on the scene, their first child. I've always thought it was important for me that they were so young as we grew up. In the truest sense, for most of my years, Dad and I have been mates to each other, rather than father and son. There were two more children, Trevor who is only eighteen months younger than I am, and our little sister Carmen. We were all crazy on sport and the outdoor life and ours was a vibrant household at all times. It was great having a younger brother with whom I could always get stuck into one game or another.

Anybody who saw me as a toddler might have bet money that I'd never make a sportsman in later life. I was born with a slight problem in my ankles and when I ran would quite regularly topple over. It must have been quite a funny sight, but Mum and Dad were quite worried at first. To overcome this clumsiness I had to wear leg braces to give my ankles some support and keep me upright. This trouble persisted into my early school days and as a result I developed quite an uneven gait.

Looking back, I see I really wasn't cut out to be a student. At my first school, Belmay Primary in the eastern suburbs of Perth, I fell into the category of 'average'—and no wonder, as I spent most of my time in the classroom waiting for the bell to ring so I could race outside and play games. But at Belmay I came under the influence of a teacher called Ken Watters. Ken was a very keen sportsman

14

and we were lucky to have him at our school because he was able to teach us the fundamentals of games. But, perhaps more importantly for me in my future pursuits, Ken imparted the first idea of a will to win in sport. In those days my interests in sport were widespread, with swimming, athletics and football just as appealing as cricket. It wasn't until much later that those other games simply fell by the wayside.

Though Dad had only a sketchy knowledge of cricket, he would always join in when we needed another 'player'. But I guess Mum's father, Len 'Pop' Halifax, was a bigger influence when Trevor and I wanted some extra guidance with our cricket. We went into things in a big way, with typical front lawn 'Test' matches involving all the neighbourhood kids. Trevor and I would spend some time preparing the sand wicket with a roller we had commandeered ... and so I began my career as a fast bowler on that strip, delivering an old tennis ball off a cramped five paces! I dug the footholds out so severely that we eventually placed an ancient mattress there—a precarious footing, but it did teach me the value of being upright at the delivery point.

Of all the cricketers who have had a bearing on my development none was more important than the big West Indian speedster Wes Hall. He was my inspiration. I jumped the fence at the WACA Ground in 1960 to watch him bowl and was struck almost dumb by his awesome aproach to the wicket and the way he could make the ball fly so fast and so far. Now of course our 'wicket' at home just had to be re-aligned to allow for a longer run-up and the lads used to rib me by saying 'Look out, here comes Wes Hall.' Others who made a mark on me were Graham McKenzie, from my own home State, Alan Davidson and the fiery Freddie Trueman. They gave me something without ever knowing it ... and whenever I think of that I am reminded of *my* responsibility to the kids of today.

Perhaps the cornerstone of my cricket career has been an appreciation of the value of good physical fitness. It came to me at a very young age through 'Pop' Halifax, whose motto ('If you can call up a second wind and be in control of your body, then your mind will be free to cope with the job ahead') has always been in my mind. Pop instilled this, and was always there to encourage me to stay with it. As a consequence I was running laps as an under-age player while the other kids were fooling around after practice sessions. I knew deep down that to bowl fast off a long run-up you just had to be fit and hard work on the training track was the only way.

15

As I said, I was no great scholar. To be honest, my desire to achieve at sports overrode such mundanities as schoolwork. At the age of fifteen I left school and began work as a clerk-storeman in a city warehouse, waiting for the next intake for a banking career. By this time my club cricket career had begun with the South Belmont club, where the coach Mick Basile was a good guiding influence. I certainly was dedicated to the game, playing for the club's junior team on Saturday mornings and one of the lower senior sides in the afternoon. It was a good job they didn't have Sunday matches or I'd have been happily at it all weekend, even at that early stage.

Mick Basile could see that I could go no further with South Belmont and advised me to join the district club, Perth. So, at the age of sixteen, I took another step as a raw youngster by playing second grade, where I remained for most of the summer. I was chosen for the first team late in the season—but there was to be no fairytale debut. In fact, I took just one wicket in my first game and very few more for the remainder of the season. I recall that I was reasonably fast, but very inaccurate. Perhaps our home wicket at Lathlain Park, which was very slow, was making me try too hard. I now know what that can do to even a mature fast bowler.

By this stage all other pursuits, such as swimming and football, were falling behind. It seemed my very being was concentrated on my advancement in the sport that was becoming my life. But I wasn't quite so dedicated that at the age of seventeen I didn't notice a rather attractive young lass in the local delicatessen one evening. It was indeed fortuitous that Mum had sent me for that loaf of bread! Helen Munsie was only fourteen then, but I was rather taken by her looks and soon found out a little about her. It turned out she lived in the house behind ours. No, I wasn't as slow as all that, we'd not long moved into a new house!

We saw to it that the relationship was given every chance to develop and it did to such a degree that we were married some three years later in 1970. Helen knew nothing at all about cricket before we met and I know it must have been very hard for her to understand and absorb all my absences through my sport. But if she did one thing it was to keep my mind firmly on the job of developing as a cricketer. Perhaps if I'd remained single, the temptation to give in to other distractions would have been too much.

At the Perth Cricket Club I met Peter Loader, the former English Test fast bowler who had come out to live in Western Australia. Peter was always there to offer a bit of advice if I needed it, but

16

above all it was he who got me chosen in the State Colts squad for extra training with the best young cricketers in the State and, of course, all the coaching that was available there. For a sixteen-year-old, mad keen to learn, that was important. My captain at Perth was a fast bowler of sorts called Kevin Taylforth, who may not have taught me a lot about bowling, but who did help imbue me with a desire to win and a hatred of batsmen.

In the summer of 1969-70, my fourth season of senior club cricket, Western Australia's two best fast bowlers, Graham McKenzie and Laurie Mayne, were away on tour in India and South Africa. This opened the way for other fast bowlers and I was determined to seize on such a golden opportunity. I was playing a club game at my home ground of Fletcher Park on the day that the State selectors were due to announce the team for the opening game of the season. My team were out on the field late in the day and the arrangement was that if I was in the team when it was announced on the radio my father would toot the horn of his car, which was parked on the verge.

Nervously I waited as the afternoon dragged on and still no sound came from the boundary. Then it happened ... the familiar sound of Dad's car horn and I knew I was in! Spontaneously the other people seated in cars around the ground began to sound their horns. It was the best tune I've ever heard. It seemed like a day or so later that I found myself making my debut for WA at the Brisbane Cricket Ground. What a thrill! At the age of twenty I was on my way up the ladder to my pot of gold. However, if I had any fancy preconceptions about taking the Sheffield Shield scene by storm, I was completely wrong. The 'Gabba wicket was dead flat and in my youthful enthusiasm I was guilty of spraying the ball all over the place. In those days I had just one thought in mind: to bowl as fast as I possibly could for as long as I possibly could.

I remember my first wicket as though I took it yesterday. It was Sam Trimble, caught in close on the leg side by Derek Chadwick. My return for the first innings was two for sixty—certainly nothing to catch the headlines—and I picked up just one in the second innings. But our captain, Tony Lock, seemed quite happy. In fact, the old campaigner was like a father to me, encouraging me to bowl fast and never criticising me for inaccuracy as long as I *was* fast. I appreciate now how right Locky was in giving a young fast bowler that sort of support. The ability to bowl really fast is the important factor and it mustn't be dulled by somebody insisting on good line and length. Anyway, as I've found, if you are really quick there

17

aren't too many batsmen around who can lash you if you do stray a bit.

You will have gathered by now I was a bit green as a bowler, more or less just running in and letting them fly as fast and as straight as I could. But if I was green as a bowler, I really was wet behind the ears as a cricket tourist—as John Inverarity soon found, to his delight. We had travelled by air from Perth to Brisbane to begin the tour, but the leg from Brisbane to Sydney for the second game was to be an overnight train trip. I had roomed with Invers in Brisbane and he had no trouble convincing me that the senior player had the choice of beds. Naturally, he chose the double bed and I squeezed into the single for the five or six nights we spent in Brisbane.

When we arrived at our compartment in the railway carriage for the trip to Sydney, Invers paused at the door, looked at me and with a very straight face said, 'Same again, pal, my first choice of beds.' Reluctantly I nodded in agreement and for the first time in my life crossed the portals of a two-berth sleeper compartment in a railway carriage. There I saw one bunk at seat level, with its nice padded back, and frantically my eyes scanned the apartment for a second bed. Quick as a flash, Invers pointed to the luggage rack and said drily, 'Sorry pal, that one's yours . . . I'll have the bottom bunk.'

My heart sank as I tried to picture myself spending a night way up there on such a narrow ledge in a rocking carriage. Finally my tormentor could contain himself no longer. When he stopped laughing he kindly explained to me that the back of the seat during the day became quite a comfortable top bunk at night. I breathed a sigh of relief.

Back to Tony Lock—he was a help to me in more ways than one. He led the team by example and his personal dedication set a standard which was hard not to follow. He spent ages just bandaging himself up to get out there and play and we all knew that at times he found it awfully hard to stick at it day after day. But he never called quits and by that example he simply hardened the men playing under him. During the hours of play he was tough and at times uncompromising, but at the end of the day's battle he'd always be the first to grab a beer and bury the hatchet for a few hours until stumps were pitched again. I can thank Locky for a few things, I guess, not the least of them being my nickname of FOT.

I've got to admit that out on the field early in my career my mind was squarely set on bowling and such a thing as fielding was quite secondary. Locky was never a great one for detail in the field (he

18

ısed to play it by ear a bit), but he occasionally did look my way in the deeps at fine leg and third man—and it seemed every time he did I was hopelessly out of position. The old fellow used to become quite exasperated with me and was wont to shout rather rudely at me in his raucous cockney voice. One day I went to sleep in the outfield once too often and Locky's infuriated reaction could have been heard in the heart of Perth a mile or so away. 'Come on, Lil,' he screamed, 'you're like a Flipping Old Tart' (or words to that effect). Whereupon our vice-captain John Inverarity, a man of letters, seized upon the initials to come up with F-O-T, which has been with me ever since.

We played 4 games on that tour and, thanks to a bag of 6 wickets in the final match in Adelaide, I finished with a total of 15 wickets. I wasn't too pleased with myself and I wasn't greatly surprised when I was dropped to twelfth man for the next game at home, a 1-day affair. Much to my delight, I was re-included in the team for the following home game, which was against South Australia, and a 7-wicket haul in the second innings helped me to amass 32 victims for the season at an average of 22.03 and a striking rate of 1 every 6 overs. That was the best for the season by a WA bowler, not forgetting that our two top quickies were away overseas.

The Australian selectors must have seen something which wasn't altogether evident to me at that stage, because they picked me to tour New Zealand with a second team at the end of the season. It was a pleasant surprise, to say the least, to have won such high honours at the end of my first season. I played in the third unofficial Test on a featherbed wicket at Wellington and took just 1 wicket, that of Glenn Turner. For the short tour overall I had 18 wickets at 16.44, averaging 1 every 5 overs. The tour was marvellous experience and I prepared for the new season (1970-71) back home feeling a far better bowler for it.

It's amazing how circumstances can affect your life. As I said, the absence of McKenzie and Mayne had opened the door for me—well, the return of McKenzie slammed the door in my face, because I had to concede the first use of the wind to him, and quite rightly so. As a consequence I endured a terrible opening to the new season. The 4 matches of the Eastern States tour produced just 6 wickets for plenty and the first game after our return home was even worse for me. It will be remembered as the 'Barry Richards Benefit', because he literally helped himself to a treble century. Again I had a poor return with the ball and when, the following week, I was dropped to twelfth man for the game against Ray Illingworth's MCC side I felt quite convinced that a bright, but brief, career had possibly come to an end.

However, circumstances again prevailed and at the last minute McKenzie dropped out. I went into the side and started with the wind. The reprieve gave me new life and vitality. The first ball I bowled knocked Geoff Boycott's cap flying . . . but at the end of the innings, all I had was that pleasant memory. I relaxed a little in the second innings—perhaps I was resigned to the fact that this could be my last chance—and I bowled quite fast and a lot better. Along the way I picked up Boycott for 9 and Colin Cowdrey for 6 and finished the match a much happier man.

In WA's next game I teamed up with Bob Massie for the first time and we picked up 14 wickets between us. I was back with the wind and bowling with all the verve and fire in the world. Wickets kept coming my way and soon I was blinking in amazement at my name coming up for the Sixth Test against England at the Adelaide Oval. It was more than I could have dreamed possible, especially after such a poor start to the season. In truth, I did feel as though my act was coming together a bit . . . most of the time I had the speed and now batsmen were finding they were having to play at more and more of my deliveries.

When I arrived in Adelaide I realised the Press were trying to build me up to be Australia's answer to John Snow in a 'bumper war' that had developed through the series. I was a little bewildered about all this, because I knew I could never win such a 'war' against a bowler as great as Snow was at that time. Fortunately Sir Donald Bradman realised my plight and went out of his way to take me aside at a pre-Test function. He said to me, 'You have been picked for Australia to bowl as you normally would . . . forget this bumper war business. Just keep the ball well up to the batsman and bowl normally and I'm sure you'll do well.' It was some of the best advice I ever received in cricket. I certainly was too young and too inexperienced to be drawn into such a feud and, quite apart from that, the Adelaide Oval wicket was about the last place you'd want to be bowling short stuff on purpose.

Allan 'Froggy' Thomson, the Victorian wrong-foot speedster, took the first over and this gave me a vital few moments in which to gain some composure. However, it did mean that I had to start off into the wind and consequently I struggled in the early overs. I had to wait a long time for my first blood . . . England were 2 for 276 when

John Edrich (on 130) edged a ball to Keith Stackpole. At the close of play that first day I had 1 for 41 from fourteen overs. The following morning I had the wind at my back and found I was able to run the ball away from the right-handers. Suddenly I was bowling with rhythm and everything I tried came off.

I picked up nightwatchman Alan Knott early and later bowled Illingworth with one that started to go away, then nipped back. At the end of the innings I added Snow and Bob Willis to finish with 5 for 84 off 28.3 overs in my first Test innings. I was beside myself with joy and must admit to having a few sips with my mate Rod Marsh that night—it was a good job we had a rest day the next day! The seventh and final Test in Sydney was one I'd like to forget. I tried to bowl too fast and lost that all-important rhythm, finishing up with just 1 wicket in the first innings and 2 in the second.

But it was the game I won't forget in a hurry. Firstly, there were nasty incidents involving the Sydney crowd and John Snow, who I must admit had bowled his fair share of short stuff to our boys on the tour. Snowy had felled Terry Jenner with a shortish one in the first innings and I was next man in after 'T.J.' was helped from the field. Soon after that things got so hairy out there, culminating in Snowy being physically grabbed and threatened by somebody in the crowd, that Illingworth led his team off the field. Finally the umpires talked the Englishmen into returning and the game continued, but it was a sad happening, a black mark on the history of Test cricket. But there was to be more to the story than that.

After play resumed I hung on until stumps and naturally was one of the first in the nets the following morning to practise my batting. However, to my surprise, Ian Chappell came up to me and told me he was grateful for the job I'd done in filling in for Jenner when he was hurt, but that T.J. was fit to resume his innings now and I could drop back to my normal position in the order.

I thought this was a bit odd, but this *was* the Australian captain. So I didn't hurry back from the nets for the start of play, preferring to use the time there having a good workout. The umpires had gone on to the ground before Ian realised I had taken him seriously and the joke was backfiring. He had to send a runner to get me back to the dressing-room in a hurry to prepare to continue my innings. Boy, was I gullible.

Geoff Boycott missed that game (Graham McKenzie had broken his arm in a one-day game between WA and the MCC a few days before), but he was still in Sydney for the match and after play one

21

day we had a chat about the prospect of my playing in England. Initially we talked about County cricket, but the long grind that promised didn't really appeal to me. In the end I settled on a contract to play as a professional in the Lancashire League for the Haslingden club. Helen and I had a lot of fun during the summer of 1971 in England and playing in the League was good experience, bowling in strange conditions. Perhaps the best lesson I learnt was the need to bowl a good line and length on slow wickets. I took only 68 wickets and Haslingden finished eleventh, but we seemed to get on well and I always go up to the club when I'm back up North during tours to catch up with my old mates and have a pint or two.

I was back in Australia for the 1971-72 season, but political pressures forced the cancellation of a planned tour by South Africa. I must admit to having mixed feelings when I heard that news . . . my memories of Barry Richards were quite fresh amd I knew he wasn't the only top-liner in their batting order. But the reprieve, if you could call it that, was shortlived because the Australian Cricket Board soon announced that a Rest of the World team would tour instead. This team, captained by Garry Sobers, boasted a galaxy of international stars and promised to be just as much a challenge as meeting the South Africans in full flight. Really, though, it was important that we had good competition that season, to continue the rebuilding of the Australian side under Ian Chappell in preparation for England in 1972.

The first international in Brisbane was affected by rain and I left the 'Gabba with just 3 wickets for 111 for the game. The second international was played on my home ground in Perth. Australia batted first, making 349 in the first day without a lot of fuss. I recall waking up the next morning feeling awful. I was so lethargic I could barely lift myself out of bed, yet I had to lead the Australian attack in a few hours.

I struggled off down to the ground, knowing I had to pull myself together in a hurry. Well, the first ball I sent down gave me just the tonic I needed. The wicket had obviously sweated under the covers overnight and was much faster than it had been the day before. That ball was just short of a length, but it flew so fast and so high to Rod Marsh that he almost needed a step ladder to bring it down.

The fourth ball simply took off and Sunny Gavaskar got a glove to it to be caught by Rod. From then on the wickets really tumbled and before the end of the first session they were out for 59 and I was back in the dressing-room with 8 for 29 from 7.1 overs next to my name. It was almost unbelievable, particularly when I recall that after 4 overs I had approached Ian Chappell and told him I wanted a spell because I wasn't feeling too good. At that stage I had 2 for 29. Ian said, 'See if you can bowl a couple more.' I agreed. The next over nothing happened, then the last 6 wickets came my way for no runs in the space of 15 deliveries. That was perhaps the fastest wicket I've ever bowled on, but on top of that the day was just right for bowling *and* there were some brilliant catches among those 8 dismissals.

I sat down in the dressing-room feeling completely drained. I had given everything in that short spell. Imagine my horror when I realised that Ian had decided to enforce the follow-on and I had to be out there firing again in a few minutes. I picked up 1 more wicket before lunch, giving me 9 for the session, and ended up with 12 for 92 for the game. On paper that was my best performance, but there have been other times when I've thought lesser figures were more meritorious. A good example was the fifth Test at The Oval in 1972, when I had to work hard for the 10 wickets I took on a featherbed track. I feel that in self-analysis you must honestly weigh up the conditions when making comparisons with performances.

I left Perth feeling that this wasn't such a bad game after all, but my come-uppance awaited me in the next international at the Melbourne Cricket Ground. And the man to deliver it was Garry Sobers. He had scored 20 not out and 15 not out in Brisbane and in Perth I'd claimed him for a 'duck' in the first innings and he'd made 33 in the second. In fact, I really began to fancy myself when I got him without scoring in the first innings in Melbourne and nearly had him caught hooking in my first over at him in the second innings. But that was the end of that. He proceeded then to play one of the truly great innings of modern cricket . . . 254 glorious runs in just 376 minutes (including two 6s and thirty-five 4s).

Quite a deal of those runs came off my bowling, I might say. Garry was in complete command of the situation and there was just nowhere you could bowl at him without getting some hammer. I place that innings in the same category as Barry Richards' treble century against Western Australia the summer before. They are the best two innings I have ever seen. Sir Donald Bradman went one higher when he summed it up this way, 'I believe Garry Sobers' innings was probably the best ever seen in Australia. The people who saw Sobers have enjoyed one of the historic events of cricket. They were privileged to have had such an experience.'

I'll remember the next game against the Rest of the World just as vividly—but for an entirely different reason. At this stage the series was tied one-all and in this game we were in full command as we went into the second innings bowling on a very flat Sydney Cricket Ground track. I was feeling very tired and was operating at not much above medium-pace and without a lot of purpose when Ian Chappell came up to me and said, 'Look here, if I want somebody to bowl spinners, I'll ask T.J. [Terry Jenner].' That really touched a nerve, pricked my conscience and savaged my pride all in one. I stormed back to the top of my mark, determined to bowl the fastest ball ever bowled to show Ian he was wrong in saying that to me.

I streaked in and let one go full bore and it really did fly to Sunny Gavaskar. However, my joy at seeing him have to hurry his shot was cut dead when a spear of pain at the base of my spine stopped me in my tracks. It was all I could do to finish the over. Then I left the field wracked with pain. The initial diagnosis was that I had suffered a muscular injury. I returned to Perth immediately, where a local doctor gave me a series of stretching exercises designed to ease a muscular injury. He made me rest for a fortnight before resuming light jogging and after a week of that I was back in the nets. It was getting close to selection time for the England tour, so I lined up for a Sheffield Shield game with Western Australia and I must confess I was no star in that one. Not long after that, though, I had passed a fairly crude fitness test and was on my way to England for a five-Test series.

It was bitterly cold at the start of the tour, but I took great care to warm up thoroughly before doing anything strenuous. Then I spent the first few sessions in the nets working at half-pace, but, to my dismay, when I started to try to build up to anything like full pace I always felt these shooting pains up my spine. I was sent to a specialist, who gave me a thorough examination, a pat on the shoulder and sent me on my way saying, 'You'll be all right . . . we'll get you there.' In the nets at Worcester for the first County game I was struck again by sharp pains each time I really stretched out. The team manager telephoned the specialist in London and was told that I was suffering from joint inflammation and that I wasn't to worry if it hurt a little when I stretched out.

Armed with the reassurance of a Harley Street specialist, I went back to the nets to give it everything. But it was no good, the pain was too great. Back in the showers I simply broke down and cried with disappointment and frustration. Keith Stackpole was an immediate source of comfort. He at least seemed to understand that I was under a lot of pressure and needed some understanding and help. Later in the piece Ian Chappell was a great support, keeping me going when I might otherwise have considered tossing it in.

I played in the following game, against Lancashire, but whenever I tried to bowl fast it just wouldn't happen. The pain was a constant barrier. In the following game against Nottinghamshire it seemed to come good all of a sudden and I was able to send down a couple of real quickies in the nets, but gradually it worsened and I was as bad as ever. It was terrible. I seemed to be more comfortable on the rub-down table than anywhere else. So the decision was taken with the specialist that when we returned to London he would manipulate my body under a general anaesthetic.

Any thought that this would be an immediate solution was put to rest when I bowled in the nets the following day at The Oval. I tried to build up some pace, but I couldn't get near it without suffering considerable pain. I went back to the dressing-room very despondent, had some physio and during the luncheon adjournment was back on the ground giving it another try. There was little or no improvement. We went straight to Southampton to play Hampshire and I was picked to play. It wasn't until the second innings that I began to get some pace without any inconvenience. The drastic treatment had worked . . . and I can tell you I had a drink or two in the coach on the way back to London after the game had finished! We went straight into the MCC game at Lord's and when I got Geoff Boycott lbw after beating him with sheer pace I was in seventh heaven.

So I was right for the first Test at Old Trafford. We went down on a 'greentop' and I have often wondered how we would have gone if my West Australian team-mate Bob Massie had been picked to make his debut in that game, rather than the second Test at Lord's. The Lord's game will always be remembered as 'Massie's Match'. . . he took 8 wickets in each innings and finished with 16 for 137 in his maiden Test. Absolutely fantastic!

Bob simply bamboozled the English batsmen with his controlled swing and cut at a lively fast-medium pace and with his occasional sorties bowling round the wicket. They just couldn't cope, it was as near perfect a piece of bowling as could be imagined. I was just privileged to partner Bob that game and to claim the other four wickets that fell for a clean sweep to the two West Australians.

Bob had literally bowled us to a memorable victory and I recall the celebrations in detail. The fact that we had a midnight appointment at a recording studio to lay down our 'hit' record 'Here Come the Aussies' put no damper on the occasion. By the time we got to the studio we were all 'nicely, nicely' and a couple of cartons of cans kept us on the boil. There were some funny moments as the recording people tried to find out who could sing and who couldn't. Those who couldn't, myself included, were placed in front of what I'm convinced was a dummy microphone. In the end it was harder work than winning the Test, but heaps of fun.

My next game was against Leicestershire, where I came up against my friend and West Australian team-mate Graham McKenzie. As planned beforehand, when 'Garth' came to the crease I gave him a big bouncer and his antics when he ducked for cover got a few laughs from the crowd at Grace Road. But a couple of balls later as I reached the top of my mark I noticed a tennis ball rolling on to the ground from a knock-up game between some kids. I veered out, bent down as if to do up my bootlaces and picked the tennis ball up, then slipped the cricket ball into my pocket and took off to bowl the tennis ball to Garth.

It was reasonably well pitched up, but it took off sharply and ballooned over Garth's head, frightening ten months growth out of him and the wicketkeeper. Way down at fine leg, Bob Massie thought I'd bowled the red cover off the ball and just the white innards went down to the batsman ... at slip John Inverarity thought the ball had gone so fast it had turned white hot! And, by freak coincidence, an amateur photographer at the ground captured the moment and my tennis ball delivery made the national Press. Garth gave a sort of sheepish grin and obviously stored it away in his memory box. A few years later in a double-wicket competition back home in Perth he brought out a tennis ball and gave me some of my own back. It certainly does come as a shock.

I must admit I wasn't beyond having a bit of a lark in some of the County games. A bit later in the tour, when we played Sussex at Hove, I spied a large, shiny red apple on the lunch table and pocketed it. The apple went out with me and I did the switch for the first ball after lunch. It landed on a good line and length, but broke up on hitting the hard turf. One piece hit the stunned Sussex batsman on the pad dead in front, while another careered on to hit the stumps. An international incident was avoided when a sharp-witted umpire threw out his right arm and called 'No apple!'

26

The third Test at Trent Bridge was drawn and we went to Headingley, Leeds, for the fourth expecting a bit more life in the wicket than had been the case in Nottingham. Headingley had been helpful to seamers earlier in the season, but, to our total dismay, we found that the Test strip was almost devoid of grass and its brownish colour was a stark contrast to the healthy green of the remainder of the square. The England selectors rushed Derek Underwood back into the side and we were never really in with a ghost of a chance on a diabolical 'turner'. It was like a minefield and certainly not a wicket of Test match standard.

So we lost and it was a bitter pill to swallow. We had been 'sold out' and that was that. A later investigation into the quality of the wicket gave the verdict that some mysterious bug had eaten the grass away ... and, funnily enough, the bug had only affected the one wicket on the whole square! That victory gave England a two-one lead in the series, which meant they couldn't lose the Ashes. At The Oval for the fifth and final Test we had an easy paced, but fair, wicket and Australia recorded a memorable victory. I believe that win was the beginning of big things for the Australian side. Ian Chappell had us in the palm of his hand, and we were the nucleus of a very good team, with youth on our side. I ended the series with a total of 31 wickets, a record for an Australian in England ... after the frustrations of the first few weeks of the tour that was far more than I could have hoped for.

There was nothing much in the way of a rest when we got back home. It was straight back into harness for a series against Pakistan. But before that started, between the beginning of November and the middle of December, I had played in 6 games and bowled a total of 207 eight-ball overs for 44 wickets. I then leapt into the first two Tests against Pakistan, when I bowled 63 overs to take 8 wickets. So, by the time I reached Sydney for the third Test I was pretty weary. In fact, in the nets the day before the game I felt a bit of a twinge in my back, so it was no real surprise to me when in the first innings my back gave way again.

I left the field and saw a doctor in the dressing-room. He simply told me I'd had enough cricket and advised me to rest up for the coming tour of the West Indies. But as the game went into its final innings, with Pakistan needing not a lot to win, I felt it was my duty to offer to bowl a bit of line and length stuff to help us defend the total. I was given the all-clear to do that by the doctors and bowled 23 overs at medium pace, just well enough to contain while Max

Walker cleaned them up with 6 for 15 from 16 overs. It was a truly rousing victory, but I was a very sore and sorry boy in the dressing-room afterwards.

Looking back, that decision to bowl in the second innings was probably a stupid mistake. We left soon after for the West Indies and I'm not sure that I was fit enough to go. But things worked out reasonably well in the early stages and I lined up for the first Test at Kingston. I bowled 32 overs and seemed to have suffered no harm, even though my back was very sore throughout. We then went to Antigua to play the Leeward Islands and it was there that I broke down completely and didn't bowl another over on the tour.

Then followed a desperately unhappy time for me as I went from one specialist to another and received one diagnosis after another. None of it seemed to make much sense to me and I certainly got no nearer to being able to bowl again on the tour.

Then I came across Rudi Webster in Barbados. Rudi is a radiologist and a former fast bowler himself. He had been in Perth a year or two before and I'd met him at the WACA Ground nets. He told me he had suffered from stress fractures in his lumbar vertebrae while playing County cricket in England and suggested that perhaps I had the same problem. So Rudi took a series of X-rays of my spine from all different angles and finally came out with the tell-tale signs of three tiny fractures on two of the vertebrae. He suggested a course of exercises to strengthen my back and stomach muscles in a last-ditch effort to make the side again before the tour was over.

So I threw myself into these exercises plus did plenty of running to build some stamina. However, I ran into inter-island professional jealousies and in Trinidad was forced to see a specialist who refused to give any credence to Rudi's findings. He made me try bowling with painkillers and, when that failed, made me submit to another manipulation under a general anaesthetic. Still my back was no better. By now three Tests had passed and my only hope was to get right for the last in Port of Spain. The tour had become a nightmare for me and there were many times I wished I could go home. But where there's life, there's hope, and I pressed on with my training routines. In the end I just had to give in and I was truly glad to get back to Perth again.

But there was no great fun for me after my return. I showed Rudi's X-rays to my doctor in Perth and his reaction was to encase me in plaster from my buttocks to the top of my chest, just to make sure that I was giving my injured back *complete* rest. So I spent a very uncomfortable six weeks, unable to do a lot of things for myself and with poor Helen virtually my servant. I had troubles getting dressed, my clothes wouldn't fit and I couldn't wash without help. It was a terribly frustrating period, even though I could appreciate it was for the best. What a relief when it was finally removed!

The doctor talked of another cast, but finally compromised (he couldn't bear to see a grown man cry, I'm sure), and for the next six weeks I wore an aluminium ribbed, webbing harness. This was just as uncomfortable and restricting as the cast had been, but at least I could take it off to have a shower. After the harness I was into a period of no more than cautious movement, which gradually gave way to light exercises, stretching and running. I was back on the road, which was great.

Then came the agonising decision: whether or not to try to pick up the strings and bowl again in the coming summer (1973-74), when Australia had 'twin' tours against New Zealand. After carefully weighing up the consequences, I opted to stand out of first-class cricket for the season. It just wasn't worth the risk of another breakdown.

There were two other factors influencing this decision. Firstly, I hadn't seen much of Helen for two years and she was pregnant with our first child, Adam (Dean, our only other child, followed a couple of years later). Secondly, I had left the bank and taken up a partnership in a contract cleaning business and wanted to be able to throw myself headlong into getting it going on a good footing. So I went into the new summer as captain-coach of the Perth Cricket Club. This came as a bit of a surprise to those who thought I was nothing more than a tearaway fast bowler. I looked on it as a good opportunity to gain some experience in other aspects of the game—*and* I had to justify my position in the first team because I had decided not to bowl a single ball that summer.

The experience was invaluable. The business of really looking for a batsman's weaknesses and setting a field accordingly was something I hadn't thought a lot about previously. It was a learning process which would stand me in good stead in the future. Having to concentrate on my batting did me no harm at all and I ended up making more than 600 runs for the season, which wasn't far behind the best in the competition. Of course, I couldn't contain myself when it came to bowling again . . . the season hadn't gone half-way before I was finally tempted to break my promise.

After getting an 'Okay, but be careful', all-clear from my specialist, I sent down just a few overs off a short run and felt none the worse for it. As the season wore on I did more bowling, but took it steadily through to the finals at the end of the summer, when I stretched out to bowl at near to my top speed. Earlier on, though, when I was bowling slower I found I had to be more accurate and do more with the ball to get wickets. So I began to really develop the finer points of the art of fast bowling, such as swinging the ball, making it move off the wicket and the other variety balls like the bouncer and the change of pace. The circumstances gave me the opportunity to really think about these deliveries and to spend the time trying to perfect them.

2. Back to the Mark

Having safely negotiated the relatively calm waters of a domestic club season, I now had to address myself to the big question of a future in first-class and then Test cricket. And it wasn't all that long before I realised there was going to be a lot of pressure on me. For a start there was a doctor who wasn't sure I'd be able to bowl fast under pressure again. All that did was sow a seed of doubt in my mind as I prepared to launch myself into a most comprehensive programme of preparation for the attempted comeback. But I was aided by the confidence of Dr Frank Pyke, of the University of Western Australia Physical Education Department, where I was to undergo my build-up. I thought I'd be able to bowl fast again—but how long would I last?

Would I bowl one over, maybe two overs and then break down again? If I did get through the initial spell, would I bowl for two or three games and then play State cricket again and do well enough to get back in the Test side only to collapse in agony during my first over? These questions and many more flashed through my mind as I drove down to the University to begin what turned out to be two months of torture. There were so many questions.

I wished I could have the answers then and there. It was agonising. Finally I resolved that I just had to throw myself into whatever work was prescribed for me and give myself every chance of being fit and ready for the comeback. As to all the questions ... in time they'd be answered in full.

Frank Pyke and his team at the University had devised a series of exercises aimed at strengthening and supporting the damaged area by building up the back and stomach muscles. They also laid down a training programme aimed at having me at the peak of fitness for the start of the season. First of all, though, I was tested and told that my fitness was extremely good. A target was set for a 20 per cent improvement all round. So I started a set of isometric exercises especially designed to complement the fast-bowling action and a most rigorous fitness campaign. It was extremely hard work in the

31

middle of that winter of 1974, but at the end of it I could see a pot of gold in the form of playing for WA and Australia again and the vision spurred me on.

Then, after about three weeks of sheer hell, I received a jarring setback. We had built up the isometric exercises to a peak, putting heavy work into the back muscles and increasing their strength and flexion most satisfactorily. However, as I strained into one exercise I fell in a heap as something 'went' in the region of the base of my spine. I collapsed on the floor in a mixture of pain and anguish. Had I reached the end of the road already? Were those questions all being answered at that moment? We stopped the exercises immediately and I showered and went home.

I was a very worried man as I waited in the doctor's reception room that evening. What concerned me most was that the pain I'd felt had been so similar to that I'd experienced when I broke down initially. What a blow, having laid off and done everything properly for more than a year! But the doctor was full of good news. He was positive it wasn't the same injury and simply recommended a week's respite from the exercises, before gradually building them up again. I wasn't quite sure whether to believe him or not, I was so despondent, but I did take his advice. When I cautiously returned to the exercises I found that my fears had been ill-founded and I soon regained confidence that everything would be all right. All I'd suffered was a muscle strain at the very base of the back.

So I continued the programme under Dr Pyke's close guidance, from now on never putting quite so much force into the isometrics. Repeated testing showed a consistent improvement and we soon went sailing past the 20 per cent target set in the beginning. That fact gave me heart and as the season approached, so my confidence grew. My preparation was punctuated by a brief trip to Hong Kong, but even on holiday I made sure the exercises were continued. Being in Hong Kong also gave me a chance to start bowling and I did so for between half an hour and one and a half hours every day. Back in Perth I was straight into training with the West Australian squad and everything was going swimmingly until I put myself under some pressure when bowling in a State trial game at the WACA Ground.

I bowled within myself in short spells only and was very happy with the way things went. The following day there was a bit of stiffness, though little in the back area, and anyway no more than you'd expect from a first serious workout in a season. But after the second day things didn't feel right at all. I felt a sort of weakness, rather than a soreness, in the back area and wasn't able to bowl at practice for three days. Even batting was a little difficult.

I was worried enough finally to go back to the doctor, who gave me the great news that I could expect that sort of reaction every time I put my back under pressure. If there was pain, he said, I was to try not to worry because I couldn't do any more damage other than further fracturing over a period of time. He suggested soldiering on, using painkilling tablets, if necessary. As a parting quip he added that if the pain became too bad he'd consider acupuncture. Lovely!

Through all of this preparation for my comeback I had been through a change in employment. Long before I had left the safe confines of my job in the bank for the world of commerce. I'd begun working with a contract cleaner and after a couple of months had bought into the business. Eventually this didn't work out, because I was having to work at all sorts of odd hours which often conflicted with my commitments with Frank Pyke down at the University. So I decided to sell out to give myself more freedom to devote all the time I needed to training. I took a job with a travel company, which I was to hold until I returned from the tour of England in 1975. After that I was out of work for a couple of months, before joining a car company.

I really appreciated the sort of support I received from Rod Slater at that car company. I had found from personal experience and from my observations of many other players in senior cricket that cricket and employment don't mix all that well. Looking at it from an employer's point of view, it must be very hard to get value out of a Test cricketer on his staff. I don't blame those employers who turn their backs when asked to give a cricketer a job one bit. The game consumes so much time and there is so much travelling interstate and overseas that it's very hard to settle down in a job. There's no continuity once the season gets under way.

Of course this employment situation can put great pressure on a cricketer. In the early days of my first-class and Test career the money we received as players was so poor that we simply had to work to cover the expenses at home. And I can vouch for the fact that there were no luxuries in our household in those days as Helen and I struggled along trying to pay the mortgage and feed and clothe ourselves and our two little children. This problem really worsened when the Australian Cricket Board began to schedule more and more Tests and tours. It was a matter of simple arithmetic—if you lose money playing one Test, then the more Tests you play the further you go down the drain. I suppose I was saved by the fact that I was able to get occasional jobs and then gradually to expand my work with advertising and promotions. Without that we'd have sunk.

My opening first-class match was to be against South Australia in Adelaide and as the day grew closer the pressure built up. Coinciding with our landing in Adelaide was the arrival there of the MCC team to begin their tour of Australia—and that meant the discerning eye of the British Press corps was added to that of the band of Australian media-men who seemed awfully interested in my well-being.

Our captain, John Inverarity, sensed that I was going to be plagued by the Press and hit on the solution: he called a Press conference. It was a master stroke. I endured a fairly hectic hour or so in a motel room and then it was all over and I was free to concentrate on the job ahead of me.

We were to bowl first and my stomach was doing somersaults as I paced around, waiting for the umpires to call into our dressing-room and the moment of truth to arrive. At last we were out on the ground and I was measuring out my run for that fateful first delivery. As I placed the marker down I looked towards the pavilion away to my left and there were a dozen or so MCC players standing and watching. That gave me a boost ... they were concerned enough about me as a threat in the Tests that season to leave off their net practice at the rear of the pavilion and come and have a look. I grinned, took a deep breath and away I went with a little prayer that everything would fall into place.

I had decided not to try and bowl fast in the opening few Sheffield Shield games. Ahead of me lay the agonising questions of when to try myself under full pressure. As I went into that first session I wasn't worried so much about how well I'd bowl, but whether or not my back would stand up to the stress and strain. I bowled mainly at three-quarter pace with a couple of quickish ones an over. In simple terms, I didn't trust my back and how far I could push it. The best way was to bowl mainly within myself and in a way that was to help me for the rest of my career. There would come a day when I could no longer tear in all day and blast out the best batsmen in the world. Then all the skills I'd learnt while bowling within myself would be worth their weight in gold. There was, after all, some silver lining behind the dark clouds that had been hanging over my head for so long.

After the first couple of overs I was overwhelmed by a feeling that everything was going to be all right, that most of my worries were behind me. I didn't bowl exceptionally well, just well enough to give me heart. In fact, I took 4 wickets in the first innings and 3 in the second—and I picked up Ian Chappell's wicket in each innings.

In Melbourne for the second game against Victoria I was embroiled in an on-field incident involving Richie Robinson. It occurred in the first innings. Alan Seiler and I had gone awfully close to colliding as he ran down the wicket for a run and I finished my follow-through. Then Richie came in after lunch and we did collide heavily as he was taking a run down to third man and I was following through.

I was upset, to say the very least. As I walked back to my mark I was fuming, I thought to myself, 'No matter what condition my back is in, I'm going to make this the fastest ball I can bowl . . . I'll let the bastard know I'm not too happy about that.' The trouble with bowling within yourself is that the slips tend to stand a yard or two closer than usual, which makes an edge off the quicker ball a tough assignment. Well, I charged in and let fly at Richie and he edged it into the slips, but to my dismay the ball went crashing through Ian Brayshaw's hands and down to third man for a couple. That didn't help matters, because I really wanted that wicket—but worse was yet to come.

The incident was right out of my mind as I sat down to relax with a drink in the dressing-room after play that day. But Sam Loxton, a Victorian and Australian selector, obviously hadn't forgotten my clash with Robinson. He came into our room and barged straight up to where I was sitting. I was just pulling off my boots when this rather belligerent face appeared before me. In his typically throaty voice Sam spat out, 'Don't ever let me see you do that again.'

I was taken aback. 'What are you talking about, Sam?' I replied. He said 'This!' . . . and indicated as though he was making a blow with his elbow. For a second I was stunned, then I replied with equal firmness, 'You should have a look at your own players before you start criticising me.'

I just laughed and Sam stalked off. Actually, it was great to hear from Sam, because in almost five years of Test cricket I reckon he wouldn't have said more than half a dozen words to me. What a way to get to know one of the men who was sitting in judgment on my bowling! Anyway, Sam never bugged me again after that . . . he must have got the message loud and clear.

Despite a rash of dropped catches off my bowling—mainly because our slips fieldsmen just couldn't cope with the change of pace when I occasionally sent down a quickish one—I was doing well enough during the next game in Sydney to think that my chances of playing for Australia that season were going along just nicely.

However, I had a little problem which had to be solved before we went as far as that. It all concerned a quibble with the Australian Cricket Board over the payment of some medical bills that had mounted up during the latter part of the period when I was out of action with my back injury. They were bills for the treatment I had received from time to time during my efforts to get back into Australian cricket.

The Board had paid my medical accounts up until the day I bowled for the first time in a club match in Perth before Christmas in the 1973-74 season, when I had stood out of first-class cricket. After that date it seemed they'd decided any medical bills were my problem—and that, anyway, I was going against doctor's advice by bowling. Quite to the contrary, my doctor had told me I could bowl in a match if I wanted to, but as long as I stopped if there was any suggestion of pain. I felt the Board could easily have found that out by asking the doctor. I had bowled in club cricket within his limitations, but the Board had put up the shutters because they said their insurance company would no longer back them.

And so began a shuffling about of doctors' bills. I sent all of them to the Board and they kept sending them back to me. The reminders would then come to me from the doctors and so on. At one stage a doctor even offered me the chance to pay his account off at a dollar a week. How embarrassing! It wasn't the amount of money, it was the principle. I'd injured myself playing for Australia and I just wasn't going to pay for the treatment that followed. I decided that the matter had to be resolved then and there, so I went and saw Alan Barnes, the secretary of the Australian Cricket Board.

I decided to get straight to the point and said, 'Look, Australian selections are coming up very soon ... you haven't paid my bills from this injury ... if those bills aren't paid in two days' time I'm not available for selection.' His comment was, 'We sent the cheque off the other day.' I replied, 'I don't know whether you've sent the cheque off or not, but what I said stands,' and walked out. The bills were paid within two days. The amount was less than a hundred dollars, but I suppose the fact that I had again become a prospect to bring money in through the gates encouraged them to settle up. The whole thing left a nasty taste in my mouth.

Waiting for the team to be announced for the first Test, to see if I'd be returning to the Australian side right off, wasn't much fun, either. For the couple of days before the names were to be announced I was quite apprehensive. I thought I'd bowled well enough, but I was afraid the selectors would be thinking 'Will he last for a full Test match?' After all, it was the opening game of an Ashes series and in those circumstances selectors aren't renowned for taking risks. In the light of all that I was thrilled when I heard I'd been picked.

It was like starting my career all over again. After all those heart-breaking experiences with the back injury, the long periods of not knowing what was wrong, the weeks encased in plaster and then wearing a harness, and finally the long period of rebuilding my strength and fitness, there I was back in the Test team.

Up in Brisbane at the final practice session the day before the Test there were Pressmen everywhere. They put a lot of pressure on me, just being there, but all of a sudden I realised, 'Hell, it's on in earnest tomorrow and I'd better be good.' Now I'd reached the moment when I'd have to decide what to do when the ball was handed to me. Should I continue to bowl with something in reserve or should I give it all, because a Test will always deserve a player's all? The way I'd been bowling in the lead-up games had been reasonably successful, but would it do at the higher level of Test cricket? Sitting in my hotel room that night I made the decision: I had to give it what I could; I'd revert to bowling fairly quickly.

As it turned out, I did bowl fairly fast in patches, but I didn't feel all that comfortable. Looking back, I thought I bowled fairly well, though mainly because Jeff Thomson was really sending them down at the other end. This was a blessing, really, because if Thommo had struggled I'm sure I'd have been battling, too. I felt a mixture of emotions ... my excitement at being back in the Test scene was tinged with distinct concern that at any stage my decision to go flat out again could result in the end of my career and even leave me a cripple for the rest of my life. That anxiety was a bit of a dampener at times.

A couple of happenings early in the game helped to take my mind off my back. We batted first and when I went in at the fall of the eighth wicket we were a shaky 229. Peter Lever was bowling and very soon I heard Tony Greig encouraging him to bang them in short at me. But 'Plank' was a bit tired and just couldn't get them up. I was playing him fairly comfortably, which seemed to really upset Greigy. 'Give me the ball ... I'll show you how to do it,' he said. Then he took the ball and slipped a couple of bouncers in at me straight away. I tried to hook the second one out of the ground, but took it on the glove and was caught behind. As I walked past him on the way back to the pavilion I said, 'I hope you can handle what you've got coming.' He just laughed.

I wasn't the only one in our tail who got the short-pitched treatment and, on reflection, these were rather foolish tactics. I don't think Greigy quite realised the implications—there's no way he and his team-mates could have known that Thommo was going to be such a force to contend with during the series. Also, the only time they'd seen me bowl was in Adelaide at the start of the season when I'd bowled only fast-medium at best. So they probably thought Thommo wasn't what the Press had cracked him up to be and that I was finished as an express bowler.

As it was, those bouncers from Greigy really fired us up and we decided then and there that, 'Okay, it's good enough for them to be firing in bouncers at our tail ... let's see how well their tail can handle some of the same medicine.' That's where the so-called 'Bumper War' started.

I don't think anybody could blame us for bowling bouncers at their top-order batsmen, but a few of their tail-enders did start to squeal a bit towards the end of the tour when we were bowling much quicker bouncers at them than they were able to bowl at our tail. Our bowlers didn't really want to be part of the carry-on that followed that first innings up in Brisbane, but we felt we had to answer fire with fire.

Out of it all, in some ironical way, Greigy emerged as something of a winner himself. There's no doubting that his antics and behaviour on the field got us riled right from the start and we probably played into his hands. We got a bit carried away with bowling short to him when perhaps we should have realised that it's awfully hard to bowl good bouncers to a man of his height. His answer was to stand back and slash at the ball and time after time it flew over the in-field to the boundary. There were some good shots, but a lot went flying over slips off the edge. Greigy also displayed a lot of arrogance, signalling boundaries himself and really carrying on out there. I became quite irritated by him. It's obvious now that it was his idea to break my concentration.

That first Test in Brisbane was really the beginning of the 'Lillee and Thomson' partnership which was to prove so fruitful for both of us and for Australia. We had actually bowled together against Pakistan in the second Test of their 1972-73 tour, but we certainly didn't set the world on fire then with just my 3 wickets between us. To be fair, Thommo had suffered a broken toe in that game and that slowed him down a lot.

Though this Brisbane Test was just his second Test, he bowled beautifully and very fast indeed. He picked up 3 in the first innings and his bag of 6 in the second was a match-winner. It was just marvellous bowling down the other end and although I picked up just the 2 wickets in each innings I was very happy at the end of the game. I had a bit of stiffness and soreness, but nothing to worry about. I thought, 'Oh well, one down ... perhaps I'll play a few more.'

The second Test in Perth was memorable for a couple of reasons. England had a couple of injuries and surprised us all by calling the veteran Colin Cowdrey out from an English winter as a replacement. Cowdrey, just a few days short of his forty-second birthday, had not played a Test since June 1971, and he went out to face our attack only four days after arriving in Australia. It was asking a lot of the man, though he'd faced some very good fast bowlers over the years and was considered one of the better players of pace. I must admit we thought it was a bit of a joke, but as it turned out he did a good job under the circumstances. He batted number three in the first innings (making 24 in 124 minutes) and opened in the second (with 41 in 131 minutes).

It was a courageous performance, though he was well padded with a thick chest guard. This gave him the confidence to let go a lot of the short-pitched deliveries that were causing all the trouble to his team-mates. I don't know what Colin's padding was made of, but the ball really flew off his chest and at times even ran down to the boundary. He was done up like a knight for a joust—and joust he did, very well indeed. However, England needed more than Cowdrey could offer to keep Thommo at bay. He really blitzed them with 2 in the first innings and 5 in the second. It was a few days after this game that the England opener David Lloyd is said to have written home to his mother, saying, 'Mum, things are looking up ... today I got a half-volley in the nets!' That reflects the intensity of the heat out in the middle when Thommo and I were at our top.

Of course, a highlight of this match was provided by Doug Walters, when he took his score from 3 to 103 in the session between tea and stumps on the second day. It was vintage Walters—and he posted the 'ton' with a 6 over backward square leg off Bob Willis on the last ball of the session. Dougy's partnership of 170 with Ross Edwards was a gem. Then, as if records were the call of the game, Greg Chappell took 7 catches for the game to set a Test record for a non-wicketkeeper. We won by 9 wickets to go 2-up in the series and again I picked up 2 in each innings and pulled up fit and well.

One England batsman who had come to Australia with a great reputation was the Warwickshire opener Dennis Amiss—a stockily built right-hander who liked to get after the bowling a bit. He had enjoyed a marvellous run of successes in series against the West Indies in the Caribbean (the first Test played early in February of 1974) and then at home to India and Pakistan later the same year (with the last Test against Pakistan at The Oval late in August). In the space of those few months Amiss had 18 innings and scored 1253 runs, including a double century and 4 centuries.

Thommo got him for 7 and 25 in Brisbane and he missed the Perth Test through injury. But, beginning with the third Test in Melbourne, I had a bit to do with his Test career slowing down and coming to a full stop a few months later. I don't know why, but in the end I just seemed to have a spell over the poor fellow. I got him for 4 in the first innings in Melbourne, but he did make 90 in the second to go within 2 runs of the record number of Test runs made in a calendar year. That mark of 1381 was set by Bob Simpson in 1964. I'll come back to that Melbourne Test, but in subsequent meetings I had Amiss for 37 in the second innings of the fourth Test, for a 'pair' in the following Test, for a 'duck' in England's only innings in the sixth and final Test and finally for 4 in the first innings of the opening Test in England later that year.

Amiss lost his place in the England team after that, though he did later return to Test cricket. Ironically, the next time I came up against him was early in 1977, when the MCC played WA in the lead-up game to the Melbourne Centenary Test. The old magic was still there and I picked him up for 9 and 29. He was forever edging the ball to the catching cordon behind the wicket. However, that was the end of my run . . . in the Centenary Test Amiss batted down the list and fell to Max Walker and Greg Chappell. But it was an incredible run of successes against the one player. Incidentally, despite his woes on the Australian tour, Dennis still managed to score a total of 1428 Test runs for the year from the beginning of February 1974 to the end of January 1975.

Back to the third Test at Melbourne. It was drawn, but perhaps we should have won. Beginning the last day's play we were no wicket for 4, needing in all 246 to win . . . when stumps were drawn we were 8 for 238. At tea we were 5 down and needed just 101 runs. I was involved in an eighth-wicket stand of 27 with Max Walker and going into the last over from Tony Greig we needed 11 to win. When I was out trying to clear the pavilion off the fifth ball the shutters went up. It had been an even, tight game and once again Thommo had called the shots with the ball. What a marvellous season he was having . . . none of the England batsmen were comfortable when he was around and Rod Marsh's gloved hands were taking a terrible pounding.

I guess I'll never forget the fourth Test in Sydney. For a start, England's captain Mike Denness dropped himself from their side. Then late on the final day we succeeded in bowling England out to win by 171 runs. That win gave us the Ashes. It was a great moment; the culmination, if you like, of all that we'd been working towards since Ian Chappell had taken over the captaincy back in 1971. It's no secret that we had a few celebratory drinks that night—Sydney town has never been the same since! Again it was Thommo who did the damage in the first innings and for the fourth successive game all I could manage was 2 wickets in each innings.

During our first innings Tony Greig and I locked horns once more. He hit me on the arm with yet another short one and I wasn't greatly impressed. Feelings ran high when we came out to bowl and I must admit I really let myself go for the first time that season. I was well pleased with the result in terms of the speed I was able to build up and the fact that I pulled up so well afterwards. I was considerably concerned in the second innings when I downed John Edrich with a blow to the rib-cage with the first ball I bowled to him. I've always admired 'Edie' as a courageous and very competent player and I was not surprised, but rather relieved, when he came back later in the innings and batted very well. He hung in there until the last few overs of the mandatory 15 in the last hour and nearly saved the game for England.

We then went to Adelaide for the fifth Test and at last I got a bag—4 in each innings, this time. It was all coming together beautifully for me, but my mate Thommo wasn't quite so fortunate. He bowled very well again in the first innings as we put England out for just 172, but then injured his shoulder in a social game of tennis on the rest day and took no further part in the series. Even so he had taken 33 wickets at the incredible average of 17.94 and without a shadow, of a doubt had been the dominating factor in the series. His blistering speed and his constant hostility just never gave the England batsmen a moment's respite. It was great fun bowling at the other end and occasionally picking up the pieces.

England had their one moment of joy for the tour in the final Test, which Thommo missed because of his injury and in which I bowled just six overs before breaking down with a bruised foot. The England batsmen came out of the woodwork, with Mike Denness and Keith Fletcher each making centuries, and we ended up losing by an innings and 4 runs. Such a comprehensive defeat did little, if anything, to take the gloss off our four-one win over England in the series. It had been a rough and tough series, with many tense moments as the 'bumper war' raged pretty well throughout. But at the end of it all there was great satisfaction. For me there was the particularly personal satisfaction that I'd been able to make a reasonably successful comeback to the rigours of Test cricket. I'd taken 25 wickets and was feeling fit and strong in my back area. Canada and England, look out!

3. World Cup and Beyond

As I packed my gear for the 1975 tour of Canada and England I felt a distinct tinge of excitement and expectation. This promised to be a real tour with a difference. For a start there was a two-week warm-up jaunt in the 'unknown territories' of North America and then a shortish stay in England with plenty on offer.

Our first job in England was to tackle the inaugural Prudential World Cup one-day series and then, after all the other countries had gone home, a four-Test series against England. There were two major challenges ahead of us—the chance to prove our ability as one-day cricketers and then to firmly establish our supremacy over England in Test cricket.

But first there was Canada. The tour opened on the West Coast in Vancouver and the setting for the first game was simply idyllic. On one side of the ground were national parklands and mountains, on the other, water. I had the game off. Though it was a very cool and crisp day I just enjoyed sitting at the ground and drinking in the scenery, while watching Jeff Thomson prove conclusively that he was well and truly over the shoulder injury he'd suffered on the rest day of the Adelaide Test. He really let them go and had the opposing players jumping around most uncomfortably. I guess it wasn't much fun for them, but we thought it was an important indication that Thommo would again be a force by the time we reached England.

During our stay in Vancouver Bruce Laird and I were taken up to the mountains to have our first feel of snow. I'd seen snow from a distance in New Zealand, but it was the first time Bruce had even seen it. Where our car pulled up we could see pure, clean snow away above us—much better than the rather dirty stuff that lay about in clumps on the roadside! So we decided to trek up a very steep trail to get to the 'real' snow we could see in the distance. I suppose we trudged over a kilometre up that trail, getting soaked through because we didn't have the right gear. However, by the time we got to within 200 metres of the fluffy white we were so exhausted we couldn't go any further. So I never did get to touch some real snow then. I had to wait until some years later in Europe.

My first game in Canada, on Vancouver Island, was rained off. All I could do was run a heap of laps as it teemed down, in a bid to keep my fitness level up. The next day we flew to Toronto, where I did play my first game, against a 'Canadian Eleven'. An interesting fact about that side was that there wasn't one Canadian in it—just one Australian and ten West Indians and Indians.

They put on quite a party for us the night before the game, which turned out to be a very good tactical manoeuvre because they beat us the next day. I don't think anybody on our side was too heart-broken about the loss because Canada was no more than a warm-up for what was to come in England. Our players really appreciated this relaxing preparation for the tour of England and I think there should be more of it . . . just a couple of weeks in a place like Canada, the United States, Hong Kong, Singapore or even South America. Obviously the cricket is not of a very high standard, but it's a good pre-liminary, and a great promotional exercise.

There was a real buzz of excitement when we arrived in England. All the other major cricketing nations were arriving for the first complete gathering of teams in the history of the game. It was a very interesting concept and all our players were looking forward to it eagerly. The timing, in the early part of the English summer, put us at a slight disadvantage, but we did have a couple of lead-up games and by the time the series began we were reasonably confident of acquitting ourselves well.

Our first game was against Pakistan at Leeds and we felt we had to win it to make the semi-finals. It turned out to be a very tight game. We were almost overwhelmed by the hugely pro-Pakistan crowd . . . one coach after another crammed with Pakistani sup-porters had come up the motorways from the Midlands. They were very vocal early in the piece when it looked as though their side might win, but when the tide turned later in the piece the dancing and flag-waving gave away to angry cushion-throwing.

Our second game against Sri Lanka should have been a mere for-mality, but we had to struggle a bit before finally putting them away. So we were in pretty good spirits when we went to The Oval to take on the West Indies in our final qualifying game. We knew they'd be tough nuts to crack and as it turned out they played well and beat us convincingly.

But the final was to be played at Lord's, where the wicket was a bit faster, and we gave ourselves a chance if we could make it there for the rematch. At The Oval we got our first taste of the fanatical, but good-spirited, support of the London West Indians. They formed swaying lines as they filed out of the ground, chanting with toothy grins, 'We killed a kangaroo . . . we killed a kangaroo . . . eee-iii-adio, we killed a kangaroo . . .', to the accompaniment of their own stylised steel band.

We travelled up to the North again for the semi-final against England at Headingley and we expected a hard game, facing the most experienced one-day players in the world. We bowled first on a greentop that seamed about all over the place. Gary Gilmour was almost unplayable, as his figures of 6 for 14 from 12 overs would surely indicate. We had them out for just 93 and it looked like a mere cake walk to victory. But again we needed 'Gus', this time with the bat, to carry us through. When he went to the wicket we had lost 6 wickets for 39, but he banged the first ball he received away through mid-off and continued to bat beautifully and win the game for us. We took great heart from that victory. The conditions had favoured England, yet we had beaten them at their own game.

There was a huge build-up for the final against the West Indies and we were keyed up, but mildly confident, as the hour arrived. The Windies batted first and early in the piece Roy Fredericks hooked me high over the fine leg boundary, but he just toppled on to the stumps in doing so and we had the early break we wanted. In fact, we progressed well to have them 3 for 50, but then Rohan Kanhai and Clive Lloyd came together to turn the flow of the game. We gave them both a chance early. I dropped Rohan from a difficult running chance at fine leg and Ross Edwards turfed Clive low down and hard at mid-wicket. Clive went on to bat superbly and scored 102 in a partnership worth 149 and finally their innings ended at 8 for 291. It was more than they should have made, but then that's cricket.

Still we thought we could get the runs, because it was an excellent batting track. If it hadn't been for some brilliant fielding by Viv Richards, which resulted in 3 runouts at the top of the order, we might well have won. The annoying thing was the way a couple of the runouts happened—trying to steal a run off a misfield. Our ninth wicket fell at 233, but still Thommo and I thought we were in with a chance. Certainly, the West Indies fans thought the game was going to end at any moment, because thousands of them lined the boundary, taking up the 'on your marks' position each time their bowler ran in to us. But as our partnership grew and the gap was narrowed, so their spirits were dampened and the chants and the banging quietened. Thommo and I found the runs were coming fairly easily as the shadows lengthened over Lord's.

Then Thommo hit one straight to Roy Fredericks at mid-off and was apparently caught. The noise of the crowd had covered a 'no-ball' call and the multitudes came streaming on to the ground to celebrate what they thought must be a West Indies victory. 'Freddo' had heard the call and he shied at the bowler's end stumps in an effort to run me out. The ball missed and went away towards the mid-wicket boundary under the feet of the stampede. Thommo and I took off for some runs. I can't recall how many we ran, it could have been 3 or 4 before we thought we'd better stop in case one of the West Indies fieldsmen had found the ball and was creeping up through the milling crowd to run one of us out. The umpires conferred and one walked up under the scoreboard to indicate that we'd scored just the 2 or 3 runs. It was hilarious, to say the least.

We still needed 18 from something like 10 balls . . . we thought we could do it. It only needed a lucky 6 to bring that target down to something within reason. Then Thommo ran down the track to hit one, missed and was run out when Deryck Murray behind the stumps rolled the ball up underarm and hit the sticks. It was all over. A memorable game had ended in a grey light at a quarter to nine.

There followed a fantastic spectacle as the West Indies supporters gathered at the Nursery End and formed a conga line to snake their way up to stand beneath the Pavilion and call for their heroes on the players' balcony. At the head of the mob was an impromptu steel band with dozens of 'players' banging together anything from two beer cans to rubbish bin lids and yet evoking a melodic tune. It was another day in cricket that I'll never forget, and it capped off a highly successful venture. I was thrilled to learn later that it was planned to make the World Cup a four-yearly event . . . I could see it was going to become a very important and most prestigious part of the world cricketing calendar.

Now for the second part of our mission—four Tests against the old foe. We ended up winning the series one-nil, more by good luck than better play. Our good fortune began with the first Test at Edgbaston, when Mike Denness made what turned out to be his final mistake as captain of an England team. He sent us in after winning the toss and that was the first time any England captain had made that choice at Edgbaston. After a good all-round batting performance we were dismissed for 359. Then, one over into the England innings there was a thunderstorm which flooded the uncovered wicket. So we tore into them on a rain-affected pitch and won by an innings and 85 runs. Thommo bowled exceptionally well in the second innings for his figures of 5 for 38 from 18 eighteen overs. One of those victims was a young fellow called Graham Gooch, playing in his first Test—and the poor chap bagged a 'pair'. What a way to start a Test career!

After that debacle, following hard on the heels of their thrashing in Australia, the England selectors made important moves. First, they sacked Denness as captain and appointed the brash Tony Greig. They also dumped experienced batsman Keith Fletcher and picked two newcomers to Test cricket in Bob Woolmer and David Steele, both of whom would have a telling influence on the remainder of the series. Most of us had expected the axe to fall on Denness and the logical successor was Greig, who had enjoyed fantastic success in Test cricket.

I must admit I felt sorry for Denness because he was such a nice fellow. Sadly, he just wasn't what I would call a good enough player for Test cricket. He'd been through the horrors in Australia, then had failed twice at Edgbaston, though admittedly the wicket was tricky. But, even so, to be dropped as captain during a series must have been a humiliating experience.

But what of the man who stepped into his shoes? I thought perhaps his aggressive attitude on the field would carry through in his captaincy, but it never really emerged. There was a lot of the traditional English approach in his leadership: wait a bit until your opponent's down, then strike hard; level off again and re-group before launching another attack when the occasion arises; then hopefully win, but if that's not to be, happily settle for a draw.

Having said that, I'd have to say that his strong competitive spirit tended to lift the players around him and get a bit more out of them. But the responsibility seemed to make him a little more conservative with his own game. When batting, he just didn't take the risks any more. When he was bowling, he seemed to cast aside the inventive and exploratory style and opted instead for more of a line and length routine. He batted a bit more as though he felt *he* had to make runs for the side to succeed and at times I thought he bowled himself rather too much. As a person he didn't change all that much with his new role. On the field he and I tended to clash, but that was part of the scenario. Off the field I always found him a good bloke.

Greigy's aggressive nature was typified by one instance when he toured Australia with the Rest of the World side in 1971-72. In the game against Western Australia in Perth he bowled a string of bouncers at our tail-enders, being particularly hard on Bob Massie. We fronted Greigy in the dressing-room while having a drink after play that day and he bounced right back.

'I'm happy to be bounced by anybody,' he said, 'so I'll bowl bouncers to whoever I like.' That's all very well, but it doesn't necessarily endear you to the opposition—not that I've ever thought that mattered to Greigy. He had something of the Australian in him: get in there and win, at all cost.

Later in his career, and particularly in his days with World Series Cricket, Greigy became less and less liked by the Australians. He became a bit more serious and some of his statements were a bit heavy. And, of course, he wasn't playing so well. He found that while you can get away with a bit of carry-on when you're making runs and taking wickets, it soon wears a bit thin when you're not. Another example of this a couple of years later was Derek Randall, the cheeky little England batsman who got plenty of laughs when he was on top, but became a bit of a yawn when his batting fell to bits.

In the second Test at Lord's, Greigy immediately lifted his game with a good 96 after going to the wicket with the score at 4 for 49. At the other end was the 'Grey Ghost', David Steele, who showed his relish for a scrap against some pretty hostile fast bowling. The pair put on 96 in a gritty stand. Steele made 50 and was a thorn in our side for the remainder of the series. He seemed to have no worries whatsoever about who was bowling, propping on the front foot the whole time and just digging in for long stays. He played more or less the sheet anchor role from number three, but that was just the stiffening that England needed. A lot of their batsmen were still a bit shell-shocked after the tour of Australia.

Steele wasn't a great player by any means, but he was a battler. He knew English conditions very well and was aware that on flat tracks all you have to do is go forward with purpose to be in command. The Lillee-Thomson bowling machine seemed to mean nothing to him and you just had to admire him for the way he fitted in and applied himself to the task. I think we struck on his weaknesses, which were the lofted hook and pull strokes, but we didn't work at them long enough. The West Indies seemed to sort him out on those strokes the following season and that was the end of him. His main problem with those two strokes was the fact that he had to go into them from a front-foot position and so couldn't control them or bring them down well enough.

Bob Woolmer was picked to fill an all-rounder's role. He was no champion with his medium-pacers, though he did stick at them admirably. However, he did impress greatly with the bat. He was one of England's better players from the viewpoint of technique, strokeplay and good old-fashioned guts and determination. Anyway, back to the second Test.

Thanks largely to Steele and Greig, England made 315. Then John Snow bowled superbly and we really had to struggle for runs. In the middle of a string of failures by our top-order batsmen, Ross Edwards made a typically gritty 99—and if ever an innings deserved a century it was that one. But they say that some 99s will be better remembered than if they had been converted to a three-figure score. I must admit I enjoyed this innings more than somewhat because I ended up making 73 not out and even figuring in a last wicket stand of 69 with Ashley Mallett.

Though they led by 47 on the first innings, England seemed happy enough to play for a draw. John Edrich, whose technique and approach to the task of batting I've admired so much, was in the vanguard with a mammoth stay at the crease ... 538 minutes for his 175 runs. Greig finally declared with England leading by 483 and the inevitable draw eventuated. But the latter stages of the game didn't pass without incident—during the afternoon of the fourth day a rather well-built young man took it into his head to shed his clothes and run naked across the ground. He was the first streaker in a Test on English soil. He showed great daring by hurdling the stumps at either end before being apprehended and led away by a couple of Bobbies.

I must admit it was rather funny at the time, but as the years rolled on and streakers became more and more frequent their intrusion onto the field of play became rather boring. Also, I always thought it wouldn't have been so bad if we'd been interrupted by naked ladies, rather than boozy, beer-gutted men. Then, one day in Perth it happened. We were playing a Sheffield Shield game against South Australia when over the fence came three naked nymphs (or so we thought). Now that *was* a hoot, especially when the police started chasing them and the girls got into top gear. The lads all took their pick as to which one looked the best and there were a few red faces about when those who had chosen the willowy brunette were later told that 'she' was a 'he'.

The third Test at Headingley was, sadly, marred by the vandalising of the wicket by a group who were trying to draw attention to the plight of a man in prison. During the night before the last day's play, which promised a thrilling battle for victory, they got into the ground and splattered oil on the wicket and hacked it up with a knife. I couldn't help thinking at the time that a knife wouldn't have done much good on my home ground wicket at the WACA Ground in Perth—maybe a coal chisel and a sledge hammer would've! It was a shame that the game had to be drawn in this manner, because we had still needed 225 runs to win with 3 wickets down and had fancied our chances of getting them. As it turned out, rain fell for most of the day anyway, so the draw was on the cards either way.

Once again, though, David Steele was a major contributor with the bat in that game. In fact, his 6 innings against us in the 3 Tests he played were: 50, 45, 73, 92, 39 and 66. Those runs were all made from the number three position against Thommo and myself in pretty good nick. England 'blooded' another player in this Test, the left-hand orthodox spinner Phil Edmonds and he bowled remarkably well. In his first Test innings he claimed 5 wickets for 28 runs and was an excellent foil for the veteran Derek Underwood, who in that game became the fourth England bowler to claim 200 wickets in Test cricket.

It was a true tragedy that politics had interfered with a Test match. I suppose my first thoughts after learning what had happened to the wicket should have been, 'What a shame the game won't be played out,' but I've got to be honest and state that inside I was screaming 'You beauty, we've retained the Ashes!' That's an indication of how strongly your feelings ride when there's an Ashes series in progress. My mind also travelled back to the same ground in 1972 and I did feel it was almost like poetic justice that the England players were robbed of what they considered to be a very good chance of winning the corresponding Test in 1975. But the less said about the implications of people tearing up Test match wickets in clandestine night-time raids, the better.

The final Test at The Oval is one I'll remember for a long, long time—mainly because we were in the field for a long, long time in England's second innings. We batted first and scored 532 for 9 declared, with Ian Chappell making a magnificent century in his last Test appearance as Australian captain. We then had England out in a hurry and enforced the follow-on with a lead of 341. However, our hopes of an easy victory were ground into the unresponsive turf of The Oval track. England made 538 in an innings lasting 886 minutes—that's more than two days and one session on top of the time it took us to dismiss them in the first innings! It was England's second highest score against Australia and the lynch-pin was the score of 149 by Woolmer. He reached his century in 394 minutes to record the slowest hundred in Tests against Australia.

You can just imagine how we were going towards the end of all that. At the grounds in England it's traditional for a five-minute bell to be rung before the start of each session of play. Well, in the end that bell began to haunt us. We'd hear it and there'd be a chorus of 'Oh no, not again!' as we'd rise to go out on the field for yet another session of torture. England's sixth wicket fell at 522 and thank goodness for that. Doug Walters cleaned up the remainder in short order and they were out by tea on the last day. This meant we had to bat for the final session. However, we were all so used to answering that bell that when it sounded to call the England fieldsmen and our two batsmen and at least half of us leapt to our feet, crying, 'Oh no, not again!'

During that marathon innings we had a fair amount of trouble with the balls being used. This wicket was hard and dead and the balls just kept on falling to bits. At one stage I was trying to bowl fast with something that looked as though it had been through a mincer. I approached umpire 'Dicky' Bird and asked him if he would change the ball. He examined it and replied that I should keep on bowling with it. I said, 'I'm not going to bowl with that thing. No batsmen has to bat with an inferior bat. It's out of shape and split and I'd like it changed.'

Dicky said, 'No . . . and will you please complete the over.' I had the feeling he just wanted to have his way and that he would change that ball at the end of the over, so I just dug my heels in.

'No,' I said, 'no way . . . you change it, I'm not going to try to bowl fast with that thing.'

Dicky bounced back, 'Please Dennis, complete the over.' Again I refused, so he called Ian Chappell up and told him he'd have a look at it at the end of the over.

Ian looked over to me and said, 'You'd better complete the over, pal.' I said I would, but only bowling off-spinners. At the end of the over Dicky said they were two of the best offies he's ever seen!

Trust Dicky to put the matter to rest in such a manner . . . he really is a very funny man, apart from being one of the best umpires I've seen in my career. He gets on very well with all the Australian players and loves to have a chat with us over a pint after play or even occasionally out on the ground, where you might make a comment and he'll come back with his thoughts on it. It's a great thing for players to feel they can relate to an umpire as a human being—though not to the extent of overdoing it. I'm sure Dicky would be the first to pull the reins—if he felt he had to. But his attitude certainly makes you feel more at ease with umpires' decisions. Mind you, it's a natural thing with Dicky. I for one wouldn't like to see all umpires trying to act the same way.

And so came to an end a tough campaign. We all thought it had been a reasonably successful tour, confirming our high ranking on the Test ladder and establishing us for once as capable exponents of the one-day game. We had gone to England feeling very raw at one-day cricket, perhaps because of a lack of experience, and were thrilled to have reached the final and gone so close to winning the trophy. However, there was a tinge of sadness for all of us when the tour was over because we realised it was the end of an era—'Bertie' Chappell was retiring as Australian captain after a record thirty consecutive appearances as skipper. His period of tenure in the job, beginning late in the 1970-71 season in the series against Ray Illingworth's England side, had been a wonderful time for Australia in international cricket.

His thirty games as captain had produced fifteen victories, five losses and ten drawn games, but you can't tell the Ian Chappell story in terms of figures alone. When he took over the side it was at a very low ebb and he assumed the role in unfortunate circumstances, replacing the sacked Bill Lawry. But right from the outset he was positive in his resolve to see us back at the top of the tree. There's no doubt he achieved that, with victories over England and the West Indies in successive home series. Ian was always a 'lead by example' skipper. Because he set such a brilliant example, and his great skills blended beautifully with a dogged determination, he had to be a winner. He was always approachable, loved a laugh and, above all, loved the guys and they loved him. Playing under Ian Chappell you always felt you were part of a *team* . . . that's the ultimate tribute to a captain.

4. West Indies in Australia 1975-76

The 1975-76 season produced a real mixed bag for me personally, but for obvious reasons it was a summer to remember . . . after all, Australia did defeat the West Indies five-one in a marvellous head-to-head conflict. However, before the series even got under way I had my ups and downs. For a start when I returned from England I had to face up to the fact that because of the pressures of Test cricket, with all of its commitments, including advertising and promotions, I was unemployed. It wasn't a lot of fun and I did feel deeply concerned about the future for my family.

Later that summer I received extremely strong overtures to up camp and move to Brisbane and play cricket for Queensland. In fact, the radio station 4IP approached me and asked me to virtually name my own price to move North. I have to admit that I gave their offer a lot of thought, but in the long term I chose to remain in Perth and hope for the best. I had a strong 'gut feeling' that I could make it on my own in my home State and for many reasons I was subsequently glad I'd resisted the temptation. My fast bowling mate Jeff Thomson, who was in his second season for Queensland, ended up striking a contract with 4IP worth a staggering $633,000 over 10 years.

That record contract put a few smiles on Thommo's face and good luck to him. My smiles came when I was named vice-captain of the West Australian side. Our regular captain, John Inverarity, was to leave Australia for England on a teaching assignment early in the season and he stood down for Rod Marsh to take over. It was a great thrill to have been recognised in such a manner by my own State and both Rod and I only wished things could have worked out better for the team in our first season. We won four out of our eight games, but finished a distant third behind South Australia in the Sheffield Shield, a bit of a let-down after having won the season before.

Our third game of the Shield season, against Victoria in Perth, was one I'd rather forget. I was bowling away against my old mate Max 'Tangles' Walker, Victoria's number nine batsman, when it hap-

53

pened. I dropped one a bit short—it came to him about chest high—and as he fended it off the ball flew from the top edge of his bat straight into his face. Tangles hit the deck like a pole-axed boxer down for the count. The only trouble was I didn't think he'd ever come up! He lay there, face down with his head buried in his gloved hands, for what seemed like a couple of minutes. And he didn't move a muscle . . . for one ugly moment I thought perhaps I'd killed him!

Thank goodness he started to move convulsively, then I heard him moan and saw him raise his head from his blood-soaked gloves. Tangles was okay! He was placed on a stretcher and carried off to be rushed to hospital where he was detained. The innings ended not long after and I made a bee-line for the Victorian dressing-room to get the latest report on my mate. To my dismay I was greeted by an extremely hostile reception. Strange to say, the loudest noise came from one of the Victorian fast bowlers who had been making a habit of purposely bowling 'head balls' at our tail-enders for quite some time. I remained in that room just long enough to give that fellow a few reminders.

Rod Marsh will have more pleasant memories about the 2 Victorian innings in that game. In the first innings he took 6 catches and in the second 5 (in all, 5 of them off my bowling) to equal the world record for the number of catches by a wicketkeeper in a first-class game. That record was held by Arnold Long, of Surrey. We had to chase 161 runs for victory and got them with 4 wickets in hand. With only a few runs remaining to knock off, John Inverarity, who had given long and distinguished service to the side, came in for his farewell innings before leaving for England . . . and was run out without scoring. What a way to go!

And so to the Test series against Clive Lloyd's Caribbean cavaliers, who a few months earlier had been our conquerors in the Prudential World Cup final. Going into the first Test in Brisbane, I summed up our opposition. I'd had a good look at most of them as a 'spectator' in the West Indies in 1973 and then had a refresher course on them in England during the World Cup. I knew they were a pretty good side who'd be hard to beat, but I felt that their style of game depended on confidence and the run of the ball and the game. In those circumstances we bowlers had a vital role to play, to get a few of their key players early, then anything could happen. And I had our guns aimed at Alvin Kallicharran and Clive Lloyd as their main danger men.

Our batting looked to have great stability with Ian and Greg

Chappell and Ian Redpath in the top half, while Jeff Thomson was in devastating form going into the series. Bowling for Queensland against Western Australia in Perth a few weeks before, Thommo had bowled as well as I'd ever seen him. It looked like being a top series between two great and positive playing sides. What a disappointment all round when we arrived in Brisbane to find that there were major problems with the wicket at the 'Gabba. As an army of men scrambled over it on the day before the Test was due to get under way, the track looked more like a disaster area than a Test wicket. It was just another example of trouble with the wicket or the weather in Brisbane and I couldn't help thinking then that any city but Brisbane should get the first Test of a summer.

Well, the West Indies won the toss and chose to bat first. What followed certainly wasn't what you'd expect on the first day of the first Test of a series which was being touted as deciding the best cricket team in the world. In no time they were 6 for 99 as their batsmen just threw everything at almost every ball. They got into trouble and then tried to hit their way out of trouble—it's inevitable that your luck will run out when you try to do that.

By far our best bowler was Gary 'Gus' Gilmour, a remarkable fact because he had such a bad case of pre-Test nerves that he couldn't sleep the night before. Neither could his room-mate, who had to keep examining a callous on Gus' left hand and assuring him that it wouldn't spoil his bowling. As that room-mate, I was rather glad Gus took 4 wickets the next day, ensuring the chance of some good sleep for both of us from then on.

Maybe as a result of that sleepless night, I didn't bowl all that well in either innings, but I did pick up 3 in each and my second victim for the game, Viv Richards, went down in the record book as my 100th Test scalp. In contrast to my forecasts, Thommo bowled only fairly well and, in fact, suffered a warning from umpire Tom Brooks for some short-pitched deliveries he sent down to tail-ender Inshan Ali in the West Indies' second innings. But the highlight of an easy victory for Australia was Greg Chappell's performance in scoring a century in each innings. It was the first time that such a 'double' had been achieved by a player in his first Test as captain . . . further proof, if it was ever needed, of Greg's great ability as a batsman.

Bolstered by an 8-wicket victory we bounced into Perth for the second Test—and how Australia came crashing to the ground, with an innings defeat early on the fourth day. Aided by a spate of dropped catches and brilliant centuries from Roy Fredericks and

Clive Lloyd, the tourists led us by 256 on the first innings. In that West Indies innings of 585, 4 of our bowlers, Thomson, Gilmour, Mallett and Lillee, all conceded more than 100 runs and Walker was hit for 99. Then we were absolutely blitzed by the cat-like Andy Roberts, who took the first 7 in our order in 14 devastating overs. It was spine-chilling savagery, the best performance by a West Indian against Australia and probably the best I've seen by a fast bowler. He was extremely quick and exceptionally accurate.

There was an interesting sidelight to this Test match. Some boffins from the University of Western Australia took the opportunity to have a very close look at a line-up of some of the world's fastest bowlers. They set up photosonic equipment on one of the square boundaries and timed us all for speed through the air. Thommo was clocked at 99.68 miles an hour, just a tick off the magical 'ton', while Michael Holding was the fastest in consistency with an average of 92 mph over a period. Andy Roberts' fastest delivery was 93.6 mph and my own was 86.4, though I had a heavy cold during the Test and consider I could have done a little better.

From there on in the series was all Australia. We hit right back after the hiding we received in Perth to win by 8 wickets in Melbourne. Thommo and I at last got into stride and cleaned them out in the first innings and then we took a lead of 261, thanks to a fine century by Ian Redpath and then a 'ton' in his maiden Test innings by a tall, bulky red-headed young fellow called Gary Cosier. Only 22 years of age, Cosier showed great powers of concentration and even dominated a stand of 114 with Greg Chappell. The powerfully built youngster really caught the eye, with his strength off the back foot, particularly square of the wicket on the off side.

My old 'partner in crime' Rod Marsh was in devastating form behind the stumps. He took 3 catches in the first innings, then had 5 out of the first 7 wickets to fall in the second innings. At that stage he had four off my bowling for the match and was staring at equalling Gil Langley's world record for the number of dismissals in a Test match. Knowing how sharp Rod is behind the stumps, you'd have thought he'd only have needed half a chance to be up there sharing that record. Well, in fact, he had two stumping chances that I'm sure he'd have 'eaten' earlier in the game—and missed them both. It just wasn't Rod's style.

Unfortunately I had to miss the fourth Test in Sydney as I was unwell. I just couldn't get myself going and I knew there was something wrong. Doctors had thought the trouble was a virus infection and recommended rest. However, on the night before the last day of the Test things worsened and when I awoke that morning I felt really ill, particularly around the chest and back. So I went to a new doctor and he administered new tests and some treatment. That meant the better part of the day being X-rayed, giving blood samples and undergoing tests. Finally it was decided I had pleurisy and I was put on a course of treatment, which thankfully had me back on deck quite soon.

Our attack of Thomson, Gilmour and Walker did wonderfully well, particularly in the second innings when the Windies were fired out for 128. Thommo bowled really quickly and claimed 6 in that innings. Greg Chappell was at his very best with an unbeaten 182 in the first innings. It was his third 'ton' for the series and seemingly the West Indies bowlers had no answer to his superb technique and his great determination. His brother, Ian, was at the centre of a rather controversial umpiring decision on the first innings. The tourists gave a great appeal for caught behind the wicket off the first ball Ian faced from young Michael Holding, but umpire Reg Ledwidge ruled 'not out'. The West Indies players just couldn't believe it and Holding took ages to come to terms with things and get back to bowl the next ball. He was obviously very emotionally upset, but he showed great maturity by going back to work and getting Ian's wicket a couple of overs later.

I was certainly in no position to say whether or not Ian had hit that one or if Ledwidge's decision was good or bad. However, the fact of the matter is that Ian Chappell was such a strong competitor that there's no way he'd have 'walked' on the appeal, whether or not he thought he was out. And I don't blame him. I think the umpires are out there to do a job and it's much better if they don't have to endure players making their decisions for them. That can throw confusion into their minds and influence them if a player who normally walks, for once stands his ground. Some umpires won't have a bar of it, either ... like the West Australian umpire who was in charge of proceedings when Graeme Watson gave himself out while playing for WA in a Shield game. The umpire considered it had not been a catch and the next break in play went to the scorers and ordered them to mark 'retired' next to 'Beatle's' name in the scorebook.

I suppose I'll always remember the fifth Test at Adelaide and I'll probably be labelled a 'spoilt child' when I give the reason. I came back in after my illness and Max Walker lost his place, but I lost my place at the head of the Australian attack with the new ball. For reasons best known to himself, in both innings Greg Chappell gave the new ball to Jeff Thomson and Gary Gilmour. We batted first and made 418, with Ian Redpath making his second century of the series, and still I had no inkling of Greg's plan to make me a first-change bowler. In fact, it wasn't until we were actually out on the ground and I was going through the motions of warming up to my task that Greg told me what was happening and then threw the ball to 'Gus'. I was most unhappy, to say the very least, firstly for not being given the new ball, but mainly for the way I wasn't told until the last minute.

Once more the Australian pacemen troubled the tourists and we led handsomely on the first innings. After a second innings declaration, leaving the Windies 490 to get for victory, we went on to win quite comfortably—but not before witnessing a magnificent innings from Viv Richards. Opening the batting, he scored 101 in 182 minutes and the knock included 17 boundaries. It was easy to see why Viv was nicknamed 'Smokin' Joe' after the former world heavy-weight boxing champion, Joe Frazier. He just came out slugging and didn't know when he was beaten ... or, rather, when his team was beaten. Richards is very powerful and when he hits you, you stay hit. And he goes after the good balls, not just the loose ones. He's a truly exciting player.

The sixth Test in Melbourne was a mere formality, it seemed, as we won outright by a massive 162 runs to clinch the series five-one. It was almost unbelievable that we could have been so dominant. I didn't think at any stage that there was so much difference between the two teams. The game had considerable significance for a few individuals. For a start Lance Gibbs bettered Freddie Trueman's world record of 307 wickets in Tests when he had Gary Gilmour leg before wicket in the first innings and later in the same innings he had Ian Redpath caught to claim his 309th and last Test wicket. Lance retired at the end of that Test and brought to a close a marvellous career. He played the game hard and well and was always a pleasant opponent.

It was also the last game (or so we believed at the time) for two big-name Australian players in Ian Chappell and Ian Redpath. Both men had enjoyed outstanding careers for their country and both had made big contributions to our victory over the West Indies. Ian Chappell was 32 years old and in his 72 Tests had scored 5187 runs, including 14 centuries, at the good average of 42.86. It was difficult to comprehend that this mighty player, captain and competitor was to be gone from the scene for ever. As it turned out, of course, he was to do it all again as Australia's skipper in World Series Cricket *and* play again for Australia in official Tests.

Not far behind 'Bertie' in ability with the bat was 'Redders', who certainly did go out on a high note, having scored 3 centuries in the 6 Tests of the series. He was 34 and had played in 66 Tests for 4737 runs at the average of 43.45, with 8 centuries. Thin, almost to the extreme of being unhealthily so, Redders was a grand competitor who was always ready for a scrap against the ball, but a real gentleman beneath it all. Australian cricket could ill-afford to lose two players of this calibre in one fell swoop. It was the real beginning of the breaking up of the great Australian team of the Seventies, which had been compared so favourably with Armstrong's team of the Twenties, Bradman's 1948 side in England and Benaud's line-up of the Sixties.

In that final Test Rod Marsh took 6 catches, 4 of them off my bowling, to end the series with 26 victims, thus equalling South African John Waite's world record for the number of dismissals in a series. Thommo ended the series with 29 wickets and I was pleased to have ended up with 27 from just the 5 Tests—9 of those victims being to catches behind the stumps by Marshy. Rod has always been a very important part of my success or failure in Test cricket. He has such sure hands, covers so much ground in width to snap up the half chances and is so helpful in offering little titbits of advice here and there, which are usually spot on.

At the end of the series the West Indies captain Clive Lloyd tried to dismiss his team's failure by claiming that competing in the English County competition had ruined his players. That may have been a factor, but certainly there wasn't a lot of discipline and depth about their game. We found that if they lost a key wicket or two they were immediately under the hammer ... they didn't seem to have any idea of consolidating an innings. They continued to attack when the battle was going against them, rather than digging in, defending and staying there. Admittedly the Australian batsmen almost invariably gave their bowlers big scores to work with and that put tremendous pressure on the Windies batsmen.

Despite the loss of Ian Chappell and Redpath, I felt that we were on top to stay for a while. We had 'blooded' some good young talent in Graham Yallop and Gary Cosier and other relatively new boys like Thommo, Alan Turner and Gary Gilmour had all blossomed over the season. Add to that our 'oldies' Greg Chappell and Rod Marsh and there was the nucleus for Australia to go on from strength to strength. As for my own position, I felt there were a few more handy years to go.

5. Pakistan and
New Zealand 1976-77

When I look back on the many seasons I've played in senior cricket, I suppose it will be hard to find a season more interesting, more exciting and more satisfying, both from a team and a personal point of view, than the summer of 1976-77. Australia played a total of six Tests against three different countries during that period, drawing one-all in the three-Test series against Pakistan, winning one-nil in New Zealand then triumphing in the fabulous Centenary Test against England in Melbourne. I played in all those Tests and must have hit a real 'purple patch', because I captured a total of 47 wickets in the 6 games, taking 10 or more wickets in a game 3 times in the space of 5 of them.

In all Test and first-class games for Australia and Western Australia during that wonderful summer I took 93 wickets from 477.4 overs at an average of 18.92. I seemed to just bowl and bowl. It was no wonder that at the end of it all I was a spent force (with a set of vertebrae to match) and had to withdraw from selection for the 1977 tour of England. But I enjoyed every minute of that glorious summer. Of course the cream on the cake was the Centenary Test victory, which I'll come to later, but I must say I got almost as much pleasure out of the fact that I was vice-captain of the West Australian team which won the Sheffield Shield-Gillette Cup double. It was the first time such a double had ever been posted in Australian cricket and there's a marvellous story to be told about the Gillette Cup victory, with two most memorable games.

I'll also deal with that story as the season unfolds. Of course this summer was also spiced by the behind-the-scenes beginnings of World Series Cricket and I was very much a part of all the secret machinations, which came to a peak as the season drew to a close. The fact that I was closely involved, and that most of the senior Australian players became privy to the WSC operation at some time during the season, somewhat puts the lie to all those claims that the 1977 tour of England was ruined by the so-called 'evil' effects of WSC. I thought we all played pretty well during 1976-77, particu-

61

larly in the later stages when we crushed New Zealand and then won the Centenary Test.

The first part of the summer was devoted to a visit by Mushtaq Mohammad's Pakistanis. Going into that three-Test series I couldn't see them being good enough to win a single Test. I thought their bowlers just couldn't dismiss Australia for reasonably low scores twice in the same match. I could see they had the potential to make lots of runs, but they just seemed to lack fire power in attack. On the other hand, I thought we'd cover up pretty well for the retirement of several senior players and still field a good all-round side. I thought we looked potent in attack and deep in batting, particularly with the return of Doug Walters who had missed the previous summer with a knee injury.

Of course, all my calculations were made without reckoning on the fact that only an hour or so after the series began in Adelaide we'd lose the services of Jeff Thomson for the remainder of the summer. Thommo seems to have had his fair share of misfortune in Adelaide. He badly damaged his right shoulder in a collision with Alan Turner as they both went for a skied catch. Then, to make matters even worse in that opening innings, we dropped one catch after another and bowled poorly to give them a chance of making a good start. Even so, we had Pakistan out for 272 and then, thanks to fine centuries from Ian Davis and Doug Walters, took a big first-innings lead.

But in the second innings we soon found that bowling without Thommo was real hard graft. To make matters even tougher for Australia, I was nursing a hamstring strain and Gary Gilmour had ankle problems. We just had to chisel away at the Pakistanis and by the time that innings had finished I'd bowled 47.7 (8-ball) overs and Kerry O'Keeffe had sent down 53. That left us a target of 285 runs to score in 319 minutes and in the end we fell just 24 runs short, to draw the game. It was quite a controversial finish.

We were 6 down (and virtually 7, because there was no way Thommo could have batted) going into the compulsory final 15 overs and we needed 56 more runs for victory. Rod Marsh and Gary Cosier were at the crease at the beginning and the end of that period and, boy, did they come in for some 'stick' from the Press and public for not risking their wickets to have a do-or-die crack at victory.

As far as Kerry O'Keeffe and I were concerned, all through the time the booing and the slow hand-clapping was going on we were right behind our two team-mates out there in the middle. Had they thrown the Test away, it would have meant we had wasted our time bowling ourselves into the ground the day before. The stakes were too high for a cavalier approach—Rod and Gary had the responsibility to win or save the match and they saw fit to save it. And when you face facts, we should have stitched the game up long before those final 15 overs. Our catching and fielding was just too sloppy for words ... plus the loss of our spearhead Thommo didn't help matters all that much.

Those matters were put right in the second Test at Melbourne, when we put the Pakistanis through the wringers and won by 348 runs. However, during this game I got into hot water over bowling bouncers. It was unbelievable, but there I was being warned in my second over (on the dead MCG track, too, if you don't mind!) for digging them in to opener Sadiq Mohammad. This was half-way through the second day, too, after we'd made 517 for 8 wickets down before declaring. I guess I was guilty of then losing my cool, but my reaction was to try to point up the futility of it all by standing at the crease and making out to bowl an underarm delivery. Then I saw a balloon blowing on to the ground and thought it might be appropriate for me to bowl with it. And at the end of it all I had a fairly interesting exchange with some of the 'gentlemen' sitting on their fat backsides in front of the Members' Stand.

After I'd had a bit of a chat with Greg Chappell things cooled down a little. I returned to the attack later to collect 6 wickets for 82, which in a way undermined the point I had been trying to make. We narrowly failed to force the follow-on and our batsmen went out there to get runs on the board quickly and set up the outright victory. In their second innings the tourists crumbled pathetically and I was more than pleased to have picked up 4 more wickets for a match haul of 10 for 135, my first 10-wicket bag in Tests. And it was a thrill to be named man-of-the-match. I had had a few points to prove, not just about the umpire's reaction to my bowling bumpers at an opening batsman. By this time I'd got well and truly tangled up with the Pakistani hierarchy because of my writings in a Melbourne newspaper.

The Pakistani manager, Colonel Shuja Ud-Din, had fired an early broadside about members of the Australian team writing for newspapers. He claimed it was 'immoral and absurd' that we had the right to write, saying it gave us a 'great psychological advantage' over his team. He then put in the barb by saying that half of us were 'illiterate'. A few days later he said that he 'loved and adored' me, so he wasn't quite sure what he was feeling. However, he must have been acutely embarrassed when his captain Mushtaq defied his orders and began writing for an opposition Melbourne newspaper. I'd say the running battle gave us Australians plenty of ammunition to fire ourselves up against the Pakistanis—it was almost a game within a game.

Oh, how the mighty fell when we played the third Test in Sydney! We just couldn't withstand a withering attack by Imran Khan, who bowled very fast and beautifully to take 6 wickets in each innings. Imran is a superb natural athlete, but on top of that he's a thinker and a fighter, too. He never gives up. He improved so much as the tour progressed that I couldn't recognise the finished product against what I'd seen of him in England in 1975. At that stage of his career Imran was, if anything, a better batsman than he was a bowler. I'd have described him then as a fair to average medium-paced bowler who could bat. But everything fell into place in Sydney and he looked to be on the springboard. After the Test, and after Imran had been named man-of-the-match, Greg Chappell rated the Pakistani's bowling as among the best performances he'd ever seen by an opposition bowler.

Thanks to Imran's brilliance with the ball and a second century for the series by Asif Iqbal, the tourists were able to cruise to victory by 8 wickets. It was the first ever Test win by Pakistan on Australian soil and they thoroughly deserved it, too. Of course, it made me eat my words right throughout the series that Pakistan couldn't and wouldn't win a single Test. And I was reminded of that more than once! After the series was over and the Pakistanis had left Australia, Asif Iqbal wrote in an Australian cricket monthly a scathing attack on me and my team-mates. He described us as 'very ugly, both in attitude and language on the field'... adding, 'I now know why your team has been called "the ugly Australians".'

Only a few days after the third Test was over there was a new challenge before Rod Marsh and me: to lead our State side to victory in the final of the Gillette Cup, to be played at the Melbourne Cricket Ground. To reach that final we had narrowly won against South Australia in the first round, then had miraculously won our semi-final against Queensland in Perth in what was immediately dubbed throughout WA as 'The Miracle Match'. When you think that we batted first in that game against Queensland, were bundled out for just 77 on a bit of a 'greentop' and then proceeded to win the match comfortably, you'll realise why that title was so univer-

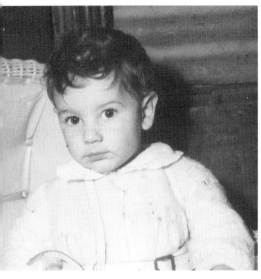

Guess who?

Mum, me, Trevor, Dad and Carmen.

At least Ron Barassi seemed to think it was funny...

A guest on the Michael Parkinson show.

Botham and Lillee swap stories.

A catch of a different kind . . . the spoils of a day's
fishing with my partner in speed, Jeff Thomson.

A rare moment with the Old Master himself . . . Sir Donald Bradman.

With a couple of old mates, Greg Chappell and Rod Marsh, after appearing in my own *This is your Life* programme.

Opposite: Advance Australia
. . . at last I'm allowed out of
hospital at the start of the 1981
England tour.

Above: Solid follow-through
during a one-day International
against England at Lord's in
1981.

Right: Back in the nets at Lord's
soon after release from hospital
in 1981 and that sunshine's a
marvellous tonic!

What's going on here?... the umpire's arm pulls me up short during the third Test against England at Leeds in 1981.

Always a magic moment . . . meeting Her Majesty at Lord's in 1981.

On your way, son . . . Graham Gooch is out for 10 in the first innings of
the first Test at Trent Bridge in 1981.

Opposite: The thorn is plucked . . . my old mate Rod Marsh hugs the ball
in his gloves after catching Ian Botham, thorn in our side during the
1981 England tour, in the fourth Test at Birmingham.

Geared up for a stint with the bat.

A typical Lillee pose, triumphant after gaining another victim.

Richie Benaud hands over the Australian Test wicket-taking record at
the MCG in the 1980-81 series against India.

Above: What better . . . a big steak and a pint to keep body and soul together during the 1981 tour of England.

Right: Yoga for a change? . . . no, I'm merely exercising in my motel room to keep up muscle tone while on tour.

That craggy face has meant a lot to me in the latter stages of my career . . . Austin Robertson senior giving Craig Serjeant and me valuable hints on the art of running.

sally applied. As we went out to defend our 'magnificent' total, three-quarters of the WA fans who had been at the ground were on the way home and as big a proportion of the local television audience had switched off in disgust.

And, just quietly, I suspect that most of my team-mates also thought the result was a foregone conclusion in favour of Queensland. After all, they had Viv Richards and Greg Chappell in their batting line-up, didn't they? Well, I thought there was just a slight chance we'd turn the tide and I was prepared to give it a go—which I shouted to my team-mates as we filed out of the dressing-room and on to the ground. Realising that something special would be required to win the match, I went for a different approach when I opened down-wind to Richards. I bowled him a bouncer, then another bouncer, then another—and was quite rightly warned by the umpire. Still, I bowled him a fourth in four balls. Two balls later he missed a straight one and was bowled.

As for Chappell, Marshy sorted that one out. He signalled for a bouncer wide down leg side, which I provided and which Greg hooked at and edged down towards widish fine leg. Trouble was, Rod had placed himself about two slips wide down leg side as I let the ball go and accepted the catch, much to Greg's disbelief. After that, we just waltzed to victory by 15 runs, believe it or not. I suppose you could have said we were simply meant to win the Cup. We did, in fact, win the final in Melbourne, but how, I'm not quite sure to this day. There were 32 903 screaming fans at the MCG—with something like 32 000 of them desperate to go away with a Victorian victory under their belts. And they should have!

Their team batted first and made the not-so-brilliant total of 164. However, thanks to some superb pace bowling by Alan Hurst and Max Walker, we were never quite in the hunt and when our ninth wicket fell with the score on 139 we looked to be gone for all money. The shouts for 'Hursty' and 'Tangles' could have been heard out on Port Phillip Bay as they tore through us. But then our last man Wayne Clark joined Mick Malone and they gradually whittled away the deficit, blessed with a little luck and charged with huge determination. Almost unbelievably we were into the final over and victory was in sight. Mick french-cut the third ball to the fine leg boundary for 4 and we were home. He'd scored 47 and taken 2 wickets—there was no doubting who won the man-of-the-match award! It was, in fact, the fourth time in some 15 months that Mick had played a match-winning hand against Victoria. A rather harassed, but good-humoured, Victorian official poked his head into the WA dressing-room to say above the tumult, 'That's it . . . we're revoking Malone's passport!'

Soon after, it was off to New Zealand for a two-Test series. For mine the tour was marred by terrible playing and practising conditions leading up to the Tests. Some of the provincial wickets were just disgraceful. You could only describe them as 'minefields', particularly one at Wellington. We couldn't do much other than have a slog and hope for the best. It was such that if you treated the situation seriously you could have got your head knocked off. Thank goodness all our batsmen were in pretty good nick from the Australian summer and the Pakistan series. I had a few problems early on, and aggravated a hamstring injury after just a couple of overs in the opening fixture, a one-day affair which we ended up losing.

Then I didn't play for almost a fortnight, until the game against Central Districts at Nelson. The wicket was diabolical, as our first-innings score of 126 would indicate. However, we did come back well to win after a sensational second innings collapse by the locals, when I picked up 4 for 9 from 7 overs. In this game we had a good look at a fellow called Jock Edwards, a chunky batsman and wicket-keeper. He scored 99, 82 of them coming from nineteen 4s and a 6! I played one more game, against Otago at Dunedin, and continued to run into some fitness and form with 3 for 18 from 10 overs in the second innings.

I'll never forget the first Test at Lancaster Park in Christchurch for two reasons. The first was that in the days leading up to the game my wife, Helen, was very sick and in hospital back in Perth. I was in two minds about dropping everything and flying home to be with her. It was a case of not knowing whether she was going to live or die. Finally her specialist spoke to me on the telephone and convinced me there was nothing I could hope to achieve by flying home. He said she'd be in hospital for a couple of weeks, but that she'd be all right. I went into the game, but with my heart not even anywhere near the cricket ground. I was very emotional, almost breaking down throughout my bowling in the first innings. It was a constant battle to stay with it—and the idiots around the ground didn't help, either. I'd sorted myself out a bit before I bowled in the second innings. Also, the doctors back in Perth had told me that Helen was on the mend. Finally I was able to talk to her myself and then I could relax a little and concentrate on the game at hand.

The second reason I'll never forget that game was because in our first innings I saw the finest partnership I've ever seen in any cricket. It was between Doug Walters, who made a record-breaking 250 in breath-taking style, and Gary Gilmour, whose 101 was simply magnificent. The two came together when things weren't too rosy for us at 6 for 208 and their stand produced 217 in 187 minutes, at that stage the highest for the seventh wicket against any country. It was a mixture of constant glorious attacking strokes and excellent defence, because there were periods when the bowlers would tighten up and get on top. That partnership enabled us to reach 552, a record score against New Zealand.

Plenty is known about the ability of Doug Walters, but what of Gilmour? He was an immensely talented fellow with the bat and the ball, as he proved many times. Sadly, during this tour he began a decline that soon saw him out of top-flight cricket. There were all sorts of unfair allegations as to why his bowling dropped off. It was even unfairly rumoured that he suffered from gout from too much drinking. In fact, it was later discovered that the poor fellow had a chip of bone floating about in his ankle. His bowling fell to bits . . . no swing, no cut and his line and length all over the place. But 'Gus' was struggling to run, let alone bowl. He had pure natural talent, but, unfortunately for Australia and for Gus, I don't think he had the true dedication required to stay at the top.

When New Zealand batted in that first Test it wasn't long before Glenn Turner was again the centre of a controversy with his Australian opponents. He seems to have a penchant for this, having crossed swords with Ian Chappell and others in the past. Perhaps he doesn't like Aussies—and I know there are a few Aussies who don't like, or rate, him all that much. I was bowling to him when he snicked one which carried low down to Rick McCosker in the slips. Rick caught it 8-10 centimetres off the ground and held it up and we all naturally appealed for the catch. But Turner stood his ground and the umpire just wouldn't give him out. There was quite a to-do and a few gave vent to their feelings. It was said that I had words with Turner, but in fact I only spoke to Greg Chappell. He told me to forget it and get on with my bowling and I replied, 'He's out and he should go.' Above all else the incident cast a nasty doubt over the integrity of McCosker, who'd have to be the most honest guy you'd meet anywhere.

Turner was a complete washout in the series. Actually he has never appealed to me as a player, though the figures may tell quite a good story about him. I've just never seen him bat well or make a convincing big score. However, though I've never rated him myself, I do know a lot of people who have. The Test ended up being drawn, but we should have won and won easily. Bev Congdon saved them in the second innings, but we dropped him so many times it wasn't funny. We also dropped other catches which could have won us the match. I bowled poorly in the first innings, perhaps because I was too worried about Helen, but a little better in the second. I ended up with just 4 wickets for 189 runs for the game and there were a few needling articles in the local newspapers.

I think I must have been pricked a little by those articles, because I bowled much better in the second Test at Eden Park in Auckland and we won it with almost two days to spare. During that match I picked up my 150th wicket in Tests and ended up with 11 for 123 for the game, a record for all countries on that ground and a record for Australia-New Zealand Tests. We had them out for 229. Then another fine innings of 64 by Gilmour guided us into a winning position. Our seventh wicket fell at 245, but we tail-enders added 132 runs, which enabled australia to lead by 148. batting a second time, the kiwis were soon 5 for 31 and they never recovered from that, despite a fine 81 by Richard Hadlee.

During our first innings a streaker dashed on to the ground and he made the distinct mistake of running straight up to Greg Chappell, who was batting at the time. Greg responded by grabbing the young man and smacking him several times on the backside with the face of his bat, much to the mirth of the crowd and the players. However, Greg's smiles soon disappeared when he was run out off the very next ball—that New Zealand infiltrator *had* done his job well in breaking Greg's concentration! Seriously, though, it can have the effect of throwing a player off the tracks when larrikins take it into their minds to intrude on the field.

6. The Centenary Tests

Surely the most momentous occasions in the long and illustrious history of England-Australia cricket have been the two Centenary Tests—the first at the Melbourne Cricket Ground in March 1977 and the second at Lord's in August and September 1980. The two matches, celebrating one hundred years of Tests on two sides of the world, were cricketing extravaganzas to be remembered forever by those fortunate enough to have been involved. And I was one of them. One of just four players fortunate enough to have been born in the right era and lucky enough to have been chosen to play in both matches. The others were my team-mates Greg Chappell and Rod Marsh and England fast bowler Chris Old.

I treasure many fond memories of those two occasions. First and foremost, the memory of two cricket matches that were filled with high drama and outstanding play. The Melbourne game had special significance for me because I ended up with 11 wickets for the Test and because Australia won the game. Remarkably we won by exactly the same margin as had separated the two countries a hundred years before. There were extraordinary personal performances from Rod Marsh, Rick McCosker, David Hookes and Max Walker for Australia, while England produced the man-of-the-match Derek Randall, and Chris Old bowled extremely well. At Lord's Old bowled well again, Geoff Boycott was England's outstanding batsman and for Australia Kim Hughes and Graeme Wood were stars with the bat and Len Pascoe triumphed with the ball.

But outside the games themselves were two grand social occasions, the biggest line-ups of cricket's notables of the present and past ever assembled. Huge inter-continental jet aeroplanes carried hundreds of former Ashes players to each of the two venues and the presence of many of the greatest names in cricket history added lustre to both events. One gala function after another set the scene for the games that followed, where the players of the day didn't fail their forefathers in the quality of their cricket. At the end of it all, when the farewells were uttered for the last time at Lord's, there was many a secret wish that some time capsule could accommodate attendance at the bi-centennial celebrations.

Having said all of that, I must be honest and admit that as the time drew close for the Melbourne Centenary Test I was a little cynical about the whole operation. I have never been one for cricket nostalgia and above all I was very tired and worn out after a long and arduous season. I was having trouble with my back and at that stage I needed another Test match like I needed another hole in the head. But when I returned to Perth after the short tour of New Zealand, only a couple of weeks before the big match was due to start, the Centenary Test fever hit me square between the eyes. It seemed the whole world was buzzing with excitement about the big event and it was impossible for me not to join in.

To add to all that, no sooner had we landed back in Perth than we were into action playing against the MCC party, who were having just the one warm-up game against WA after a tour of India. WA could easily have won that game which ended up being drawn. Most important, I guess, the game gave us our first look at Derek Randall. I was most impressed by what I saw. Randall is only a little fellow, but didn't he time the ball well . . . he slammed us for a couple of beautiful 4s as soon as he came in in the second innings. And his antics out in the middle were something to behold. As we crossed paths at the end of one over I made a comment to him to the effect that I liked the carefree confident way he played the game. Randall just gave me a cheeky Pommy grin and said, 'Maybe I haven't much ability, but I've a lot of guts.' He was to prove his 'guts' quite soon.

Again in that MCC game I was able to claim Dennis Amiss' wicket in both innings and perhaps as a result of that continued weakness for a fast one outside the off stump, he was dropped down the order for the Centenary Test. That move worked. Amiss got amongst the runs in the second innings of the Test and, with the help of Randall, went awfully close to engineering a remarkable victory against huge odds. In general terms England put up only a fair performance in that Perth match, but they had just come from the slow wickets of India and I knew we could expect much more from them when the acid went on at the MCG the following week.

On our arrival in Melbourne five days before the Test was due to begin, it was immediately quite obvious that much work had been done in preparation for the big occasion. Of course the official planning had begun many months before. Hans Ebeling, the former Australian player and Victorian official, gets the credit for spawning the idea of a major celebration, and it was soon obvious that the marketing and merchandising men were all set for the best cricket show on earth. We were taken straight off the plane to the Victorian Cricket Association reception at the MCG and any doubts I might have had about the magnitude of the occasion were brushed aside that night. Over in one corner were Harold Larwood and Bill Voce chewing the rag about old times together, in another old sparring partners and mates Dennis Compton and Keith Miller ... then I recognised Sir Len Hutton, Cyril Washbrook, Trevor Bailey, Peter May and my old pal John Edrich. All it needed was a tallish, fat doctor with a dark bushy beard to really top things off! I half expected him to walk into that room at any stage, such was the atmosphere of the gathering.

I can remember being overcome by a tingling feeling, a sensation almost too much to comprehend at the time. But that sort of feeling, which I suspect was experienced by many others, set the scene for the whole celebration. I'm definitely not keen on official functions, perhaps because I've been to so many, but I just couldn't help falling into the swing of things with the line-up of functions laid on in those magic few days in Melbourne. In fact, there were a couple of times when this part of it all actually threatened to take over from the main reason that we players were all in Melbourne. However, as the hour drew nigh for the game to get under way we all realised the true significance of the role we were about to play. So, too, did the people of Melbourne who were magnificent in their support—aided, I have no doubt, by several thousand people who had travelled interstate to witness history in the making.

The morning of 12 March produced grey skies, but these weren't enough to keep the crowd away. When the final count was taken on that magnificent first day it was revealed that 61 316 people had gone through the turnstiles, the forerunner of a marvellous gross attendance of just a tick under a quarter of a million. I've always reckoned there would have been an even bigger attendance on the first day if it hadn't been for some Melbourne radio disc jockeys telling listeners to their morning programmes that it looked as though there could be a shortage of room at the ground. They'd been fooled by an unusually heavy rush of early arrivals, people obviously keen to avoid a crush with parking and public transport at an hour closer to the start of play.

Tension built to fever pitch as Greg Chappell and Tony Greig went out to perform the toss. The first blow was landed by England

71

when Greig called successfully and he then raised a few of the pundits' eyebrows by sending Australia in to bat. While our openers prepared themselves in the depths of the dressing-room we watched as former captains of both countries walked on to the ground and were introduced to the huge crowd. That was a good touch and really set the scene. The significantly pro-Australian crowd sat on the edges of their seats no doubt waiting for their team to do its bit ... but how we let them down! Both our openers were gone with just 13 runs on the board and we struggled desperately to reach the 100 mark and were finally dismissed for a meagre 138 three-quarters of an hour after afternoon tea.

It was a disastrous start which seriously threatened to ruin the game as a contest and a spectacle. I am sure the importance of the occasion had a lot to do with the way we fell in such a hole. There were a lot of very nervous strokes played and perhaps Tony Greig had this in mind when he decided to put us in. Still our supporters didn't desert us and when we went out to bowl for the hour or so that remained before stumps there was tremendous cheering and chanting as Max Walker and I threw down the gauntlet to the England openers. I thought we bowled pretty well, too, but at stumps England were looking all right at 1 for 29. Somehow most of us felt we'd still give them a good run for their money. Maybe we wouldn't dismiss them for less than our total, because the pitch was evening out, but we felt they wouldn't lead by too much.

The Englishmen were all smiles after play that day—as they should have been, after all there was no indication then of what was going to happen the next day. Like the proverbial pack of cards, they collapsed in a heap and were all out for 95 soon after lunch. Their top-scorer was Greig with 18 and only 3 others reached double figures. As 'Tangles' and I started to get a run on immediately play resumed the crowd in the outer rose magnificently to almost carry us on their backs. I ended up with 6 for 26, the best figures of my Test career to date, and Tangles took the other 4. So half an hour after lunch on the second day both teams had concluded their first innings, Australia leading by 43 runs. The match was then set for anybody to win.

When the Australian second innings scoreboard showed 3 for 53 with Rick McCosker unlikely to bat because of a broken jaw received while batting in the first innings, I thought perhaps we were going to hand the game to England on a platter. However, a good stand between Ian Davis and Doug Walters saw Australia out of immediate danger. The departure of Davis brought David Hookes to the crease. It was Hookes' maiden Test, but you wouldn't have thought so as he pulverised 5 boundaries off successive deliveries by Greig. That just about brought the house down. He scored 56, but better batting was to come from my mate Rod Marsh. He had already eclipsed Wally Grout's record for the most dismissals by an Australian wicketkeeper in Tests ... now he set out to play the innings of his lifetime.

With a little help from Hookes, Gary Gilmour and me he guided the Australian score along to 353, but then he looked in danger of running out of partners. It was then that Rick McCosker answered his country's call and went out to join him at the fall of the eighth wicket, his broken jaw wired up and his face shockingly swollen. Rick went out against all doctors' advice in one of the most courageous efforts I have ever seen. A further blow to the face could have resulted in unbelievable damage, but he was prepared to take the risk. My eyes welled up with tears as I saw him walk out on to the MCG and you could hear the crowd gasp at the mere sight of him. He scored just 25, which won't amount to much when people look back on the scoresheet, but it was a truly great performance. He helped Rod to a fantastic century and the 54 runs they added was about the difference between the two sides in the final analysis.

Thanks to that rearguard action we were able to declare and set England the seemingly impossible target of 463 to win. Then this wonderful game entered its final, fascinating stage with England making a bold attempt to buck the enormous odds and win. Enter Derek Randall, playing his first Test against Australia. The perky little fellow, who'd done so much to impress me during the MCC game in Perth, far more than realised my expectations of him with a sensational innings of 174 which went awfully close to being a match-winning performance. Sure, we dropped him a few times— but that didn't make an ounce of difference to him. He just kept on attacking and carrying the game right up to the bowlers. With Dennis Amiss he added 166 for the third wicket and England inched closer to the target as the final day progressed, being 2 for 267 at lunch.

There was no doubting Randall's ability with the bat in his hand as this innings unfolded, but I must say that his antics during the whole game started to wear a bit thin on me. I remember making a comment to him at one stage after he'd given me a little bit of verbiage. 'Just remember,' I said, 'that it takes more than one innings to make a career.' I'm sure Randall would remember that. Perhaps those words have hit home to him since, because he has had such an up and down career. It is all right to be chirpy and carry on a little when things are going your way, but it's a bit dangerous to keep at it when they're not. Then it can work against you with the selectors and the public.

It can also give your opponents something to work on. We've always thought he was a very nervous character and have worked on this theory, encouraging him to carry on as much as he likes to possibly get his mind off the job of batting and making runs. His cheeky antics always made me try that bit harder when bowling against him. I thought perhaps if I could sit him on his backside a few times it might take some of the cheek out of him, but it only seemed to encourage him and make him worse, if anything. But there's no taking it away from Randall, he's an entertainer ... and the sad thing is that he's probably appreciated more in Australia then he ever has been in his home country. After his Centenary Test innings I made the statement that he was the most exciting English player I'd seen since Colin Milburn and I've been truly surprised he hasn't gone on with it.

During the lunch break, with the game beautifully poised for a great finish, we were reminded that at afternoon tea we'd have to line up on the ground to meet Her Majesty, The Queen. Her attendance at the game complemented the occasion beautifully. Well, I decided to capitalise on the situation. In for a penny, in for a pound ... I would ask her for her autograph. I asked the twelfth man during lunch to make sure to put my autograph book and a pen in my blazer pocket, so I could have it at the ready for the line-up later. As the Queen met the player next to me, I reached into my pocket and brought the equipment out. Then Greg Chappell introduced me to Her Majesty.

I bowed most respectfully and then from behind my back I produced the book and the pen and stuttered out, 'Would you mind autographing this for me?' She was obviously taken aback. She smiled embarrassedly, paused and said, 'Not now.' With no disrespect, I wondered, 'If it can't be now, when will I ever get it ... you surely won't be coming in for a drink after play.' But as it turned out, that was by no means the end of the matter. It was followed up by a cricket official, who got in touch with her aide and she signed a photograph taken of the incident. It is now one of my most prized possessions.

At afternoon tea the game was still delicately poised, with England 5 for 354, needing 109 runs with an hour plus 15 eight-ball overs to play. They were still in with a chance, Greig and Alan Knott both under way and each capable of winning it off his own bat. The Queen left not all that long after the break with her team looking good. The minute after she left we started to get the breaks and we'd won it in an hour or so after she'd gone. I recall one of the lads rationalising it his way, 'We were simply being very courteous to her . . . letting her see England in control then wiping them out the moment she left the ground!'

The game ended when I trapped Knott in front. Australia had won by 45 runs, exactly the same margin as in the first ever Test a hundred years before. The significance of that coincidence escaped me at the time, but the more I think about that game the more miraculous I think the result was. Naturally I was ecstatic at the realisation that we'd won, but I was totally exhausted. It had been a long, hard season for me and the second innings of the Centenary Test had been particularly trying. I'd bowled 34.4 overs and was close to collapse at the end of it. Yet I'd taken 5 more wickets for a match total of 11 for 165 and I derived immense personal satisfaction from that feat.

In fact, I was suffering from more than exhaustion at that stage. My back was in a bad way again. I had complained of this to my doctor in Perth earlier in the season and a new series of X-rays were taken of the lumbar vertebrae. When I returned from the New Zealand tour more X-rays were taken of the area. This time it was found that a new fracture had developed. The doctor advised me not to go to England with the 1977 tour. It was his opinion that I would almost certainly have broken down completely at some stage during the tour. He told me he felt that if that happened it would spell the end of my bowling. So in the midst of the euphoria of our memorable Centenary Test victory and my personal triumph I had to announce that I would be unavailable for the England tour.

Looking back on it all totally dispassionately, the Melbourne Centenary Test was such an outstanding success in every way that its counterpart at Lord's some three and a half years later was on a real hiding to nothing. There was just no way that any other cricketing event could have measured up to the Melbourne celebration. Even the weather, which isn't always that reliable in Melbourne, played its part to perfection . . . it rained during the match, but on the rest day, and no harm was done to the smooth operation of the game.

Every social function went like clockwork, the crowds were magnificent and the result of the Test an absolutely unbelievable repeat of that first Test a hundred years before.

So the organisers of the centenary of the first Test ever played on English soil (incidentally, that original game was played at The Oval) had a tough act to follow. Still, as we left for England and another most significant piece of cricketing history, I was not alone among the players past and present who looked forward in eager anticipation. We were convinced that even if the result of that first ever Test at The Oval—a win to England by 5 wickets—might not be repeated exactly, then at the very least the organisation and spectator support would not pale in comparison with the splendid Melbourne Centenary Test. Sad to relate, we were all a little off the mark. Things just didn't fall into place, one way and another, although it was a most memorable occasion still and I wouldn't have missed it for anything.

It was never going to be an easy matter for Australia to perform well at Lord's because we hit England in the middle of our winter and had just a limited line-up of matches in which to find form and acclimatise. Along with the West Australian members of the touring party I had spent a lot of time preparing myself from a fitness point of view, but as far as bowling was concerned the best I could do was work out off a short run on synthetic indoor surfaces. Then matters worsened for me when I was hit by a virus a week or so before we left. This not only took the edge off my fitness, but also limited the number of cricket workouts I was able to have before flying out.

Obviously we were a sadly under-prepared lot when we landed in England. The senior players all realised that we would struggle against any opposition we met because they would be well into the swing of things and playing as well as they were going to be that summer. As the tour progressed and we performed accordingly rather poorly some of the younger players started to panic a bit. Little comments were made, like trying to tell senior players how they should be bowling, which would have been unheard of on a normal tour. The more experienced players weren't all that concerned—we knew that we would rise to the one big occasion of that out-of-season tour, the Centenary Test.

During one of the lead-up games, against Surrey at The Oval, Greg Chappell made public his feelings about County sides not making a contribution to games against touring sides by making occasional declarations. It has been a gripe of the Australians over

76

the years that we have to make all the running, while the County sides simply play for a draw. That's a sad trait of English cricket in general, even in Test matches. Anyway, it was bad luck for Greg, because his outburst did stir Roger Knight to make two declarations to his one and we ended up losing the game. We had a few laughs about it and so did Greg, but the hope was that the point he made just may have been appreciated by a few County captains. Let's face it, touring sides are there to entertain the public, but there's not much entertainment if there's only one side trying to make a game of it.

Our next three-day fixture was against Lancashire, and that meant coming up against our West Australian team-mate Mick Malone. Mick's a bit of a practical joker and he brought to the ground a very lifelike rubber snake which had some property that kept it moving a bit after you dropped it on the ground. Not many Australians are too happy in the presence of snakes, but English people are petrified just at the thought of them. All they hear is the untrue statement that if you are bitten by one you're dead within a minute.

So we had a bit of fun with Dicky Bird, who was one of the umpires, placing it strategically in his room a couple of times. It must have passed out of Dicky's mind when, as twelfth man, I brought out a sweater for Ashley Mallet—with the snake wrapped up in one of the sleeves. As the snake fell out 'Rowdy' screamed with fright and dashed from one end of the wicket to the other. Dicky later confided to me, 'As soon as I saw it I was trying to work out which part of the fence I could get over quickest'.

I suppose it's not all that often that I'm lumbered with the drinks waiter's duties, so when I am it offers the lads a chance to get a few back on me. Later in the Lancashire game I was quietly resting in the back of the room while our boys were out on the field when one of the lads on the balcony called out that Greg was rather agitatedly calling for drinks and I'd better hurry. I hadn't been following the game closely and wasn't aware that there was only half an hour or so to go before the end of the session. There I was at the end of the over strolling on to the ground with a tray of drinks. Greg saw me coming and waved me off, telling me just what I could do with my drinks. But rather than that, I decided to hand them out to the members sitting along the fence in front of the pavilion. They thought it was great!

From Old Trafford we went straight into the first of two one-day

Prudential Trophy matches. Once again the old story came up about the Aussies being bunnies at one-day cricket. We made a bit of a mess of those two games, losing by 23 and 47 runs, and the British Press went for our throats, saying we were outclassed and out-generalled once more. Let's get this straight, once and for all, we'd much rather three, four and five-day games. We aren't all that keen on one-day games, but playing against England it runs deeper than that—we just aren't prepared to play at their game. We hate the way they send their men to all points of the compass as soon as the first half-attacking stroke is played by one of our batsmen.

That's why the circles were devised in one-day games when World Series Cricket got under way and it was interesting that when the Pommies came to Australia in 1979-80 they refused to play with the circles. On one occasion during that tour they even had every fields-man *plus* the wicketkeeper on the boundary to ensure a victory. The circles force captains to keep men in reasonable field placings throughout the game and I think that makes for a far better spec-tacle. I look back on those two and one-day games, at The Oval and Edgbaston, and I recall some ridiculously defensive fields set by Ian Botham, even though England had us by the throat. Trouble is there's no bonus for getting a side out and when you play the way the Pommies do, perhaps the introduction of such incentive would help make for a better game.

Anyway, I think the gap between Australia and England in one-day cricket, no matter what the local rules, has been closed. We're now playing much more one-day stuff at home. After all, it's experi-ence that counts. Only a few years ago, while the England players were having their fill of three different domestic one-day compe-titions, we Australians were experiencing very little of it. Fortunately for Australian cricket, though we are getting more one-day games, we're not being swamped by the effects of limited-overs play. Surely the real test of a cricketer and a cricketing nation comes at the Test match level. That's not to say there isn't a place, at this stage, for one-day games in world cricket . . . there is, but let's keep things in perspective.

Our final match leading up to the Centenary Test was an absolute disaster against Nottinghamshire at Trent Bridge. We went down by an innings and 76 runs, the worst defeat an Australian side had suf-fered in a County game this century. So we went to Lord's with a tarnished reputation and were given little hope of winning. This was reflected by the London bookmakers' opening quote of seven-to-one, framed after we'd lost the second of the one-day internationals.

After the loss to Nottinghamshire *and* the suggestion that Greg Chappell may be unfit after injuring himself at Edgbaston we drifted out to ten-to-one. There's no doubt the bookies got a little carried away, because we were a fairly promising side although we were out of season and had had very little practice. Also, the Test wicket would be different from anything we'd played on so far.

Anyway, we were all convinced that we'd be lifted by the import-ance of the occasion and do much better. I thought the odds of seven-to-one and the whisper of tens was absolutely ridiculous. It took very little talking to convince the lads to chip in and put a fairly substantial amount on ourselves to win with a covering bet on the draw. We were very happy to take the odds. We were, in fact, very, very confident of winning the match, though Ladbrokes couldn't have known that. And, after all, those odds were set in a four-horse race . . . the wicket, the weather and the two teams.

Back in London for the build-up to the Test we found a wonderful gathering of some two hundred past players at the Russell Hotel and the same nerve-tingling atmosphere we'd experienced at Mel-bourne. The first official function was held at Lord's and after mingling with the greats in the Long Room it was upstairs to a sit-down dinner. However, to my dismay there was no after-dinner speaker at this most auspicious occasion and the night ended up a bit of a damp squib. Of the two other later functions, perhaps only the Lord's Taverners dinner held a candle to the series of outstand-ing get-togethers in Melbourne—and I thought England was the home of the after-dinner speaker! But the Taverners did put on a great show. J. J. Warr (England) and Bill O'Reilly (Australia) spoke superbly and, of course, Harry Secombe and friends were in irrepressible form. It was a night to remember.

There was a tinge of sadness about the naming of our side for the Test. Jeff Thomson was twelfth man and I think everybody, especially myself, felt pretty sad to see him carrying the drinks. This great player suffering such an indignity. Thommo's morale was rock bottom as a result and I'm sure he just couldn't wait to get home. I thought he'd bowled pretty well in the early part of the tour and later in the piece none of us had bowled all that well. But it was de-cided to take two spinners into the game and Len Pascoe and I got the nod ahead of Thommo. There was the inevitable talk about this being the end of the road for Thommo. I just couldn't swallow that. I thought he still had something to give an Australian side, particularly where the wickets were hard and helping the quicks a little bit.

It was no fault of the players that the Centenary Test at Lord's wasn't as memorable a game as its Melbourne predecessor. Sadly the weather was the culprit, with almost ten hours lost to rain in the first three days. That made it extremely difficult for either side to force victory, though I thought we played well enough to deserve a win. Greg Chappell won the toss and we batted first, moving on through numerous frustrating rain breaks to reach 5 for 385 before declaring. Nursed along by Chappell, Graeme Wood posted the first of three centuries scored in the game. But better was to come from the bat of Kim Hughes, whose century, spread over the first three days, included a smorgasbord of delightful strokes.

Hughes had to wait until late on the third day, too, because of a long and controversial delay while the umpires allowed the ground to dry out. Ironically, the weather was good that day, but water running off the covers down the slope had saturated the bottom uncovered part of the square. We wanted to play, England didn't and the umpires ruled the ground unsafe until we finally resumed at 3.45 p.m. It was a tragedy that play had been held up for so long. There were thousands of people waiting outside the ground and those inside the ground became angrier and angrier as the sun shone and yet nothing happened. I didn't think the offending area of the ground was bad enough to hold things up as it did. In my opinion play should have started somewhere nearer to midday.

What amazed me was the fact that no effort was made to work on that wet area and improve it until the last moment, when some sawdust was spread on the worst parts. Surely the ground staff could have been doing something during those long hours of waiting. When England had looked like beating Australia in the fifth Test at the Oval in 1968 a massive mopping up operation got the ground fit for play on the last day. But the state of the game shouldn't have come into it . . . this wasn't a series decider with the Ashes at stake, it was a celebration with great potential for spectator involvement. Sure there was a lot of interest in who won, but not enough to be pedantic about a small wet spot on the field and keep people waiting for most of the day. It was farcical.

As the delay lengthened, so did the anger of the crowd fester. In the end there was an ugly incident which must surely haunt the MCC forever. The umpires, Dicky Bird and David Constant, were making their way back through the milling members with the two captains after their umpteenth inspection when they were jostled by some angry MCC members. The incident was captured on television and it was the worst thing I've ever seen at any ground. And by the members at Lord's! After all the things so pompously said in the past about the behaviour of us Australians . . . put under the same sorts of pressures they proved themselves to be worse. I lost a lot of respect for them in that one ugly act.

There's no doubt whatsoever that Bird and Constant were badly shaken. They were under enough pressure as it was with the crowd, the Australians and even the officials after their blood for not getting the game under way. Out on the field later in the game Constant seemed to be the worst affected. Some of our players said he actually had tears in his eyes on more than one occasion. Off the field I found out that Dicky Bird wasn't himself, either. Not long after the incident I came up behind him standing outside the umpires' room, which isn't far from the visitors' dressing-room at Lord's and tried to give him a fright by shouting 'Snake'! There was just no reaction and I couldn't understand . . . until I walked past him and all I could see was a glazed look in his eyes. Nothing was registering with him. He was in a state of shock.

When we finally were able to get a good crack at England on the Monday after the rest day they cracked up badly and had to struggle to avoid the follow-on. I was delighted to pick up the first 4 in the order, but it was Pascoe who did the damage with 5 wickets for 59, career best figures. He bowled very fast and straight, with 4 of his victims going to leg before wicket decisions. Then Australia went all out for victory, with Hughes dominating proceedings a second time. He was right in his element, dashing down the wicket and thrashing the England bowlers all over the place—one of his more effervescent efforts landing on the top deck of the pavilion. It was scintillating stuff and it's worth noting that Hughes, who scored 84 and probably threw away the chance of a rare double with a century in each innings, had batted on each of the five days of the game.

The Australian declaration left England the challenge of scoring 370 runs in 350 minutes, but they chose to turn a blind eye to the prospect of a memorable victory and the game ran out a tame draw. Geoff Boycott used the situation as a chance to get some batting practice and, accompanied by plenty of jeers and slow hand-clapping, ground his way to his nineteenth Test century. Along the way he went past Sir Leonard Hutton and Sir Donald Bradman in the all-time Test aggregates list to move into fourth place behind Sir Garry Sobers, Colin Cowdrey and Walter Hammond.

So the Centenary Test at Lord's had ended up a fizzer, mainly because of the weather, but I've often wondered whether a start a couple of hours earlier on the Saturday would have given us the chance to force a victory. Out of that short tour had come a lot of good. First the maturity of Hughes, with some top-quality batting in the latter stages. He began the tour terribly and soon was at a very low ebb in confidence. Then he had a stroke of luck in the first one-day international. He was dropped in the slips early and went on to make an unbeaten 73. He followed that up with 98 in the second one-dayer, missed out twice against Nottinghamshire and then won the man-of-the-match award at Lord's. Allan Border also showed he had the potential to become one of the greatest left-handers Australia has produced. Border has a great knowledge of the game, too, and shows real leadership potential.

Graeme Wood also came under notice and his century in the Test was a very good hand. He is a very well-equipped batsman, but too often lapses in concentration have cost him his wicket. With the help of Greg Chappell he surely learnt a few valuable lessons about making big innings. I predict a very bright future for him. Also coming from the tour was an indication that perhaps Wood and Bruce Laird would provide Australia with its most reliable opening pair since Simpson and Lawry, with Wood the left-handed strokeplayer and Laird right-handed and as solid as a rock.

Then there was Len Pascoe's bowling. In the Test he demoralised the England middle order and spearheaded a collapse that cost the home side their last 8 wickets for 68 runs. Powerfully built, aggressive and totally dedicated, Len looked to be set for a great career with Australia. However, he slipped out of the front line not long after with knee problems.

At the end of that short tour we returned home to prepare for twin tours of Australia by New Zealand and India, quite confident that at least the batting side of things was in good shape for some years to come.

7. The Birth of World Series Cricket

It is a generally held opinion that World Series Cricket was spawned only a few months before news of its existence shocked the cricket world to its core during the Australians' tour of England in 1977. In truth it had its genesis in the steamy confines of the visitors' dressing-room at the Brisbane Cricket Ground in the early stages of the 1974-75 season. That was when Austin Robertson and I first became involved in a business arrangement, which in fact backfired on me at that particular stage, but which led to the development of a strong friendship that mushroomed to the boardrooms of television magnates and the backrooms of a clandestine operation to sign up the world's best cricketers for a commercially promoted competition.

At the time I first met him, Austin (who had carved out a name for himself as a champion Australian Rules footballer) was working as a sports writer for the *Daily News*, Perth's afternoon newspaper. Cricket was his game in the summer and he had accompanied the WA team on its Eastern States tour and was probably clacking away on his typewriter in the Pressbox above the dressing-room at the 'Gabba when the telephone rang and the caller asked for me. He identified himself as Frank Mills from the Australian Broadcasting Commission and said he was planning a documentary programme on fast bowling, following up some frank comments about the attitudes of fast bowlers in a book I had published called *Back to the Mark*.

The subject matter was the intimidatory nature of fast bowling and the idea was for me to be interviewed and to bowl at the former Australian opening batsman Keith Stackpole in the nets. He told me it should take the best part of a morning. I wasn't breaking my neck to do it, but I asked, 'How much are you prepared to pay?' Mills said he thought the ABC would go to $200. I was reluctant to just say 'yes' then and there and perhaps miss out on a bigger fee that could be gained by negotiation. A thought flashed across my mind. Earlier in the tour Austin had said that if I ever wanted any help with this sort of thing he'd be pleased to do the negotiations. 'Hang on,' I said, 'I can't really talk a final price with you ... but my manager is here at the ground and I'll get him to speak to you.'

I put the phone down and dashed upstairs to the Pressbox to bring Austin down to speak to Mills. On the way down I gave Austin a rough idea of what I was expected to do and said I'd like him to handle the negotiations. It turned out the two knew each other because Mills had previously worked in Perth. I heard Austin say, 'Well, let's get down to the nitty-gritty ... Dennis will do the job, but how much are you paying?' I had made the mistake of not telling Austin that I thought it was worth more than the $200 being offered. 'Fine,' he said, 'that's okay, Dennis will be there ... goodbye.'

With a big smile Austin hung up and turned to me. 'There you are,' he said, 'I've just organised your first job.' He then gave me the details of where and when, which I already knew. 'But how much?' I asked. 'Oh, $200 ...' I just looked at him and laughed. 'Look Ock, that's great,' I said, '$200, less your per cent, means you owe me money!'

So began a relationship which was to blossom over the years and have an enormous bearing on the history of cricket. Austin's deep involvement in football back in Perth, coupled to the fact that we were based too far away from the 'big smoke' of Sydney and Melbourne, meant that little happened immediately in our relationship as player and his manager. That came a little later, after Austin had retired from football early in the 1975 season. His club in Perth was running a testimonial for Austin and it was at one of the functions for the fund, with a guest appearance by Paul Hogan and Strop (John Cornell), that destiny took a hand. Cornell had grown up in Western Australia and during that time he and Austin had become very good friends. John could see that his mate was languishing and suggested he make the move to Sydney, 'where the opportunites are far greater'.

So, in November of that year (1975) Austin packed up and went to Sydney where he moved in with Cornell. I'll come back to that, because meanwhile there had been two other significant happenings in the story of the development of World Series Cricket. The first occurred in the Australian team dressing-room at the Sydney Cricket Ground after we had defeated England in the fourth Test of the 1974-75 tour to clinch the Ashes. To say that we had a celebratory drink in the rooms that day was an understatement! I reckon I was as high as a kite before I'd even had one, but much later in proceedings I found myself talking slightly incoherently with some friendly chap and espousing my theory, rather strongly, that we cricketers were grossly underpaid.

The fellow hadn't introduced himself, but it later turned out that he was a journalist from Tasmania. He casually dropped a few questions into our conversation and the next day a story appeared in the Tasmanian Press, which later came to the mainland, quoting me in no uncertain terms. I had suggested that players be put on a salary, rather than a match payment situation. There was so much cricket on, we were making a huge commitment, yet were getting next to nothing in return. My idea was that players receive $25 000 to $30 000 to play for Australia for as much of the year as the Australian Cricket Board wanted them. I said the players should be put on contract, so they'd have some security. I was back in Perth the next day when details of the article reached the ACB hierarchy—and it turned out they weren't too impressed by my ideas!

I was playing in a club game the following Saturday when I saw, to my surprise, Ray Steele, one of the top ACB officials who lived in Melbourne. 'G'dday "Cast",' I said with a smile. But Cast wasn't smiling.

'I'd like to see you after play,' he said. He went, but was back in the social clubrooms when I came in after showering and dressing. He took me aside from the other players and told me the Board was not happy with what I had said in the newspaper article. I told him that basically the reason I had said it was because *I* wasn't happy with the Board . . . and 'I think you'll find most of the other players aren't, either.' He then warned me 'as a mate' to be very careful about what I said in future with regard to the subject.

A subject as serious as the matter of the players' livelihood when faced with a heavy commitment to the Board and the rising cost of keeping the house and home running with little or no other income, doesn't die as easily as that. Ian Chappell was in no mood to let the players suffer as we were. He was the architect of a meeting towards the end of the 1975 tour of England. Present at the meeting were the members of the touring party, the team manager Fred Bennett and the ACB chairman, Tim Caldwell. The idea was for the players to open their minds and for the two officials to convey their thoughts to the Board on returning to Australia.

We put up something like twenty suggestions, all to do with pay and conditions. One suggestion was that the players receive a percentage of the gate, even just five cents per head at the gate which the public would know was going towards payment of the players. Another was that Test players be put on contract with the Board, much the same as my suggestion which had gone into print. Others were more general thoughts to be aired at a Board level. The two officials smiled at the end of the meeting. They said our thoughts were great. 'We'll work on them for you and you should get a few of them when we take them to the committees.'

We heard no more about it. That was the annoying and frustrating thing. We just never seemed to be getting anywhere in our efforts to get a better deal with the Board. At times we felt we were making some headway, then all of a sudden a brick wall would appear at the end of the passage. Always that brick wall was there and it seemed a waste of time talking to them about anything.

They made statements about trying to get closer to the players and, sure, they were talking to us—but they weren't moving a finger to implement any of our suggestions or trying to help us out in our situation. In the end they initiated captains' conferences, which led to the formation of the players' committee, but from what I've seen of it, it's been little more than window dressing. So there was considerable discontent building up among the senior Australian players, who were honestly feeling the pinch and certainly making no headway. I do feel, though, that officials are trying more to communicate with players these days.

As the 1975-76 season progressed, with no significant change to the players' lot, Austin Robertson was quietly settling in to a new life in Sydney. Initially he didn't do a lot ... a bit of freelance writing, a few bit parts in the Paul Hogan Show and generally assisting Cornell wherever possible. Then there was a fateful discussion over a glass of white wine one night. Austin said to Cornell that what he was interested in was sport, first and foremost, and secondly that he liked the challenge of television. From that discussion came a suggestion by Cornell that they set up a small sports packaging company. (Austin later told me that, as a bait for Cornell, he had said he could get both myself and Rod Marsh for him to manage.)

I remember the call coming from Austin in Sydney during a game in Perth early in 1976. My first reaction was to say that I was really quite happy doing it all myself at that stage, that it was a bit of a struggle but I was fairly satisfied as things were. I added that unless Cornell had something in the pipeline for me there was no point in committing myself to their management. Austin's response was to say, 'Give him three months to see how things go and if you aren't happy call it quits.' And he pointed out how successful John had been in the management and direction of Paul Hogan, who had emerged as a top Australian comedian. He also pointed out that John really knew the market value, whereas I might sell myself short with national advertisers in particular. Cornell would mean more money to me, even though I'd have to pay a commission.

I agreed to give it a try. Soon afterwards I was playing in Melbourne and Austin arrived to virtually take over my affairs for a couple of weeks. He got down to re-directing my phone calls, taking care of the little things and leaving me clear and free to throw myself into just playing cricket. That really impressed me, because things were getting a bit hot with promotions at that stage and I just wasn't getting enough time to myself. By now John and Austin had other irons in the fire with John Newcombe and snooker star Eddie Charlton on their books. In fact, 'Newk' and I did some ads together at one stage. The company called 'J.P. Sport', an offshoot of 'J.P. Productions' (after the initials of John Cornell and Paul Hogan), was off the ground.

At this stage Austin was actually living in Cornell's home in Neutral Bay and it was on the occasions when the two were embroiled in late night chats that Austin began to sow the seeds which later grew into World Series Cricket. He plugged away at John about the ridiculously small amounts of money we leading cricketers were receiving for our really solid commitment to the Board. Austin told me he hit Cornell with the fact that I'd received about $8000 for something like eight months cricket and that, because of cricket, I was virtually unemployable. There was the occasional employer who gave me a chance, but if it hadn't been for bits of promotional work here and there I just couldn't have coped with a family on my overall income.

It seems that Austin had hit a nerve with Cornell. The next thing I knew Cornell was in Perth to do some appearances with Hogan at a city hotel and I was called to meet them in their suite at the Parmelia Hotel. I'd spoken with John on the phone, but I'd never met either him or Hogan. As I walked into that room I did expect 'Strop' (the half-wit character played by John) to jump out of his chair, the jaw to drop and a sneaky laugh to follow. But John immediately impressed me as being very sharp, on the ball, full of ideas and eager to do something for me, being my manager, but also for other cricketers. The cricketers' lot was so bad that something had to be done about it ... it was as though it had become a crusade for him and it certainly didn't appear to me that he wanted to make anything out of it personally.

Paul Hogan didn't say much in the early stages of our meeting, which lasted an hour or more, but later in the piece he did have quite a bit to say. As things began to roll along towards the formation of World Series Cricket he remained closely interested, though obviously he couldn't do a lot because of time commitments. John asked me a series of questions about how much cricketers were paid and how much time they had to put in each year. I told him all I knew and added that I thought it was diabolical and that I was fed up with it. Then I said to him that I thought it would be possible to get together a group of players from Australia and another from around the world to play a series of matches, just three or four, at the end of an Australian season. The players involved could receive good payment out of the gate, the television rights and sponsorship and this would allow the senior Australian players to get a reasonable return from a full season, which in turn would take the pressure off the Australian Cricket Board.

My original concept was for a one-day competition only, strictly worked in conjunction with the Board, but simply aimed at relieving the Board of the burden of coming up with more money to satisfy the needs of senior players. I envisaged it being run along the lines of the World Cup, which we'd played in England in 1975, but just between two sides and played in Australia. I suggested that as Australia was doing so well in the international scene, people would like to see us pitted against the very best team that could be lined up from the rest of the world. Of course things changed dramatically before World Series Cricket actually came into being. I suppose I must bear some of the responsibility for what actually did transpire, but I hasten to say I have no regrets whatsoever.

I told John I thought I could get at least three or four top Australian players to be in it, as easily as flicking my fingers. I knew too well the ones who were really unhappy about the money they were getting and the conditions. John had listened intently to my proposal and said, 'Leave it with me.' The following day he got back to me and said, 'I'm really excited about this . . . have you ever heard of a guy called Kerry Packer?' I had to admit that I hadn't, so John explained that he was the head of a big media chain in the Eastern States and that his interests included the Channel Nine television network. He added, 'Well, I've spoken to Kerry and this idea sounds like it could be a reality . . . I'll get back to you on it.' He hung up.

A major step down the road to World Series Cricket had been taken.

When John returned to Sydney he and Austin thrashed out a lot of things before the proposal was put to Packer. I soon learnt that Kerry wasn't a man to do things by halves, that he wanted to go into it boots and all. Never mind my idea of a few sponsored one-day games, he told John he wanted to go the whole hog and play Test matches as well as one-day games. So my almost altruistic motives had been swept aside, but I was relieved to learn that it was planned that there wouldn't be a clash with the traditional Tests. So when it came back to me the concept was quite different from my first thoughts—but I liked it. I realised that the organisation would have to be done without informing the Board, because previous approaches (and there had been more than one) for the establishment of one type of professional cricket contest or another had all been knocked on the head by the Board.

So began the mammoth task of setting up a completely new cricket entity. It was well past the halfway mark of the 1976-77 season and the plan was to launch World Series Cricket in the 1977-78 season. So much had to be done in a short time. First, the players . . . I was in for sure, but we needed other big-name players. I gave Austin and John a list of players I thought should be recruited, marking against the names those who I thought would be certainties to join. The initial target was Ian Chappell. Even though he had retired from Test and even first-class cricket, he was still young enough and good enough to step back into a top-flight international scene. It was my duty with the Australian players to make the initial contact and to introduce them to Austin and John, who had the job of signing them on.

I organised a meeting between Ian and the other two in Sydney. As in almost every other case, all I said was, 'I can't tell you what it's about, but these blokes want me to introduce you to them so they can put a proposition to you . . . I don't want to influence you one way or another.' I made that last point quite clear to each of them. A lot asked if I was involved and I always answered that I was. To those who didn't ask, I didn't volunteer any information. Some rang me back afterwards to discuss things before making their decision. Ian Chappell, in his own way, jumped at the proposal and left the meeting with a verbal undertaking that he would be involved and that he would captain the Australian side.

He also indicated that he felt his brother Greg would be very interested in such a proposal. Not very long after that Austin and John turned up in Auckland, New Zealand, where we were playing the second Test against the Kiwis at the end of February. They had come for one reason: to sign up Greg. Again I made the first approach. Greg asked me what it was about and I gave him an inkling and told him of my own involvement. The three had their meeting and Greg indicated that he would join, leaving the other two and returning to his room. Then Austin, John and I went for a meal in the hotel restaurant. Not long after a message came out for the team physio—Greg was in his room and wanted a sleeping tablet. We looked at each other and grinned. The Australian captain certainly did have a lot on his mind!

It was a great relief to me to hear that Greg had readily said 'I'm in!' I knew we were on the road. It was decided that while the two were in Auckland for a couple of days they should talk to Doug Walters, but we obviously didn't want to attract attention to such a meeting. Austin and John were dismissing their visit to Auckland on the pretext that they were making arrangements with me to do some television work in Sydney, which was true. But for them to be seen having a meeting with Doug was a different matter. I hit on an idea. Out the back of the dressing-room and about three doors down was the ambulance room, which never seemed to be used. I sent Austin and John down there and told them to wait until Doug arrived.

I gave Doug a quick run-down on the proposal and off he went down the passage to the ambulance room. Doug later told me how it all unfolded. He had walked in to the room and seen these two guys sitting there like a couple of idiots. He'd already met them as my managers at the hotel the day before. John spoke first. 'G'dday Doug,' he said. 'Look, I didn't want to ask you in front of the other fellows . . . but could you lend me a couple of bucks?'

Doug said he'd reached instinctively towards his pocket and replied, 'Oh yeah, sure . . .' before realising he'd been sucked in well and truly when the other two burst out laughing. They then explained the proposal to Doug and without even giving it a second thought he said, 'Count me in.' When I heard that Doug was in I knew we had a goer. We had four whom the others would follow if they were approached.

That had transpired on the second last day of the Test and Austin and John were due to go home later that day. John came up to me and explained the plan to offer big winner-take-all incentives for the teams in World Series Cricket. He asked me if I thought that all that money would make any difference to the players' attitude towards winning. I said I wasn't sure. 'I'll tell you what,' he said, 'I'll pay you $50 for every run you make over 20 when you bat in this innings.' I was due in soon and when I did get out there I worked awfully hard to score 23 not out—and, boy, was I upset when Max Walker got out. When I came off the field Austin told me that they had to leave for the airport in forty minutes and they'd pay me $200 for every wicket I took before they left. By the time they'd gone I had 4 wickets. Not a bad way to earn $950! I then realised they had been conducting an experiment with me the guinea pig!

8. Putting the Show on the Road

The Centenary Test in Melbourne, a couple of weeks after the New Zealand tour was over, gave Austin Robertson and John Cornell a golden opportunity to get down to some solid recruiting. By this time Ian Chappell had finalised the list of Australian players he wanted and most of them were in Melbourne either as members of the Centenary Test team or as recently retired Test players. I had to hustle Austin into hiking Max Walker to the top of the list when I learnt he had been made a huge offer to leave Victoria and return to play for his home State of Tasmania the following season. So big Max was approached in all haste and he signed on with a toothy grin. There were no problems at all in getting the players to have a chat with Austin and John, who let me know after each interview that they'd received a favourable response.

Some players had responded by saying, 'Yes . . . where do I sign?' right on the spot, but most took time to mull it over, perhaps have a discussion with their wives. In the case of Rick McCosker, his wife Meryl was even flown down from Sydney to have further talks. Each of us was fully aware of the need for absolute secrecy. There was one funny story regarding this as player after player was being signed up. Among the Australians approached I was the one common denominator . . . they all knew I was involved, but they hadn't a clue whom among the others had been privately approached and signed up. Because of the strict security precautions, none of them dared to ask another if he was 'in'.

Obviously Rod Marsh was one of the most important players on the list, but it just so happened that he was one of the last to be signed. In fact, it occurred during the lunch break on the last day of the Test, with England batting and making a most earnest endeavour to snatch the Test from us. Rod told Austin he'd be in—and dashed off to join the other players going out on to the field for the mid-afternoon session. As the Australians took up their positions, with Rod behind the stumps and Greg Chappell at first slip, Marshy found he couldn't contain himself. He turned to Greg and said out of the corner of his mouth, 'Well, pal, looks like this is about the last time we're going to be standing out here for a while.'

Greg, as poker faced as ever, replied 'What do you mean?' Marshy frowned. 'You know bloody well what I mean,' he said, breaking into a grin. Even among the closest of friends, the individuals weren't saying a thing to each other.

As the whole thing unfolded before my eyes I felt both delighted and excited at the prospect of the new venture. As to my own contract, I thrashed it out with John Cornell. A figure was agreed upon and a three-year term stipulated. I was twenty-seven years old at the time and I really didn't think I'd be playing much over the age of thirty, so I was happy with a three-year term although I knew a lot of the others, particularly the younger ones, had signed on for a three-year term with a two-year option. I was very happy with the situation, because I could see that the level of promotion World Series Cricket would receive through the Channel Nine network must result in a healthy spin-off for all the players in the more commercial side of its operations. It did work out that way too, though I hasten to say that similar opportunities would have come my way if I'd remained a senior player with the Australian Cricket Board.

So you can see that throughout my stay in Melbourne for the Centenary Test I was busily involved with the recruitment of players for WSC. I lined up one interview after another for Austin and John and was often the bouncing board for talks with those players as they made up their minds to join and as they mulled over the pros and cons after they'd signed up. Once again, though, the extra involvement had no detrimental effect either on my game—I did take eleven wickets for the match—or on the performance of the Australian side, which won the game in grand style. However, at the end of the Test I announced that I couldn't make the forthcoming tour of England because of troubles with my back, which became worse and worse as the season progressed.

As luck would have it, I was signed on by Channel Nine in Sydney to be their resident expert when they brought a telecast of the series in live from England. This meant being in Sydney for each of the Tests. All of this plus work I did for the Channel Nine programme 'A Current Affair', had been lined up by John Cornell as part of the management arrangement which was now well and truly flourishing. Being in Sydney so much during the winter of 1977 enabled me to sit in on many meetings during which the planning of WSC was finalised. I was convinced it would work and work well, despite all the inherent problems. I was present when subjects such as the construction of portable turf wickets were thrashed out ... and if that was possible, then anything was possible. Of course there were times when I wondered if we'd ever get over all the hurdles in time for a kick-off at the start of the following summer, but as time went by I developed great confidence in the people involved.

I was really looking forward to the new happening for many reasons. I'd enjoyed playing for the ACB, but I believed, as did a lot of the others, that the time had come for a change. We all believed that what we were doing would benefit the players of the future in many ways, both financially and in the terms of their playing conditions ... whether WSC kept going forever or there was eventually a compromise. Actually, it was my hope right from the outset that there would be a compromise, be it in four or five or even ten years' time.

When that compromise came my hope was that all we had done would be the platform for players to benefit forever and a day. Even if the establishment of WSC meant the end of my Test career as such, of my aspirations to join the immortals, I didn't care because I believed so strongly in the concept. I also believed what we were doing was for the good of the game and the players in the long run. And Helen was right behind me.

Immediately after the playing of the Centenary Test the England captain Tony Greig went to Sydney and had a meeting with Kerry Packer. He was signed on as captain of the World Eleven and was immediately given the job of selecting the players he wanted and helping with the recruitment of those men from all over the world. The matter of the choice of these players was completely out of my hands, though I did have several discussions with Kerry during my stays in Sydney and the subject of the overseas players was high on the list of priorities. As it turned out Pakistan were touring the West Indies, so Austin flew over there with a briefcase full of contracts to sign up four West Indians and four Pakistanis. From there he went to England to line up the South Africans and the Englishmen who were wanted.

One who was approached but didn't go on with it was the England opening batsman Geoff Boycott. He was spoken to during the Centenary Test and in fact gave his word to Kerry Packer that he was 'in'. But then he said he wanted to be captain of the World Eleven—or to be able to name the captain of the team. The man he named as the only captain he'd play under was Ray Illingworth, a

94

rather ironic choice in the light of future relationships within York-shire County Cricket Club! Boycott also saw problems with our hastily prepared contracts, in which the end of the WSC period and the beginning of the new English County season clashed slightly. He wasn't happy and wanted to discuss it further. He wasn't given another chance. Another to be approached but not play for WSC was England's fast bowler Bob Willis. He virtually said 'yes' but then went to the English cricket authorities and something happened to help Bob stay with traditional cricket. He has come through as a shining light for having rejected the WSC overtures.

Kim Hughes has claimed that he was approached by WSC, con-sidered the matter and then declined. Quite naturally his comments made me raise my eyebrows, because I'd had something to do with the recruitment of every Australian player and I had no knowledge of Kim ever being approached. I have checked and re-checked with all those empowered to make an approach and to my knowledge none was ever made. It is true that he was approached by Austin Robertson before WSC had even been thought of with an eye to J.P. Sports acting as his manager. Hughes' advisers looked at the man-agement proposition and then declined to go ahead with it. All I can think is that Hughes must have confused that approach as having come from WSC.

What of Kerry Packer, the man in the background who was more or less pulling the strings of the whole operation? I first met him in the Channel Nine studios in Sydney while I was doing one of the telecasts for the Test coverage from England. My first impressions of him were dominated by awe at the physical size and appearance of the man. Partly because of that and partly because of the sort of guy he is, he really does hold your attention. There's no doubting that he's a great lover of sport and I was astounded to learn in my many talks with him during that winter the real depth of his techni-cal knowledge of the game of cricket. He has theories about the game which could only have resulted from far-reaching analysis over many years. And it's not just cricket . . . it's golf and tennis and just about any sport you want to talk about.

We had many lengthy discussions on the telephone during those Test match telecasts. Some of the 'chats' lasted from the minute I'd gone off air after doing the lunch-time comments through to a few minutes before I had to prepare for the afternoon tea comments. And sometimes he'd have been on the line for an hour before lunch and then again after tea. He'd ring me from home and we'd both be talking while watching the game on television. His comments about what was happening in the game were spot on, I couldn't help but be impressed by the fellow. He had his opinions, but he wasn't the sort of guy who wouldn't listen to your side. I admired him for that. He could so easily have told me to jump, but he always gave me the impression that he was treating me as an equal. I found him a very, very likeable man.

I can imagine he'd be a tough customer in business. That must have been a big part of his success story ... in the same way his toughness showed the way in the success of WSC. It was important that he didn't crack under all the pressures we met. I'm sure he was deeply involved in the whole concept and an example of that was the way he insisted on rules being made for the fitness of the Australian players. He didn't want anybody to be able to fire a shot at us at any stage because we were seen to be cruising, so he talked to me a lot about fitness and related subjects and then laid down the law for his players. We all had to pass fitness tests before the start of each season. In fact, Gary Gilmour failed the test coming into the second season and was warned that if he didn't improve he'd be fined. He improved.

Incredibly the security cover, now involving many people, lasted until well into the Australians' tour of England. When news of the venture finally broke, at a party in England thrown for the Aussies by Tony Greig, I think we all felt a sense of relief. We'd been sitting on a time bomb. The break came about a week before it was planned to release the news through the proper channels. I was in Sydney at the time and I escaped a lot of the flack, which seemed to be centred squarely on the players in England and Kerry Packer himself back in Australia. From my point of view it was something of an anti-climax, because it wasn't known at that stage that I was one of the players initially involved. Not that I was complaining, mind you! The early release made no difference to the organisation of things, but it certainly hotted up my lot.

I was flat out just helping some of the players and protecting them as much as possible under the fire all round them. They were constantly being 'spooked' by cricket officials and the media over their decision to join WSC. It was a torrid time, being away from the nerve centre in England and being able to do little about it. We had to battle hard throughout many a long night and with one phone call after another, trying to control the threshing beast over in England. This was often after having worked half the night on the television cover. After that Austin, John and I would often talk right through until daylight and then fall asleep absolutely exhausted. I remember talking to Clive Lloyd, who was in hospital having some work done on his knees, and to Viv Richards, who was as strong as an ox ('Don't worry, man, we'll be all right, man') and trying to catch Alvin Kallicharran. 'Kalli' was hiding from our phone call because his resolve was being eroded by the Warwickshire County Cricket Club.

We had to stand firm in the crisis and keep the players with us. I was the liaison man ... I had to be, because none of the players really knew Austin or John or even Kerry very well, if at all. It was no use any of them ringing the players to tell them not to worry. I had to be the strength of that part of the operation. The players had to be able to relate to somebody. We all knew there'd be an explosion once the news got out, but I don't think anybody, those right on the inside included, forecast the dimension of that explosion. The antagonism of the Press, for example, was far greater than we had expected. It was totally one-sided and unfair. They called WSC a 'circus' right from the start and hacked away at the players and undermined their morale relentlessly.

All through it they never bothered to try to get the players' side of the story. The journalists just wrote what they thought, shooting at the players from a distance. I found their attitude very upsetting because I felt I'd bent over backwards to help the Press in every way before WSC—and this was their way of saying 'Thanks'. The least I'd expected from them was to be given a fair hearing. I guess a lot of the Press hostility stemmed from the fact that WSC was being backed by another media magnate in Kerry Packer. It gave them a grand opportunity to chop away at him as much as at the cricketing concept. No doubt Kerry'd hurt a few people's pride over the years. There was a vested interest involved and I've no doubt whatsoever that there were cases of writers operating under editorial direction. There were a couple of exceptions in the Australian Press, to be fair, but they were few and far between. As a result of those attitudes I must admit I've since been cautious with Press contacts.

As the time got closer for the new concept to get off the ground I was based mainly in Perth. Most of my attention was directed to an effort to get myself fit and ready for the season. A good deal of the others would be match fit because of their playing involvement in the northern summer but I had a lot to do to catch up. I was occasionally consulted by the WSC hierarchy in Sydney when it was thought perhaps I could add some special expertise. Back in Perth

I soon found that in some quarters I was no longer a 'desirable'—and this was before even a ball had been bowled and when very little was known publicly about the WSC concept. A lot of people I had thought were friends simply didn't want to know me.

In fact, there were many instances where they'd duck or turn their heads when they saw me, pretending not to have even noticed me. For example, I was in a suburban supermarket doing some shopping one day when I saw a cricket colleague with whom I'd played in club sides for years and whom I knew very well. I was just about to wave to him and say 'hello' as we approached each other down the aisle, when down went his head and he tried to pass me without stopping. As we drew level he still had his head down and I decided to put him on the spot. I said quite loudly, 'How're you going, Barry?' He looked up, a stunned look across his face, and stammered out, 'Oh Dennis . . . how are you?' Then dead silence. There followed a conversation lasting several minutes, during which I asked him one question after another and he barely even answered. Barry obviously just couldn't wait to get away from me and, sadly, that sort of reaction was not a rare occurrence.

But on the other hand, there was an incredibly positive reaction from many others who were excited by the news and were desperately keen to know what WSC was all about. Because of all this mixed feeling I went through a very emotional period for the couple of months leading up to the first WSC game. There was just one hassle after another . . . we couldn't get proper practice facilities, we weren't allowed to play club cricket and we were clearly ostracised after being so much a part of the heartbeat of West Australian cricket. On top of that there were legal problems and one ugly incident followed another.

Through all of this the Melville Cricket Club, its players and officials, was magnificent. To them I was still Dennis Lillee, a cricketer and a friend who had come to their club and done the right thing by them. There were none of the sideways looks. They genuinely wanted to know what was going on in this new venture of mine and were at all times fully supportive. They also wanted me to play club cricket for them and in fact made themselves quite unpopular at the WA Cricket Association committee table for their outspoken standpoint. It was wonderful to have this pocket of support. I couldn't judge the reactions of players and officials of other clubs, because I just wasn't involved with them.

When the Australian team returned from England late that winter all the WSC players very quickly formed themselves into a little team within a hostile cricket world in Perth. We had to. We trained together exclusively and tried to keep each other going in the face of the constant fire all round us. Austin Robertson arranged physical fitness work for us at the University of Western Australia Physical Education Section.

We actually practised our cricket on park wickets, malthoid surface or whatever, getting down to it whenever and wherever we could. We'd practice occasionally at the cricket club grounds, but on their malthoid wickets. There'd be Marsh, Malone, Edwards, Laird, Trevor Chappell, Langer and myself, for example, working out in one of those nets and people would stop and get out of their cars to watch us. I think they understood it was us against the cricket world, so to speak, and I could feel their support and their interest.

9. The First Supertests!

Finally World Series Cricket got off the ground on time and without too many hitches. The fact that it did and that it ran as smoothly as it did was something akin to the eighth wonder of the world. When I think of all the numbers of people involved in putting the traditional game on the road each year, I'm lost in admiration for the small bunch of dedicated workers who gave their body and soul to getting WSC moving. Obviously there were teething troubles as it all unfolded in that first season and on many a night the midnight oil was burned to have things just right before the next day dawned. In a major change from the original concept of having just Australia and a World Eleven, it was decided to make the West Indies a team on their own for the Supertests. Then the West Indies players would go into a pool for selection of the World Eleven. And to give the players on the fringes something to occupy themselves, a second Australian team was engaged in playing up-country games. This meant a further rash of signings.

The fact that the cricket was of such a high standard was amazing, because we Australians in particular had a most limited build-up. I think it was all to do with the wonderful atmopshere of anticipation which was pervasive when the players assembled in Melbourne about a fortnight before the season was due to begin. We knew that we were about to take part in a most historic happening and that we were a very important part of it all. The fortnight was dedicated to getting as much practice as possible on the turf wickets at the Moorabbin ground (home of the St Kilda football and cricket clubs). We all realised that within the space of those two weeks we had to cram in two month's normal practice and be prepared to go into an international confrontation without the value of a couple of club and first-class games to run into form.

That took some coming to terms with mentally. Also I'm sure that some of the players just didn't get sufficient practice during that period to prepare themselves adequately, and consequently their form suffered for the whole of the season. And another big problem with being a WSC professional was the fact that if you lost form you couldn't just drop back to a club or state game to find some touch . . . you could only go back to playing in country areas against world-class players on wickets that weren't always the best. To complicate matters even further, there were no proper turf practice facilities available where you would spend a few hours working on technique and hopefully bring yourself back into form.

There were problems here and there regarding facilities, yet nobody ever complained seriously. It was such an exciting venture, and I guess we just floated along enjoying every minute of it and glossing over the little setbacks. Things like the situation in the first season when we had to travel on match days from the Old Melbourne Inn on one side of Melbourne to VFL Park way on the other side of the city in little vans. It was a long journey in terribly cramped conditions, but the guys didn't seem to mind. We knew that the administrators were doing their best and we had to do the same just to keep up with them. The whole atmosphere rekindled my interest in top cricket and I know I wasn't the only one to be overcome by that feeling. It was like taking on a new sport where you could see exciting new challenges. I loved it.

Above all, for once, all the players were able to communicate with the administrators and if a decision was to be taken it was taken immediately. There were no communications barriers as we'd known them with the Australian Cricket Board and no great delays while the cumbersome systems went into motion. Austin Robertson was the link-man between the players, the umpires and the administration and he was always there to clear a path for healthy communications. I guess I had a bit to say about a few things, perhaps my biggest beef being the poor quality of the run-ups on most of the grounds in the first season. At times I was ploughing in through sand—and my bowling relies so much on the speed and the balance of my run-up, gained from a firm grip with my spikes.

I understood that the run-ups weren't good because there just hadn't been enough time for the grounds to settle down to withstanding the rigours of cricket. Let's face it, it was something of a minor miracle that we had any grounds at all . . . the Showground in Sydney, VFL Park in Melbourne, Football Park in Adelaide and the Gloucester Park trotting ground in Perth. None of them was a cricket ground, yet we were able to play on acceptable facilities in such a short preparation time. The wickets during that first year were nothing short of miraculous. Even though in the main they had little

101

grass and played rather slowish, the fact that they were even play-able at all was real fairytale stuff. And I can say in all honesty that one track we played on at the Sydney Showground in that first season was the best cricket pitch I've ever played on, anywhere.

The man responsible for this major miracle was John Maley, a quiet and unassuming former club cricketer from Western Australia. He put in as much time as anybody and more than most in heading up the preparation of the playing surfaces for WSC. He started from nothing at most grounds and through his knowhow and hard work, plus the loyal and dedicated support of his 'team', he produced the goods. If he hadn't WSC could have failed ... it was as simple as that. The quality of the wickets was so important. If they had been really bad there would have been terrible complications for the bats-men against the sort of bowlers who were assembled. Maley made fairly flat wickets, which I guess didn't help me a lot but which were good enough to form the basis of a good game of cricket. As the second year of WSC progressed he made better and better tracks and I've nothing but praise for John.

As the time drew near for the opening game of our new cricket competition we were all increasingly apprehensive. Would every-thing work out the way it had been planned ... would the wickets be satisfactory ... would anybody bother to come and watch us ...? Those and many other questions almost haunted us as the hours ticked by to D-day. It was how I'd imagined people involved in a stage production would feel leading up to the opening night. I spoke to many people about the coming first day, asking all and sundry how they thought we'd go from every aspect. By far the most positive was Kerry Packer. He was particularly confident that we'd do well right from the start. Even so, he was noticeably nervous. We players were most concerned. It was important to us that people were there to see that first day.

Its history now that on the first day out there at VFL Park just over 600 people turned up. Those few were really lost in the grand-stands in that vast arena and I must admit the sight was really de-moralising. However, things gradually improved as the season wore on until the real turning point came with the advent of night cricket under lights at VFL Park on 14 December 1977. After that memor-able night we began to draw significant crowds and we knew we'd cracked it. But the absolute moment of truth was the first game under the new lighting at the Sydney Cricket Ground in the second season. I'll never forget that night. People had to be turned away at the gates because the ground was full with more than 50 000 people inside. It was a marvellous sight.

I recall going upstairs to the official area to share the moment with Austin Robertson, John Cornell and the others. It was about seven o'clock and as I looked out of the back of the pavilion my eyes just popped as I saw thousands and thousands of people lined up away from the gates and trying to get into the ground. There were hordes of people and cars as far as the eye could see. As I looked out in the gloomy light I got a tingling feeling through my body.

About an hour later John Cornell came down to the dressing-room and grabbed me and said, 'Come with me, mate.' We walked upstairs to the official area, out through the front and down to where Kerry Packer was sitting with some friends and some people from Channel Nine. John sat next to me and after a few lingering seconds drinking in the sight before us he said, 'Have a look at that . . . we've made it!' Kerry turned and with a broad grin said, 'That's it . . . we're right.'

The turnout that night and on subsequent nights early in that season convinced everybody that now there really *was* a contest between WSC and traditional cricket in Australia. We had won against the greatest odds, against an absolutely hostile Press. The public had been told time and time again that WSC was bad cricket, or 'circus cricket' as they called it—but the people had had the courage to have a look for themselves, maybe at first on television, and then later at the grounds, and now there they were in their masses. I was convinced then that establishment cricket had started its downhill slide in comparison. We could look at their attendances against ours and notice clearly that things were running our way.

I knew then that WSC was a success and that as time went on we'd go from strength to strength. There was talk of packaging it for America and there were other things in the pipeline. I felt strongly that if WSC had gone into a third year one result would have been the ruin of establishment cricket as we knew it in Australia and the gradual strengthening of WSC to a point where it would stand for ever. And I was confident that the players were in a strong position, where they would remain, as a result of what had transpired. At that point I enjoyed a rather rosy realisation of the whole thing I'd some-how put on the road in a conversation with John Cornell and Paul Hogan not much more than two years before. But accompanying that feeling was a frightening concern that cricket as I had known it, which had provided a nursery for my own development, would

103

possibly slowly disintegrate. I feel sure now that there was an alternative plan.

During the tenure of WSC we came in for a lot of stinging criticism and a constant flow of harping from the Australian and British Press. But I single out as the most hurtful the suggestions (and there were plenty) that our games were 'rigged' and that we weren't bowling bouncers during the twilight and night periods of day/night games because we had an agreement not to endanger each other. There was nothing further from the truth on both counts. To deal with the 'rigged' accusations first, I objected so much to that being said or written because it was tantamount to calling us all cheats. It is true some of the games were awfully close, but you'll find that in any grade of one-day cricket there is a high percentage of fantastic close finishes. In fact I I've had a few laughs when we've been involved in close one-day games since the compromise and I've shouted 'it's rigged' at a tense point in proceedings.

The WSC games were some of the best cricket matches I've ever played in, certainly some of the hardest fought. I know I speak for all the Australians when I say that we were representing Australia as of old and were just as desperate as ever to win against two great teams, the West Indies and the World Eleven. The competition was intense, and you had to be right on your mettle just to stay with the sort of opposition we met game after game.

I remember one pre-match team-meeting in Canberra where we all took a close look at our performances, which hadn't been so good. Ian Chappell had called a breakfast meeting, which posed its problems for me as I rarely have breakfast on tour and *never* rise early. Ian told us we weren't playing too well and asked us man by man to try to tell him why. The subject was thrown around for a while, then I had my turn. 'Everybody must realise,' I said, 'that we're playing for Australia ... commit yourselves accordingly. After that, you're playing for yourself. Those who don't want to toe the line should pack up and go.'

As to the talk of not bowling bouncers in indifferent light, remember that most of the tracks we played on were so flat that it was pointless trying to bowl a bouncer. Secondly, if you did bowl one you were simply asking the batsman to help himself to a four or even a six.

So you can imagine why most of us developed a certain hostility to the Press. Of course we did notice a gradual change in the attitudes of the media in general as it became obvious that WSC had arrived and was there to stay. For a change we were given some prominence in the reporting of our games, and here and there a few nice things were said and written about us. But Kerry Packer had always contended that 'In the end, whether the Press like it or not, the people out there with their bums on seats and those watching us on television will decide if WSC has been a success or not.' And he was so right.

The first Supertest, Australia and the West Indies opposed at VFL Park, had special significance for us all, being the beginning of a new era in international cricket. It was a truly hard-fought match, with the game poised to go either way right to the bitter end. Australia led by 42 on the first innings, despite the fact that three of our top batsmen failed to score. We did very well to bowl the West Indies out for 214 on an easy-paced wicket, but then we failed to capitalise on that advantage as we fell again to the pace trio of Roberts, Holding and Daniel. Still, the West Indies needed 237 for victory and when we had them 7 for 190 we were in with a great chance of winning the first ever Supertest. But Deryck Murray and Andy Roberts made the most of the lucky breaks and carried their team to victory.

I think the significance of the occasion warrants the listing of the players of the two sides in this game, the maiden WSC Supertest. For Australia: Ian Chappell (captain), Greg Chappell, Rick McCosker, Ian Davis, David Hookes, Doug Walters, Rod Marsh, Ray Bright, Dennis Lillee, Max Walker and Len Pascoe. For the West Indies: Clive Lloyd (captain), Roy Fredericks, Gordon Greenidge, Viv Richards, Jim Allen, Collis King, Deryck Murray, David Holford, Michael Holding, Andy Roberts and Wayne Daniel.

In the second Supertest in Sydney, the West Indies mounted a four-man pace attack and we struggled right from the first ball. Mind you, things could have been a little better if David Hookes hadn't been downed trying to hook a short one from Andy Roberts in the first innings. Hookes was on 81 and going beautifully at the time. He didn't bat again in the match. In fact, he didn't play again until the final Supertest of the summer. We trailed by 85 on the first innings and without Hookes in the second there was only token resistance and we ended up losing by 9 wickets. Big Joel Garner bowled very well throughout the game.

The third clash in Adelaide, the final in the series against the West Indies, produced the first Supertest century. And, fittingly, it came from the bat of Ian Chappell. In fact, there were two more 'tons' for the match—106 from Bruce Laird and 123 from Viv Richards, who had previous scores of 79, 56, 88, 5 not out and 9. Australia led by 243 on the first innings, thanks to a bonus bowling effort of 5 for 20 from Greg Chappell. The West Indies never really recovered from that big deficit and Australia ended up winning by 220 runs. That meant we'd lost the series two-one, but as the first game could have gone either way we thought it wasn't a bad performance against such a great all-round side.

Then all the overseas players went into the melting pot for the choosing of the World Eleven for the final three Supertests. Such was the might of the West Indies party that six of them were picked for the first encounter in Sydney. Unfortunately I had to miss this game because of an ankle injury sustained when playing a one-day game in Perth. For the fourth time in four Supertests Australia batted first and for the third time out of those four games we led on the first innings. The margin was just 14, thanks to another fine, fighting Bruce Laird century. The little fellow really was stamping himself as a great player of fast bowling. But then once more Australia had a disappointing second innings with Andy Roberts and Joel Garner cleaning us out for just 128. So the World side won, but they did lose 6 wickets in making the 145 runs for victory and again we lost no heart from the defeat.

However, we were to take a real thrashing in the following game, the one and only Supertest in my home State. The wicket at Gloucester Park in Perth was as flat as a pancake ... and that's not to detract from the brilliant innings made by three World Eleven batsmen. Openers Barry Richards and Gordon Greenidge got stuck in and they stayed and stayed and stayed. Greenidge made 140 and Richards 207. The first wicket fell at 369, but there was worse to come for us as Viv Richards followed with 177. It was close to a waste of time trying to get them out, but I did end up with 4 wickets—for 149 runs! It was purely a matter of buying wickets.

They made 625 and we were away to a terrible start at 4 for 73 before Ian and Greg Chappell put on a few. Greg ended up making a masterly 174. We made 393, which isn't a bad sort of innings in normal circumstances. However, it was just 24 more than the World Eleven had put on for the first wicket. We followed on in very forlorn fashion and ended up losing by an innings and 73 runs. We were really down on our uppers after that loss, but better things were to come in the final Supertest at VFL Park. Again the wicket was a featherbed, but this time we batted first and put on the big score of 538 for 6 declared. Greg Chappell continued in his grand form

106

with a majestic 246 not out and Rick McCosker at last hit his straps with a solid 129.

There was more quality batting to come in this game as the mighty Viv Richards hit up his fourth century of the six-game Supertest summer. What a player! Still we led by 104 runs on the first innings, but things didn't look too good when we were 4 for 34 in the second innings, then 6 for 98. Then David Hookes, back in the side after his injury, chimed in with his second half-century for the match to somewhat right the ship. We led by 271 going into the last innings and Max Walker and I had the final say of the season. We picked up 5 each as the World Eleven were knocked over for 230 and Australia won by 41 runs.

Again we'd lost the series two-one, but again we thought that given an ounce of luck it could have gone the other way in Australia's favour. So for the summer we'd won two and lost four playing against two teams which boasted many of the world's best players of the day. So it was quite a good year from an Australian point of view . . . remembering that first David Hookes, then Bruce Laird and Ian Chappell had missed games because of injuries suffered against the West Indies speedsters. From my own point of view it had been a battle on easy pitches against some absolutely top-flight batting. My 21 wickets, hard-earned in 5 Supertests, had come at 36.43 apiece. In the International Cup one-day series we played off the final against the West Indies on a fast and good wicket at Sydney. We did very well to knock them over for 124 and were cruising at 3 for 76—but then we lost our final 7 wickets for 23 runs and were a sorely dejected lot at losing that one.

And so the first season of World Series Cricket was over and we could all look back on a remarkably successful opening. I am not denying for one minute that we'd had our problems—you'd have to expect some, mounting a programme such as that from scratch—but in the circumstances all went very well. It was a tough schedule for the players, but we had been paid much better and had enjoyed the challenge. Above all, perhaps, we had enjoyed the spirit of adventure that was attached to that first year. And coming out of that wonderful summer were many innovations that would remain with the game for all time, not the least of which was night cricket. If the opening gambit for WSC had been a qualified success, there's no questioning the fact that cricket at night under lights with a white ball had been a huge unqualified success, one of the great revolutions in the history of the game.

10. Supertests, 1978-79

No grass grew under the feet of the World Series Cricket administration during the winter of 1978. They had been reasonably satisfied with the performance in the opening season, but much had to be done to refine the 'product' before the onset of the second season. From a player's point of view perhaps the most significant happening revolved around the law courts, where it was resolved that WSC players should be permitted to practise and play with their respective district clubs. This was a most important factor in our build-up for the new season, because those first few weeks of practice and match play on turf wickets are vital to a cricketer's form in the firing line of international competition.

The administrators also saw fit to make some subtle changes to the competition format for the new season. For a start they decided to field the World Eleven as a separate entity, without the bolstering lent to it in the first season by the West Indies players. This made for a true three-cornered competition. It also meant the recruitment of more players to fill the World Eleven ranks and the result was the arrival of two very good players from South Africa, all-rounder Clive Rice and fast bowler Garth Le Roux. There were a couple of new faces in the West Indies camp, too, and Australia landed a rather interesting recruit in Kepler Wessels, a left-hand opening batsman. Wessels was born in South Africa, but had come to live in Australia in the hope of playing Test cricket for the country.

The idea with the new competition was for each team to play the other once, with the team leading on points after the qualifying round going straight into the Supertest grand final and the other two playing off for the right to the other grand final berth. This season we played Supertests on just the two venues, VFL Park in Melbourne and the Sydney Cricket Ground, which, in a unique arrangement, had been made available to WSC as well as for traditional cricket games. That meant we were guaranteed good wickets and, happily for me, good run-ups each time we played Supertests. The Sydney Cricket Ground Trust also made a solid commitment by installing a marvellous lights system to accommodate our day/night matches. So all the players looked forward to the new season with some expectancy ... having been through the first shake-down season and ironed out the bugs, the new summer should be a breeze. And it was.

The 1978-79 WSC season hit off with a Supertest between Australia and the World Eleven in Melbourne and we faced a line-up that read like a who's who of world cricket. So you can imagine we were absolutely beside ourselves with glee when we bowled them out for just 175 runs. However, this new fellow Le Roux, with his huge frame and his sling-shot delivery style, grabbed 5 wickets cheaply and we were soon out for 150. How deflating! Only Ian Chappell with 48 went within a bull's roar of getting on top of the attack. After that we fell further behind and finally lost by 102 runs. Wessels made a very promising 46 in our second innings and showed that he was a very determined customer who loved batting and making runs.

The two visiting sides met in the second Supertest in Sydney and the World Eleven showed what a formidable line-up they were by humbling the mighty West Indies in an innings defeat. Looking down that line-up, the World side had Test century-makers down to number nine and an attack which always had something in reserve. It was a daunting thought going into a game against them ... in this second year I always had the feeling they were an almost impossible nut to crack. Australia met the West Indies in the third Supertest at VFL Park and this produced the first drawn game after nine Supertests. Wessels lived up to all his promise with a century in the first innings, while David Hookes reflected what many people thought was his true ability with a good 116 in the same innings.

However, when the West Indies batted Lawrence Rowe made a big century and guided them to a lead of 53 on the first innings. It had been a good innings by Rowe, but from Australia's point of view he could have been out on a number of occasions and we could have led comfortably on the first innings. In our second innings we battled on manfully on a track that was difficult for batting and finally Ian Chappell was able to declare at 9 for 304. We had just 57 overs at them in the final innings and on that wicket the draw was inevitable. That put us into the qualifying final against the West Indies in Sydney, the winner earning the right to meet the World Eleven in the grand final.

At last we hit our straps! The West Indies batted first and spinner

Ray Bright bowled magnificently to bag 6 wickets on a track that was seaming about a bit. David Hookes again came to the fore when we were struggling at 3 for 17 and as a result of his dogged 69 we led by 22. Then it was my turn to produce the goods . . . a return of 7 for 23 as the Windies went tumbling for just 89. I'd been rapped on the finger by Andy Roberts while batting and was well fired up when I came out to bowl. It was possibly the fastest I bowled in WSC games. So we strolled to victory by 10 wickets and set about preparing for the big challenge in the grand final.

There was a considerable build-up for this match. Tony Greig was at the head of the list, becoming increasingly more outspoken about his team's chances of winning as the day drew closer. Greigy hadn't been playing well enough to gain a regular place in the World Eleven throughout the season, but he was back in for the final. And how he was chirping! He made statements about how he was going to make a century, that I wasn't good enough to take any wickets and how his mate Garth Le Roux would get a heap of wickets.

Well, he was right on one count, because Le Roux did give us a hard time, taking 5 wickets in the first innings and 4 in the second. However, despite Le Roux's excellent performance in that first innings, we did manage to lead by 4 runs. That could have been a whole lot better as their ninth wicket fell at 104 and they went on to make 168, thanks to Le Roux and Derek Underwood.

And Tony Greig's century? Well, he fell approximately 100 runs short of his loudly proclaimed promises. If ever I was going to do something it was to put egg on Greig's face and the scoreline read, 'Greig, caught Marsh bowled Lillee . . . 0'. Just to rub some salt in his wound, I overturned his predictions even further by taking 5 wickets in that innings. In our second innings Hookes was once more the hero with 96. This young left-hander from South Australia had shown immense talent in his short time in international cricket and what a tragedy it was when his game subsequently fell apart at the seams. Perhaps in his enthusiasm for the big time he made the mistake of letting things get out of perspective a bit. However, I do believe that he is young enough and good enough to come again and once more be a force to be reckoned with in international conflict.

So, we led by 223 when the World side began the final innings of the series and we actually had them rocking a bit at 4 for 84. In fact, we were always looking as though we might knock them over and win this vital match. But Barry Richards made a century, a good century in an innings which could have ended well short—and that would have given us our chance. He and Mike Procter, who'd had a pretty good season with the bat, put the matter beyond doubt with a stand of 91 and we finally went down by 5 wickets. It had been a match full of needle after all the drum-beating beforehand. Ian Chappell and Tony Greig were constantly at each other's throats and there were nasty scenes after the game was over when Ian wouldn't acknowledge Greigy.

For my own, I was involved in an incident with Le Roux. He bowled me a 'bean ball' and hit me flush on just above the groin. I reacted by calling him a few things, all of which apparently were heard by viewers of the game on television through the ground microphones. The big fellow made no effort to apologise, so when I later caught up with him I thought I'd better put my point again. 'If you want to play it that way,' I said, 'be careful because I'll make sure that I can do it as well as you.' Pregnant pause. 'But,' I added, 'I'm quite happy to forget it now and shake hands.' We shook hands and that was the most sensible thing to do.

In the International Cup one-day series this season there was a best-of-five final round and Australia won the right to play off against the West Indies. We were off to a flying start after Kepler Wessels scored a great century and we won the opening game comfortably. The second game was a tight go with the Windies winning with only a few balls remaining. In the third clash Wessels continued in his grand form with a 70 (following 136 and 40 run out) and we made the good score of 6 for 200. However, the West Indies' batting was too strong on a good wicket and they won with 3 overs to spare. We batted even better in the fourth game, making 240 from our 50 overs and we fancied ourselves to win this one and go into the deciding fifth final. However, we didn't bank on being defeated on a technicality. The West Indies in fact scored 8 for 228 from 41 overs and won the game on a better scoring rate. It was a very controversial finish. A decision on the rules of play was made during the night session of play and conveyed to the West Indies camp, because they were off the field, but not to Australia, who were on the field. Our understanding was that the game would be played out to the finish, regardless, and proof of that was the fact Ian Chappell bowled David Hookes in preference to myself in what turned out to be the closing overs. It was a misunderstanding, I guess, but it did leave a bit of a sour taste in our mouths when the game ended and we were informed we'd lost on an inferior scoring rate. So the Windies won the series, three-one.

111

11. WSC in the West Indies

Almost immediately after the last ball of the final Supertest had been bowled we left for the West Indies on what turned out to be World Series Cricket's swansong. Looking back on that tour, you certainly couldn't say we didn't go out with a bang. What had promised to be an exciting and challenging conflict in the Caribbean turned out to be a nightmare, thanks to the people on the other side of the fence, the West Indian spectators. More than once during a string of riots and ugly incidents I literally feared for my life. And I must admit I came away from the 'island paradise' convinced that if I ever went back it would be with great caution.

Nobody could have predicted what eventually tore the tour apart. It opened in such pleasant and happy conditions at Kingston, Jamaica, with the first Supertest in which we were thrashed by the West Indies . . . and perhaps there was a moral in that! Even though we bowled them out for 188 in the first innings we were never in the game, scoring just 106 ourselves in a miserable first-innings effort that lasted only 37 overs. It was the old four-pronged pace attack again and our batsmen just wilted under the pressure. In that innings there was the rather unique situation of having the three Chappell brothers in the side *and* following each other in the batting order. Trevor opened with Bruce Laird, then came Ian and then Greg at number four. Mind you, I should point out that they scored just twenty-seven runs between them, which is even more unusual.

Of course in this game I was in tandem with Jeff Thomson once more. He'd been to the courts in Australia to win the right to play for WSC and finally was permitted to strip in the West Indies. It was great working with him again, even though he was under-prepared for all the bowling that was asked of him. He bowled with great fire in the Trinidad game and I must say that his presence was heaven-sent for me—and the side, of course. He had a quiet opening, picking up just the one wicket in the first innings and the two in the second at Kingston. That second innings was dominated by big Clive Lloyd's flashing blade. He hammered out 197 in grand style and the

112

game completely slipped away from us. We even had to endure a partnership of 226 between Clive and Andy Roberts, who made 89, before finally ending the West Indies innings. Again our batsmen were no match for the Windies speedsters and we lost by 369 runs.

The second Supertest was at Bridgetown, Barbados, and this time we batted first and got away to a good start and it was our turn to take a good lead on the first innings, thanks to a good all-round performance. Then Ian and Greg Chappell batted beautifully in the second innings and when our innings closed we had set the West Indies a target of 357 for victory. Thanks to lion-hearted Lenny Pascoe we made good early inroads into the West Indies second innings, having them 3 for 47 at one stage. But it was at the fall of that third wicket that the crowd troubles had their beginnings. Gordon Greenidge was given out caught behind by Rod Marsh off the bowling of Pascoe and he registered strong disapproval with Douglas Sang Hue's decision. The way he carried on as he left the field really got the crowd going against us and the umpires. He really should have taken it on the chin and walked off, right or wrong.

Then a good partnership between Roy Fredericks and Viv Richards took the total on to 133. But that was the time for the trouble to really start. Lenny had Fredericks leg before wicket and, unfortunately as it turned out, Freddo stood his ground a bit and showed his disgust at the decision of Ralph Gosein. Freddo's reaction, plus the fact that at 4 for 133 their side was in grave danger of losing the game, combined to bring the big crowd to the boil. They began by shouting and jeering, then started to pelt the ground with bottles and we were encouraged to leave the field rather hastily to preserve our good looks. As a way of saying to the crowd 'Don't blame the umps, they're all right,' I put an arm around Douglas Sang Hue as we walked off and pretended to kiss him on the cheek. That landed me in hot water with the tour management for 'having incited the crowds'. Freddo and Greenidge also were hauled over the coals for their dissident reactions to the umpires' decisions.

Some fifty minutes after we'd left the field the umpires tried to resume play, but when Clive Lloyd and not Freddo came out with Viv Richards to continue the West Indies innings the riot started all over again. The umpires then abandoned the match. We were absolutely heartbroken, because we really only had to break the Richards-Lloyd partnership to win the game. Bearing in mind that they were still 234 runs short of the target, I reckon we would have levelled the series in that final period of play. At that stage it seemed to me that there was something suicidal about visiting teams doing well against the West Indies in the Caribbean. We were playing our hearts out to beat them, but as soon as we looked like achieving that goal we'd put ourselves in danger with the irate crowds.

The third Supertest at Port of Spain, Trinidad, must rate as one of the all-time great matches ever played. The advantage swapped and changed about throughout a gripping game. We batted first and were immediately confronted with the situation of being 5 out for just 32 runs and at that stage you could have got any sort of odds about an Australian win. But through some remarkable personal performances we recovered to record an amazing victory. There was no greater contribution to that win than Bruce Laird's 122 in the first innings—in the circumstances surely one of the best innings you could ever wish to see. I was out there with him for a while during the latter part of it and I can assure you that it really was tough going. However, Bruce was in complete command and I couldn't help thinking that he came of age during that innings. He later received the highest accolade . . . master batsman Viv Richards saying to one of us, 'Man, I wish I could bat like that!'

So out of the ruins came a first-innings total of 246 and thanks to a determined 5-wicket effort from Thommo we led by 16 runs on the first innings. When Greg Chappell came to the crease at number four in the second innings the Australian score read 2 for 0. Now it was Greg's turn to play an innings worthy of a man considered to be one of the best two or three batsmen in the world. On a wicket taking spin he made a memorable 150 and, thanks to that great knock, when our innings ended the West Indies needed 299 to win. It was nip and tuck all the way, with both teams always seeming to be in sight of victory.

The game was one of the most physically and mentally exhausting I've ever played in. I was nearly out on my feet near the end and had to leave the field. As I flaked out on the rub-down table in the dressing-room I thought, 'That's that, we can't win from here.' However, I was brought to my senses some five minutes later by the jubilant yells of our physiotherapist Dave McErlane, telling me that Lenny Pascoe had taken the last wicket and we'd won. I'd bowled 31 overs in that second innings and during that stint I learnt another facet of bowling when I switched late in the piece to bowling fastish off-breaks and leg-cutters with good results. But there was no better result than that memorable victory, which squared the series and gave us great hope for the remaining two Supertests.

The fourth Supertest at Georgetown, Guyana ... well, I wish I could forget it altogether, but I guess the memory of it will be with me until the day I die. In fact, I can say without a word of a lie that at one stage I thought that game was going to produce the very day that I died. The most terrifying experience of my life came soon after three o'clock on the scheduled first day when people who had paid good money to come into the ground lost patience at the thought that they wouldn't see any play and began to riot. It was a shameful performance by a band of screaming banshees, but it was sparked by the ridiculous decision of the officials to allow people into the ground when it was obvious even before the day dawned that there was no hope of play because there'd been so much rain the previous few days.

The playing area was saturated, but hordes of people had been allowed to pay to get into the ground. The umpires made several inspections, each time deeming the ground unfit for play and each time reporting that they would inspect again later. By about three o'clock the mob had had enough and all hell broke loose. At the time we were sitting around the dressing-room, filling in time as you do in those circumstances. We could hear the crowd yelling and carrying on outside and then a bit of bottle throwing started—but none of us imagined what was to come next. The next thing I knew, somebody yelled, 'Come and have a look at this!' We all rushed to the windows of the rooms to see a whole fence about three metres high and with huge uprights being rocked violently by thousands of angry spectators.

Suddenly the whole section of fence gave way ... that was a signal for more fence to collapse and for thousands of people to pour on to the ground and rush towards our pavilion. At this point people in a grandstand opposite started tearing huge sections of seating from their mountings and throwing them over the edge of the stand and on to the people milling below. Soon bottles, bricks and rocks started crashing through the windows of our rooms and I thought to myself, 'This is it, son ... you have had your chips!'

We all took stock of the situation very quickly. We were in trouble, big trouble. We grabbed our helmets and bats and headed for the safest possible corners of the room. There were glass fragments flying all over the room and some of the West Indies players, who were in their dressing-room, were hit, receiving slight cuts.

There was a tremendous din from the shouting and screaming people outside and I knew we were in extreme physical danger. As

I looked around me in the confusion, there was a sea of scared faces. Then my eyes fell on the countenances of the two umpires, who had simply come into the dressing-room to see Ian Chappell and had been trapped in with the rest of us. Had the mob broken in, which I felt was what could happen at any moment, and caught them in there with the players, anything could have happened to them. Just looking at them cowering in the corner, I have no doubt whatsoever that they were really fearing for their lives. Mind you, so was I!

If the riot squad had not turned up at that very moment, there was no telling how far the hostile crowd would have gone. They had already started trying to set fire to one pavilion and were in the midst of ransacking the pavilion in which we were cowering. I'm sure we would have been the next to go. We were all extremely relieved when we realised the riot police were getting on top of the situation.

It had been a terrifying experience, one I'll never forget. Naturally that night there was a lot of discussion about what had happened and the question was raised about the sanity of continuing any form of cricket in Guyana. We decided quite smartly that the only way we'd play any more cricket there was if the riot squad was at the ground the whole time. Even then I'd think twice about it . . . and only agree if I could insure myself for a million dollars for the duration!

We asked ourselves why would such a cricket-loving people as the West Indians are be prepared to cause so much trouble at a cricket ground? We came to the conclusion that on that day all they wanted, having paid out their money, was to see play—and the prospect of no play was too much for them. The riot had caused more than $20 000 worth of damage, which WSC had to guarantee to the local officials before a decision to call the game off was reversed and it was decided to play it as a three-dayer. That decision meant there really wasn't enough time for a result on a wicket that played very well after all the rain. Greg Chappell followed up with another fine century as Australia scored 341, then Collis King was a century-maker for the West Indies in their total of 476. Thommo was in the wickets again with 4 for 84.

The tour almost ended early for me when I broke down a week before the fifth and deciding Supertest. It was my old back which had given me so much trouble during my career and it occurred when we were playing a series of three one-day games in Trinidad. I started bowling in the first of these on the Saturday and the first two deliveries went by without a hint of a problem. Then

116

it hit. As I bowled the third delivery I felt an excruciating pain on the right-hand side of the lower spinal area. It seemed to affect the whole of my back and left me barely able to walk or bend. I tried to finish the over, but it was hopeless and I left the ground: I felt as though something was out of place, as though I'd pinched a nerve, but a series of pushes, shoves and stretches by the physio made no difference.

As you can imagine, many things were going through my mind ... Was this, after all, to be the end of my career?

I was examined then by two doctors, one an orthopaedic surgeon and the other a neuro-surgeon. The former said I had a slipped disc and the latter said it was strained ligaments. Both men said it'd be at least three weeks before I'd be mobile again, so arrangements were made for me to fly home early on the following Tuesday morning. I was despondent at the thought. However, for one reason or other things began to improve and I was so much better by Monday night that the flight was cancelled. Instead it was decided that I should fly to Antigua with the team to see if a few more days' rest would be enough to bring me up for the Supertest, due to start on the Friday. The pain was gone by the Wednesday and I was able to do some exercises and go for a long run along the beach. On Thursday, much to my surprise and that of the rest of the touring party, I was able to train at the nets and prove my fitness for the match.

As it turned out the final Supertest was a fizzer and the series ended all tied up at one-all. Greg Chappell made another century, his third in three matches, as we limped along to 234. Then we had to work awfully hard to dismiss the Windies for 438 and from then on we battled along for a comfortable draw. Rod Marsh posted his first WSC century with just one over remaining, and this, of course, in his final innings for WSC. Once more Greg Chappell was in the runs in the second innings, scoring 85. He ended the 5 Supertests with 631 runs at the magnificent average of 63.10. I was very pleased to pick up 4 wickets in the one West Indies innings, to end up the top wicket-taker for either side with 23 wickets at 28.39 for the series.

I looked back on that tour with mixed feelings. The riots, the tight schedule and the fact that it came hard on the heels of a really tough summer back home certainly coloured my time in the Caribbean. At the end of the last Supertest I felt enormous relief at the thought that I had a five-month rest coming up. My next thought was 'Thank goodness I didn't take up any of the offers I'd received to play in the coming winter in England!' I just wouldn't have been able to do any of them justice. I felt reasonably well within myself physically, but I mentally flopped after that final Supertest . . . and that night I joined the others in letting off a lot of steam!

12. The Way Back

During that tempestuous tour of the West Indies we heard the first murmurings of a compromise. We were told that Kerry Packer had been approached by members of the Australian Cricket Board with a view to bringing both camps together in the interests of Australian cricket. The idea was put to us as a group of WSC players in the Caribbean and we had a meeting to discuss it from all angles. We were asked to thrash out all the points which we as players thought should be included in any compromise agreement to protect our own interests. Naturally we wanted to avoid going back under the auspices of the Australian Cricket Board only to find ourselves no better off than we were before we left to play with WSC. We also wanted to protect ourselves against victimisation of any sort after a compromise.

We thought as a group that it was pointless going back just for the sake of going back. Ground had to be seen to have been made by all the players—yet when we looked back on it much later, we weren't too sure that it had. We didn't gain as much as we perhaps wanted, probably because in the end we wanted the compromise enough, just for the sake of cricket, to be prepared to accept less than our original demands and ideals for fear of jeopardising the negotiations. There was a strong feeling within the ranks of the WSC players in the West Indies at least that we should go back for the sake of cricket, but that was not unanimous. At the meeting Ian Chappell conducted an open forum. Everybody was encouraged to have his say without fear and the meeting certainly wasn't dominated by the senior players. There were a few who weren't happy at the prospect of a compromise, but who went along with it rather than rock the boat.

We then put our thoughts forward and then waited to hear what had transpired. As it turned out we heard nothing more until the final announcement and I certainly had no part in the negotiations. There were strong fears among the WSC players surrounding future team selections. We wanted to be sure that Australian teams would always be picked on the fairest method: that of merit, with no player held back in his progress because of participation with WSC. As one of the senior members of the WSC player strength, I wasn't all that bothered personally about this point because I felt sure that if I performed well enough I'd be picked. I felt mainly for the younger players, who had it all ahead of them. It would be tragic if their futures were jeopardised because of their past involvement with a breakaway group.

My private hopes at that early stage in the compromise discussions were for the well-being of cricket as a whole. As I have said before, from the very beginning of the split in Australian cricket I had hoped that at some stage the two groups would get back together again. I thought then that perhaps it would take four or five, even up to ten, years for this to happen. I must admit I didn't think there was any way it could have come about so quickly. My hope was that if there was to be a compromise then the good work we'd done for the lot of the player would be carried through. Mind you, I often wonder about that—for four seasons since WSC began, players under the Australian Cricket Board hadn't had a single raise in their *basic* payment. It finally improved in the 1981-82 season.

I was deeply concerned about that sort of thing—that once we got back together the Board would tighten its grip on the players all over again—and here it was patently happening. Let's face it, that doesn't make a huge difference to players like myself or Greg Chappell or Rod Marsh, because we earn extra money through promotions and advertising. It's the guys who give up their jobs and their future prospects in employment to make a full commitment to Australian cricket who must be considered when it comes to the review of incomes. Cricket has become a nine-months-a-year proposition for us. In most cases other jobs are absolutely out of the question for Test team regulars. These players need to be paid properly and their pay scales need to be reviewed on a more regular basis than once every four or five years, which seems to be the attitude of the Board.

Sadly I feel there is once more a real gap between player and administrator. We are told there is no gap, simply because once or twice a year players' representatives meet with Board members to air their grievances. It is not enough, and it never will be until notice is taken of the important issues raised at these meetings.

During the days of WSC we moved strongly in the direction of the formation of a players' association to guard against our voice ever being heard merely as a whisper. I strongly supported this association because I feared we'd be brushed aside in any compromise. However, it was impossible to get this point through to the players who had stayed on the traditional side of the fence, and when the compromise went through the players' association gradually disintegrated. Now the Board holds the whip hand. They say that they are trying to get closer to the players and I feel nowadays, talking to some of the younger administrators, it is so. The Board has now appointed Bob Merriman as the player/admin. co-ordinator and he is very keen to do the right thing by both parties.

While Kerry Packer and the senior Board officials were closetted in their compromise conferences I left for a holiday in Britain and Europe with Helen and our two boys. As it turned out our stay in England coincided with the staging of the second Prudential World Cup one-day competition. The Australian team under Kim Hughes had of course been picked without drawing on WSC players and as such wasn't rated a chance against all the other nations at full strength.

It was sad to reflect upon this fact in the light of our magnificent performance in the inaugural competition back in 1975. Still, I knew all the Australian players pretty well and it was natural for me to be very interested in their progress and while in London I even wrote a series of articles for one of the London dailies.

The Aussies were to play their first game of the series at Lord's against England. Though as a WSC player I suppose I wasn't 'part' of that team, I felt very close to the boys going into that game. Above all, I was an Australian and I desperately wanted them to do well, so I decided to send them a telegram wishing them all the best for the game and for the whole series. I wanted to send it on the morning of the game, to arrive an hour or so before play was due to start. I even went to the trouble of ringing the Post Office to find out how long it would take to get there, so I could lodge it at the right moment. They promised me it would take no more than half an hour from the time I'd lodged it to delivery at the dressing-room door. So I wrote it out . . . 'Best of luck for this game and the series. Dennis Lillee' . . . and sent it with an extra half hour to spare.

I was going to the game, so I decided to go up to the Australian dressing-room before play to say 'Hello' and wish them luck personally as well. That plan was a disaster. First of all I couldn't get into the ground. I knew some tickets had been left for me, but when I got to the Grace Gates and asked the fellow, whom I'd seen so many times before on other tours, if he had them, he replied, 'Most certainly not!' His aggressive reaction almost floored me.

I regained composure and said, 'Well, could you have a look at your tickets inside to see if there's something been left?' He responded haughtily, 'I can guarantee you there has been nothing left in that name.' End of conversation.

I could see I wasn't doing much good there, so I went back outside the gates and waited until I saw somebody I recognised. Finally I saw Geoff Wilkins, the fellow who had organised all the hotels and internal travel arrangements for touring sides for the Australian Cricket Board. I explained the situation to him and he gave me his ticket to get in and I passed it back out again. So I was in. There was no doubting the implications of that little episode at the gate: as a WSC player I was taboo! There was proof of that in the fact that I later found out that my friend *had* left an envelope with tickets in my name at the Grace Gates. However, that was only the start of my troubles that morning. I then went to the back of the pavilion and walked up to the fellow on the door, whom I'd seen so many times before, too.

I introduced myself as Dennis Lillee and told him I just wanted to go up and see the boys in the dressing-room and say 'Hello'. 'You can't go up there,' he said gruffly, 'you haven't got a tie on.' I was a bit upset at this stage. 'Look,' I said, trying hard to control myself, 'I used to play . . . all I want to do is go in and wish them all the best for the game.' He was stony faced. 'Rules are rules,' he said.

I wasn't to be outdone, so I went and borrowed a tie, put it on, and managed to get into the holy sanctuary where a naked neck is a sin. Up those stairs I went and knocked on the door of the Australian dressing-room. The room attendant answered and when I asked could I come in he said, 'I'll have to see the manager.' That's fairly standard procedure, but when David Richards came to the door and saw me his reply wasn't what you'd call standard procedure. 'Oh, I'll have to go and ask the captain about that,' he said.

I said, 'Okay' and the door closed in my face. As it did a chill went through me as I thought about the problems to come in a compromise with WSC, if there was to be one. As a former player I should have been welcomed into that room. I mean, I've never known a former player to be knocked back if he asked the manager if he could go in and see the boys. This was a real indication of the animosities which existed. A couple of minutes later Kim Hughes came to the door and said, 'Come in . . . great to see you . . . what are you doing . . .?' and so on. He was really pleasant.

We had a chat for a while and then I saw Kevin Wright, a club-mate back home, and we had quite a warm talk about things. As I did, I caught eyes with a few of the other players, who made it quite clear they didn't want to be seen talking to me.

Then I said to Kim Hughes, 'Oh, by the way, did you get my telegram?' He replied, 'No, not yet.' I said that was strange, because I had been guaranteed by the Post Office that it would be there definitely an hour before play. He repeated that it hadn't arrived yet and I resumed talking to Kevin Wright. Less than a minute later Kim came up to me and said my telegram had arrived. I must admit I did for moment have the distinct feeling that it had arrived earlier, as planned, but that he hadn't wanted to read it out to the team. Then I went out on the balcony where all the players were watching the game and stood behind them. 'How're you going?' I said, 'Good luck for this game and the tour.' Not one of them looked back. Rod Hogg and Alan Hurst half turned, but gave no reaction. I turned on my heel and walked straight out of the room.

It certainly wasn't the reaction I'd expected from the players and with the talk of a compromise in the background I must admit I was deeply concerned at that point about how the players would handle a coming together. Of course, I can now realise the invidious position they had been placed in because of the official attitude towards WSC. Just a few weeks after that most frustrating and disillusioning day at Lord's the compromise was in fact announced in a joint statement by the Board and WSC. My initial reaction was, 'Gee, that's great!' It was certainly what I'd wanted, to get things back on an even keel and get Australian cricket going in the one direction again.

However, lurking behind my delight in hearing the news was a gut feeling that there were going to be a lot of problems, that there'd always be a shadow hovering over all players who were involved with WSC. And to this day I'm positive that's the case. I thought those problems would lie with the officials, rather than the players and the public ... and as it has turned out, I was right. As far as the public was concerned it was just water under the bridge. In the first season after the compromise things were just the same as if there'd never been WSC.

As to the players, well everything went very smoothly considering the fact that only months before we'd been placed poles apart by frightened officials. At the club level there were no problems whatsoever and at a Sheffield Shield level there was no doubt in my mind that the players all tried their hardest to get things going and there wasn't even a hint of the fact that there'd been a split. Occasionally there was something brought up as a joke, but we were out there playing for Western Australia and that was that.

In fact, I remember going down to the WACA Ground for my first State squad training session for a couple of years and it was as though I'd just picked up from the day before. Of course the main matter for conjecture in the WA camp, as I guess it was in the Australian team, was who'd be captain. This one resolved itself in the State side because Kim Hughes was away leading the Australian team on a tour of India and didn't return until after the season had begun. In fact he didn't play in a single Shield game that summer because of the international schedule. So Rod Marsh was named captain and rightly so. This subject raised its ugly head the following season, but I'll come to that later.

Of course there was much speculation as to who'd be named captain of the Australian team. Greg Chappell had been captain before the WSC split arrived to change things rather dramatically, Kim Hughes was the incumbent and, as I said away performing that duty in India. To add to the confusion Ian Chappell, who'd retired from the position in 1975 and then quit Test cricket altogether in 1976, had captained the Australian side in all WSC games.

Ian Chappell soon put himself out of the running and so it was a choice between Greg and Kim and there was quite a degree of lobbying from each camp. Above all I think we WSC players thought this would be a test of the nature of the thinking of the Australian selectors and the ACB, because we felt that Greg was the most logical choice, even though Kim held the job at the time. Finally the selectors made their gesture towards a happy compromise by naming Greg to lead the side. The WA captaincy was a different story, however, and it caused many problems.

13. Re-building

After my prolonged holiday in the Northern Hemisphere I returned home with the batteries fully recharged and ready and rearing to go in the 'great compromise summer'. The season of 1979-80 promised a twin series against the West Indies and England, Australia's two most formidable opponents. A twin series was nothing new to me, because I'd been through it all in two home seasons of World Series Cricket. However, for the WSC players chosen it would mean diving headlong into a fourth series against the West Indies in the space of two years. And that was a daunting prospect, because we all knew and appreciated the many strengths and few weaknesses of their marvellous line-up.

Above all, I think we were aware of the great potential of their pace attack and we knew that, if anything, they'd be more dangerous than ever on the Australian wickets that season. We were also aware of the fact that it was the first 'full', for the want of a better word, tour of Australia for the Windies since we'd drubbed them five-one here in the 1975-76 season. A lot of water had flowed under the bridge since then and I'm sure the members of the 1975-76 touring party who were still in the 1979-80 team, and there were eight of them, had a major mission on the tour: to erase the memory of that hiding with a comprehensive victory in the three Tests and the one-day series.

As it turned out, we did have our troubles with them, losing the series two-nil after the first Test was drawn. Perhaps we would have lost that one, too, had captain Clive Lloyd been playing. He had a knee operation in Sydney the day before the game started in Brisbane and didn't even arrive in the northern city until the last couple of days of the game. Still the game was evenly poised throughout and in the end a tame 'Gabba wicket won the day.

From the Australian viewpoint perhaps the highlight was the way Bruce Laird handled the blistering West Indies pace attack. This little fellow has all the technique and courage in the world and is ideally suited to coping with fast bowling. He was dead unlucky not to record his first Test century in the first innings, being out leg before for 92. In the second innings he batted beautifully again in scoring 75. Those knocks set the pattern for a great season for my West Australian team-mate.

Greg Chappell also began the season in top form with 74 in the first innings and a century in the second. That knock was a fine example of applied concentration and it helped to put the match out of danger for Australia. Kim Hughes also made a fine second innings century, but the innings of the match came from 'No. 1' Viv Richards. Struggling throughout with a leg injury, which in fact plagued him right through the tour and caused him to go home to the West Indies rather than tour New Zealand, Richards showed great application and was typically ferocious in striking the ball when it was there to be hit. He made 140 and it was the beginning of a golden series for him, with scores of 96, 76 and 74 to follow in Tests . . . a total of 386 runs at the average of 96.50!

Actually by the end of the tour I'd just about seen enough of Viv's brilliant strokeplay. In thirteen Supertests and three Tests since the beginning of World Series Cricket in 1977-78 he had made 27 journeys to the crease against us for a total of 1634 runs at the healthy average of 65.36. He'd scored five centuries, seven other half-centuries and had been dismissed for less than ten just twice.

It's great to see such a fine player in action—but I sometimes wished he was getting a few more of his runs off other bowlers! Viv has a typical happy-go-lucky West Indian character by nature, but underneath that exterior is a very determined fellow. He's always very fit, he loves cricket, he loves life and music and a good laugh. He is basically a quiet guy, though I've found you can get into a conversation with him and end up having a very interesting discussion. He's a most likeable person.

The only criticism I could possibly have of his batting is that I think he has often jeopardised his wicket early because he has tried to assert his authority from the very first ball. You can't always do that and hope to get through the initial period of onslaught. I get the feeling that if he goes out to simply build an innings, no mere mortal gets his wicket until maybe he has had enough. If he is in that ultra-aggressive mood and succeeds in getting through that initial burst, he will normally settle down to pick up the remainder of his 100 or 150. What I'm trying to say is that if he had the real determined staying power of a Boycott or a Greg Chappell, goodness knows how many runs he'd make.

But then, perhaps his attitude of 'Get right in there and demoralise the bowlers and then it becomes easy,' is a major part of his success story. He's very strong to anything pitched short, particularly on the leg side, either pulling or flicking the ball away. If anything, we've often thought that if we've had a chance against Viv it was on the off side—not that you could ever call him weak on the off side. However, during the 1979-80 tour we saw plenty of evidence that he had become a stronger off-side player. He had developed an exceptionally good off and cover drive range. I don't freak out when I'm faced with the prospect of bowling to Viv. In fact, it's a challenge to take on such a great player and I've always bowled at him with hope of getting his wicket.

When I first bowled to him, I used to adopt the attitude of 'It's him or me' and I tried to knock him over. But now I approach the task with part of my mind and actions trying to skittle him and part trying to dry him up and encourage a rash stroke. Mind you, it's not easy to dry him up. In a way it's more of a mind game than a physical conflict when I bowl at him these days. It just doesn't pay to try to bounce him out—unless you're really quick or the wicket is really fast and bouncy. Jeff Thomson has always believed Viv was a chance with a fast bouncer and in the third Test of the 1979-80 season Lenny Pascoe stirred him up with a string of very fast bouncers. If you bowl short to him you've got to be prepared to cop it if the ball doesn't get up high enough, because he pulls very powerfully and very safely. Generally with Viv, you've got to concentrate on a good length. But he's a great player, he really is.

So the first Test was drawn with honours fairly even. In this game I had just one knock in the first innings and was out leg before wicket to Joel Garner without scoring. What's so unusual about that sort of a result from a Lillee visit to the centre, you might ask. Nothing . . . except for the fact that in that brief stay I had made Test cricket history by using an aluminium bat for the first time. I am involved as a partner in the development and marketing of a bat made of modified aluminium tubing and quite naturally I wanted to use the bat in a Test, firstly to try it out and secondly to make people aware of its existence.

My use of the bat in this game passed without incident or comment, though I suppose the brevity of my stay at the wicket could have had something to do with that. But I do remember the reaction of wicketkeeper Deryck Murray and some of the other close-in fieldsmen when aluminium met leather for the first time in Test cricket ... their faces registered bewilderment and when they realised what was going on they simply laughed at the new sound. When the innings was over I recall thinking that if nothing else the aluminium bat was off the ground. Of course our thinking with the development of the bat wasn't aimed at Test or even first-class cricket; we reckoned it was a piece of equipment ideally suited for use by young cricketers in practice and in under-age games and perhaps by older players in the country or in a social cricket atmosphere. The cost of willow bats has escalated to such a degree that we thought we were moving into a corner of the market with an almost indestructible bat that would price competitively.

If the West Indies players laughed at the use of the aluminium bat in Brisbane, then the Englishmen just about cried when I took it out in the following Test, the first against them, in Perth. My decision to use the bat again was described as everything from 'a publicity stunt' to 'absolutely stupid'. Sure I wanted to show the bat to the public and let them see for themselves that it was a good invention, but it was not a stunt. I liken my use of that bat to the case of a willow bat maker inventing a new sort of blade with, let's say, a scoop out of it or holes through it or whatever, and getting one of his contract players to use it in a Test match. That's just what I did. It was the fact that my bat was made of different material that caused the uproar.

I had used the bat in Brisbane without questions being asked and indeed people in authority had told me there was no reason why I shouldn't use it in Perth. Well, I faced a couple of balls in the first innings without comment, then I hit one through extra cover for three off Ian Botham. The ball was thrown back and Mike Brearley, the England captain, came up from his position in the slips to examine it. He then said that my bat had marked the ball and even showed me a mark on the ball in an effort to support his opinion. I could see, from long experience, that the mark he was talking about was an old graze which had been repaired by rubbing perspiration into it and had gone back to the pinky colour of the leather. I told Brearley that if my bat had made a graze on the ball it would have been a grey-yellow colour from the paint on the blade. And I added that, as a bowler who had patched up a few grazes in his time, I knew I was right about that mark.

Brearley's reaction was to complain to the umpires. They conferred, then said that they felt my bat was damaging the ball and told me to change it. Just then Rod Hogg, our twelfth man, appeared

You just can't win them all.

The beginning of the so-called 'bumper war' in the 1974-75 England tour of Australia.
I'm about to be caught off the gloves after copping a short one from Tony Greig in the first Test at Brisbane.

It can be hot and hard work—thank goodness there's a bit of shine left on the cherry!

In centre stage with the bat
during the fabulous Centenary
Test at the MCG in 1977 . . .
Tony Greig's not too interested
in my style!

Right: Kids . . . I love 'em all.

Above: What a catch! Gary 'Gus' Gilmour wraps his claws around a hot one from Viv Richards in the first Test of the 1975-76 series against the West Indies, in Brisbane.

Right: It's curtains for West Indies opener Gordon Greenidge in the first Test at Brisbane in 1975-76.

Opposite: See you later, Michael . . . the off bail goes and Holding is on his way in the sixth Test of the 1975-76 series at the MCG.

Now here's a story in two distinct parts . . . first, I manage to get one into the ribs of that magnificent England batsman John Edrich. However, I have my turn at suffering the pain—and a slight difference of opinion with England's Keith Fletcher. It turns out I'm not completely without friends out there—and David Lloyd (at right of picture) is certainly feeling sympathy pains.

Right: At Lords in 1975.

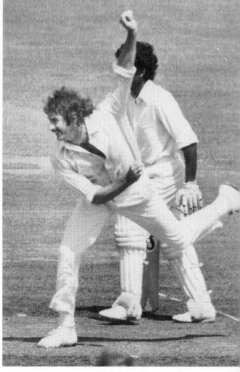

The Dennis Lillee action . . .
(a) before, (b) after,
(c) lefthand profile.

It's late in the day on the opening day of the first Test against the West Indies at the MCG in 1981-82. The master batsman is out and the West Indies are four for ten. *Below:* My moment of personal triumph is shared by the boys.

Perhaps the speed won't be quite
right, but I'm certain of plenty of
bounce . . . time out for a lark at the
MCG.

It's no wonder I enjoy playing at the MCG—those guys in the outer make me feel a giant at times.

Comment by leading cartoonist Bill Mitchell . . . after the aluminium bat incident during the first Test against England in Perth in 1979-80 and below, after England's cricket authorities refused to put the Ashes on the line for the three Test twin tour of Australia in 1979-80.

The meat in a fair old sandwich—on my right Sir Garry Sobers,
to my left Greg Chappell.

With Rod Marsh.

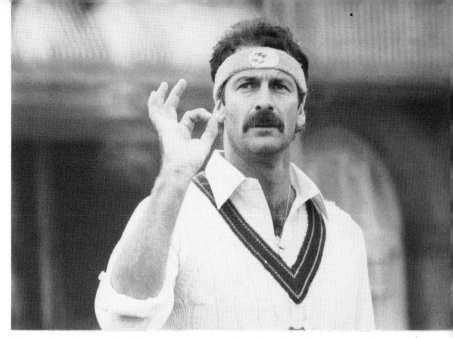

The modern-day warrior of the green sweat-band . . . the author looks the part in
England in 1981 with the latest headgear, bearing his personal logo.

Soaked Aussies flee rain. Australian cricketers—(left to right) G. Wood,
R. Bright, D. Lillee, T. Alderman and B. Laird—flee the soaking rain as they
arrive at Parliament House, Wellington, New Zealand, for a civic reception given
for the two teams before the start of the first 1982 Test. Continuous rain had
been falling for the past four days.

What a way to relax on tour—New Zealand 1982.

on the field with a willow bat, but I didn't like it or want to use it. I wanted to have the position clarified, so I left the field. As I walked towards the dressing-room I saw a WA Cricket Association official in the crowd and asked him what was my position. He told me I was within my rights to use the bat. Despite that I walked on into the dressing-room and in my confused state of mind was about to change the bat for a willow one when Rod Marsh said to me, 'What are you doing?'

I replied, 'I'm going to change my bat.' He said he thought I was within my rights to continue using it.

'Damn it,' I thought, 'he's right.' I grabbed the aluminium bat again and walked back out with it. I went straight back to the crease at the non-striker's end and waited for the game to continue. However, the umpires told me I couldn't continue until I'd changed the bat. I said, 'Look, I'm ready to continue.'

The reply came firmly 'No, no, you can't continue unless you have a willow bat—and if you don't get one we'll retire your innings.' Then I saw Greg Chappell coming out with a selection of bats and I thought, 'Well, obviously I'm not going to win out here ... and if I'm retired I'll harm the team.' That's when I became so emotionally upset, knowing that what I was doing was within the laws of cricket and feeling that I was being 'got at'.

So I flung the bat away. Perhaps I shouldn't have done that, but at the time all I could think of was that I was being victimised. And to this day I still believe that the willow bat manufacturers had a hand in what happened out there that day. There was a funny sequel the next day when Greg Chappell took the bat to the nets to give it a try himself. I never asked him what he thought of it and he never volunteered an opinion. How does it play? Well, I'd have to say it doesn't hit the ball quite as sweetly as a good willow bat and there is a bit of a noise problem (which has since been solved to some degree). Would that fateful three have been a four with a willow bat? I'm not convinced it would have. I still have that bat. It's signed by the Australian team from that game *and* Mike Brearley and his England team.

The twin series this season were intertwined ... the first Test against the West Indies, the second against England and so on. However, I'll deal with them series by series for the sake of ease in following the summer through. In the second Test against the West Indies at the MCG we were well and truly cleaned up. The track was uneven and their fast bowlers just knocked us over with their relentless attack on the stumps. The two different paces of the track seemed to worry our batsmen more than it did the West Indies, possibly because they tend to hit through the ball whereas Australians are inclined to wait on it a bit. The West Indies won by ten wickets and it was their first ever Test victory on the Melbourne ground.

The Adelaide wicket for the third Test was a beauty. My first impression of it was that we'd certainly see a lot of runs made on it and we did ... by the West Indies batsmen! Once again our bats crumpled under the pressure of these four fast bowlers, who seemed to fire at us like a new cannon ball. They operated as a wonderful team, each taking the pressure off the other by always being ready to come in and fire away at full tilt. Roberts, Holding, Croft and Garner ... all right-handers but each with something slightly different to offer: Roberts, cunning and clever variety at high speed; Holding, blistering pace and remarkable accuracy; Croft, a different angle from his delivery wide of the crease and the ability to straighten one up; and Garner's great height giving him extremely awkward bounce.

I only faced them towards the end of an innings and I certainly spared a thought for those who had to go in and face them fresh and with a new ball and the track at its liveliest. How much easier a fast bowler's job would be working in a 'pack' like they did. Over the years I've worked with one, maybe two, speed partners and we've really had our work cut out keeping the pressure right on top-flight batsmen. As a result we've often had to bowl long, hard stints to help chisel out a batting side. But the Windies line-up, with the possible exception of Croft, worked in short, sharp bursts and that certainly boosted their performance. The evenness in their attack in the 1979-80 series is reflected in the fact that in six innings not once did a bowler take more than four wickets in an innings.

My admiration for Bruce Laird's work against these speedsters was heightened by the way he tackled them again in Adelaide with 52 and 36 in two low innings scores. In the first innings we sat in stunned amazement as we witnessed Greg Chappell being dismissed first ball, edging a brutish lifter from Roberts to Garner in the gully. We had become so accustomed to Greg churning out runs that we just couldn't believe what we were seeing as he walked back, upright as ever, to the pavilion. But the highlight of this game was a gem of an innings from Clive Lloyd: 121 that was full of all the grace and ease and yet mighty power that has characterised this great player's career. We all thought that would be the last time 'Groover' would play Tests in Australia, but fortunately there were more to come. He'd have to be one of the best, as well as the nicest, players I've come across. The West Indies' winning margin of 408 runs in this game was a record for them against Australia.

During that game I was fielding at deep mid-on when a cracking West Indies drive struck a seagull that had landed and was sitting in the deeps. The bird was dazed and I acted as ambulance driver, taking him (or her) over to the boundary by the sightscreen and handing it into the custody of an interested spectator. I didn't hold out much hope for the bird, he looked well and truly past it to me. But apparently this fellow nursed the bird back to health and he took off later in the day to rejoin his mates in the outfield, proving at least that seagulls believe lightning doesn't strike twice on the same cricket ground! The commentators in the nearby ABC broadcast box saw the bird take off and dutifully reported that 'Mr C. Gull had fully recovered and was fit to resume play!'

As a result of my humble involvement in the whole performance I received numerous letters from children and some from adults, among other things, welcoming me to the Gould League. It was the second time I'd been called upon to do the good Samaritan act for a stricken seagull, the first time being in Perth during the second Test against England in 1974-75. On that occasion I fancy the poor bird didn't recover and return to the fold. Remarkably, it was the second time I'd seen a bird hit by the ball on the Adelaide Oval. The first time had been a few years before in a Sheffield Shield game between WA and SA when John Inverarity was batting and a Greg Chappell delivery hit a bird in flight and deflected the ball on to the stumps. Inverarity left the field in a dazed state, unable to realise quite what had happened. But then the wicketkeeper found a freshly dead bird, the umpires added two and two together and Invers was recalled from the dressing-room to continue his innings.

So we suffered severely at the hands of the West Indies, but in the meantime we exacted some punishment ourselves from the hapless Englishmen. I can tell you, the three-nil result in our favour against England was very satisfactory in the circumstances. We had to scramble a bit to win the first in Perth, helped along by a fine 99 from Kim Hughes in the first innings and 115 from Allan Border in the second. Border had to fight back strongly after being hit and cut over the eye and he was giving every indication of developing into a very good Test batsman. The mercurial Ian Botham took 11 wickets for the game and was named man-of-the-match, but I thought that Geoff Dymock gave just as good a performance with the match figures of 9 for 86 (6 for 34 in the second innings).

In the twilight of his career Geoff really did enjoy a great season with his left-hand medium-pacers. He moved the ball consistently and confused the right-hand batsmen with his angle across them to the slips. Geoff's great ally was always his ability to bring one back in to the right-handers; it never left them happy about leaving balls outside the off stump. In fact, 'Dimmers' cost Geoff Boycott a century in the second innings when he wiped out the last three batsmen in such a hurry that 'Boyks' was left lamenting on 99.

It was the second score of 99 in the match and that started an incredible run of scores in the late nineties in the three-Test series. In the second Test there were two scores of 98 not out, from David Gower and Greg Chappell, while in the third Test Graham Gooch was incredibly run out on 99. As for me, all I did was give the scorers the pleasures of writing in the second innings the line they'd so badly wanted to see: 'Lillee . . . caught Willey bowled Dilley . . . 19'.

The Sydney second Test marked the return to Test cricket of Ian Chappell. He'd retired after the West Indies tour of Australia in 1975-76, but of course had been back in the international scene subsequent to that as Australian captain during World Series Cricket. To see Ian come back into the hurly-burly of international cricket at the age of thirty-six—and not just stagger back, but make a great contribution, particularly in a couple of one-day games—was a tribute to the man's ability and determination. He played the second and third Tests against England and the third Test against the West Indies. He didn't fare too well against the Windies, but in his farewell Test match he performed magnificently, making 75 and 26 not out. At the end of that game he decided he didn't really need all the pressures of top-class cricket and finally called it a day.

In fact, Ian's 42 in the first innings of the second Test at Sydney was our top score and without it, goodness knows where we'd have been. He fought magnificently to hold our innings together after we'd skittled England for 123 on a rain-affected wicket. In a way England deserved to be in strife because Mike Brearley had agreed to play in conditions which we thought weren't good enough and the avalanche of wickets that followed didn't abate until the fourth innings, which fortunately was ours. The wicket didn't have that much devil in it, but there was always a bit of movement. Finally Greg Chappell and Kim Hughes mastered the conditions in our second innings with a solid stand of 105 and we won the game by

132

6 wickets to clinch the series, our first win over England since 1975.

A good first innings score of 477 in the third Test in Melbourne was good enough to give us a comfortable victory and a clean sweep over England. Once again Greg Chappell was in the runs with 114 in the first innings and 40 not out in the second. It was a memorable game for me, because for the second time in successive MCG Tests against England I bagged 11 wickets. I've got to admit that on this occasion there was always a bit in the wicket for me. If it hadn't been for Ian Botham's slashing maiden century against Australia in the second innings we might have won by an innings. As it was we strolled in by 8 wickets.

And what of Botham? He'd come to Australia with a great reputation as one of the finest all-rounders the game had ever seen. He certainly bowled very well, with 19 wickets from the 3 Tests. I was impressed with this part of his game. He was competitive, always trying something. His batting left a lot to be desired and even in that final century a lot of luck went his way. But he's that sort of player who gets out there and gives it a real go and I could see that if he came off a couple of times in a series he'd be a very dangerous customer.

We World Series Cricket players had our doubts about all the re-markable figures he'd produced in those two years when a lot of the world's best cricketers were tied up with WSC. He did give an indication of being a very good player, but perhaps not quite as good as his figures before this tour had shown. More of him later!

In the World Series Cup one-day series we failed to make the finals, which were won by the West Indies narrowly over the top qualifiers England. I was interested to note that England left Geoff Boycott out of their side for the opening one-day game, but when he came in for their second game he proved to be a new man with the bat. He approached his job with an aggression I've never seen in him and he produced a string of successes—68, 105, 68 and 86 not out—and ended the series with 425 runs at the excellent average of 85.00.

He tended to let himself go loose, probably because these one-day games don't count in career averages. But to be fair to the bowlers he came up against, the wickets were very, very flat and decidedly favoured the batsmen. Also the white ball just doesn't offer the same amount of swing and cut as we'd been able to get from the red ball. It was tailor-made for batting and Boyks took full advantage.

So another busy season had come to an end and I was reasonably happy with my own performance with the ball. I'd taken 23 wickets against England and 12 against the West Indies for a total of 35 from 6 Tests. I'd also been the leading wicket-taker in the one-day series with 20 victims. Thankfully it had been a remarkably smooth return to playing under the banner of the Australian Cricket Board. But the interwoven pattern of the twin Test series left me a bit cold. It was hard to settle down in a flowing sense against one country. But I must say, after careful assessment, that I am in favour of having two teams on tour in the one season.

It gives the public the chance to see more players in action in the one season and, as it turned out in 1979-80, two teams of beautifully contrasting styles. I looked forward to the possibility of future twin tours with the three Tests against one country being played in succession, followed by the three against the other. But I also looked forward to a full tour of Australia by England to give us a good chance of regaining the Ashes. England won't put the Ashes on the line for anything less than a four-Test series, which means in these circumstances that to get the Ashes you have to win them on English soil. The Ashes must be played for in Australia as well as in England, otherwise the contest is biased towards England. The summer of 1982-83 will be an Ashes series as Australia will be playing five Tests against England.

14. To Pakistan, 1980

I once promised myself that I'd never go on a tour to Pakistan or India—and yet here I was, on a plane and on my way to Pakistan for a three-Test tour, full of mixed feelings and with a real knot in my stomach. Why wouldn't I want to go to Pakistan? Simple ... I'd been to the West Indies in 1973 and when I'd recoiled in horror at a few of the privations we met there I'd been told by some of the seasoned campaigners that they weren't even a patch on conditions in some parts of India and Pakistan. That was enough to convince me that Pakistan was no place for a fast bowler well into his thirty-first year to be peddling his wares. I'd been told living conditions were terrible, there was a good chance I'd pick up a disease which could affect me for the rest of my life and, above all, the wickets would in no way favour my bowling.

To cap that off, things were pretty turbulent on the political scene in Pakistan and all sorts of stories were coming out of the country about the dangerous state of affairs. And, of course, the Russian presence in neighbouring Afghanistan was only heightening those problems. It seemed like no place to be, so I decided to make myself unavailable for the tour. I reckoned it just wasn't worthwhile. But then a couple of things happened to make me change my mind.

First, an Australian Cricket Board representative, Fred Bennett, had made a tour of the area and thoroughly inspected the conditions the team could be expected to meet on a tour of Pakistan. And he had reported back to the Board that we could expect very good conditions everywhere we went, with top-class accommodation and most acceptable playing facilities. Then I heard that Jeff Thomson and Len Pascoe had pulled out; if I did, too, the attack would be awfully thin.

So I said 'Count me in,' and was on my way with, as I said, some considerable misgivings. We flew straight to Bombay, arrived there about 6.30 in the morning and booked into a hotel near the airport because we had to leave later that day for Karachi. The first thing we all did was race for the dining room to have some breakfast. Now

135

I'd decided before leaving Australian soil that I would combat the dreaded disease problem by taking great care with my liquid and solid intake, sticking to the sort of things that would be least likely to cause problems. So, this is what I had for breakfast: Two cups of coffee, two slices of toast and butter (not too happy about the butter, either) and two soft-boiled eggs. It was one of the smallest breakfasts I'd ever had in my life! But I wasn't taking any chances.

After that everybody decided to take a bus ride to the Wankhede Stadium where it so happened India were playing England in the Jubilee Test. We were itching to get into cricket and what a way to start. But on the long bus drive I saw my first glimpse of the true poverty that I later found abounds in India and Pakistan. I must admit it wasn't quite as bad as I thought it was going to be—nothing much worse than the shanty areas in the poorer parts of the West Indies. At the cricket ground food presented a problem, because none of us was game to eat what was put on for the players there. We were told that the nearby Sheraton Hotel had fresh meat every day, so most of the group walked over to have a hamburger, returning to watch the last hour or so of the cricket. All along the streets there were pitiful beggars, but again it wasn't quite as bad as I'd expected.

We arrived in Karachi late at night and when we all fronted for breakfast the following morning I stood back—I just wasn't prepared to put my system to the test so early in the tour! But I broke down at lunch and had a chicken omelette. It was as good an omelette as I've ever had and I think that meal was the turning point for me with the Pakistani food. I decided that the food at the good hotels wasn't going to give me any problems and adopted my full diet without giving it much more thought. But that day we had our first shock at the playing and practising facilities we were to meet. We went to a ground which could only be described as something like a paddock out the back of beyond with a wicket that was no more than rolled out clay. Needless to say I trod warily.

There was one thing I hadn't done before leaving Perth, which had to be seen to right away. Because of a tight business schedule I hadn't had a medical examination and the Australian Cricket Board was demanding that every player be given a clean bill of health. So I submitted myself to a check by the team doctor on tour, a tremendous guy called Hugh Torode, who was a great help to us throughout our stay in Pakistan. He said, 'There's nothing wrong with you.' But team manager Fred Bennett opted for a second opinion, so it was arranged that the hotel doctor should give me a going over. It was quite an incredible experience. First he weighed me and the result was twelve and a half stone ... I thought I'd lost a bit of weight over there, but a stone and a half in two days was a bit much! As he went through the remainder of his tests I wondered how accurate they'd be. Somehow I passed with flying colours.

Our early preparation for the tour was seriously hampered by the weather. There were no nets available because of all the rain and we were restricted to running, exercises and fielding routines. Greg Chappell and I stood out of the opening game against the President's Eleven at Rawalpindi. We watched an hour or so of the play on the first day, then returned to the team hotel for an easy day—and to prepare ourselves for a special duty when the boys returned from the ground. We were to perform a ritual duty as drink stewards for the others. We had brought with us a ration of Australian beer under the guise of medical supplies for the tour. After each day's play those players off duty had the job of providing chilled beer. The job involved filling a bath with ice and getting the beer to just the right temperature.

During this game we had the first attack of diarrhoea within the group. Perhaps we hadn't been quite careful enough after all. Greg and I spent some time lounging around the pool during the game. That was great for getting a suntan, but hopeless for swimming ... well, there was no water in the pool! But back in Karachi for the first Test, there was water in the pool and in fact we were right on the harbour, which turned out to be a saviour in terms of team entertainment. On our first day we went out on the harbour in an old sailing boat across to a rocky island where we caught some crabs and had a crab and fish lunch along with a few drinks. We were looked after admirably by the Pakistani crew, who also cooked the lunch, and the boys voted it one of the best outings on any tour. We repeated the dose more than once during our times in Karachi.

The first Test was on us, after just the one warm-up game. Test match days in Pakistan start very early indeed and we had to leave for the ground at 8.30 each morning. That didn't go down too well with yours truly. At the ground I walked out to have a look at the wicket only to find it absolutely devoid of grass—not one single blade on it. We won the toss and batted on it, which was a blessing because it turned from the start and promised to be a nightmare for batting as it broke up later in the game. But we really struggled, despite a fine 85 from Kim Hughes, and were all out for 225 early on the second day. During that day I discovered the most fanatical, stupid crowds in cricket. The Pakistanis are unbelievable. They threw oranges, rocks, glass and other missiles at me while I was fielding on the boundary . . . and laughed to boot.

There's no doubt the wicket was made to be of no help to our fast bowlers. There was absolutely nothing in it for Geoff Dymock and myself. The ball didn't swing, it didn't deviate off the wicket and there was absolutely no lift available. To make matters worse, the ball was like a tattered piece of rag after three or four overs. I reckon it was the slowest wicket I've ever played on. And the other two Test tracks turned out to be just the same from a fast bowler's point of view. This one was a little different because it turned, albeit very slowly and irregularly. But I must admit that in the Karachi Test I simply didn't bowl well. I was short of a run and I was struggling to breathe, as I was pretty well throughout the tour in the very hot and humid conditions.

At stumps on the second day Pakistan were in command with Javed Miandad and Majid Khan going along beautifully. I wasn't looking forward to the third day at all, but as it turned out we had them out for 292, thanks to persistent spin bowling by Ray Bright, who finished with seven wickets. Majid's 89 was a great innings in the circumstances.

What a fine player this fellow is. He's just all class and, as with most champions, he has so much time to play his shots. Of all the fine stroke players I've seen in Test cricket, he'd have to be one of the best. A full array of shots and a beautiful caresser of the ball through the gaps in the field.

We were goners at stumps on the third day at 6 down for 90. The rest day followed and I remember talking to Pakistan's fast bowler Imran Khan that night. He told me that grass had been cut off the wicket because Geoff Dymock and I had taken so many wickets in Australia that season. And he told me the other wickets we'd meet in the Tests would be exactly the same and for the same reason. Imran said the locals were afraid that if they gave us wickets which suited our pace bowlers, we'd do better than theirs. He was disenchanted, of course, because while the wickets took the sting out of our pace bowlers they also gave him no chance to prove himself. I felt awfully sorry for 'Immie' . . . he was considered one of the best fast bowlers in the world and yet his own country wouldn't give him the chance to prove it. But he told me Pakistan were desperate to win the series and that was the price to be paid.

I kept a diary of the tour and was getting a bit down in the dumps at this stage. This was my next entry, 'Must practise off-spinners over the next few days.' The Pakistanis cleaned us out without much trouble the following day, with spinner Iqbal Qasim taking 7 wickets for a match total of 11. The following Test was in Faisalabad, which would rate as the worst place I've ever seen . . . filth, mud, flies, the lot. I gave the guest house where we stayed a one-star rating, only because I could see the star through the ceiling at night (not really!). But first things first, so I went and had a look in the kitchen at the guest house. There was unbelievable filth and slime everywhere and it was open to the elements with no protection from airborne germs. There were flies everywhere and it stank like nothing I'd ever smelt.

A fellow called Zeb from an international hotel chain was to come from Karachi to do the catering for us in Faisalabad and he was going to bring a team of workers to clean up before he got on with the cooking. I made the statement that there was no way the kitchen could ever be cleaned enough to make food preparation safe. It looked as though I *was* going to go home a couple of stone lighter! But then we had a stroke of luck when a wealthy fellow who lived next door to the guest house realised our plight and offered the use of his own giant kitchen. He also made his lounge-room available to us and to facilitate our regular treks to and from the guest house he had his workmen knock a hole through the twelve-foot high brick wall separating the two properties. As it turned out we ate like kings and I put on a heap of weight!

The first day of the Test was washed out with the ground an absolute quagmire. But the sun was very hot and drying and there was no doubt we'd get a start the following day if that weather persisted, so we all went for a good run. I needed it, too, because I was eating very well and not doing enough bowling. Play started a little late the second day and again we won the toss and batted on the plumbest wicket imaginable. We batted right through that day and the next. During the scheduled third day, when a few of us were practising on a wicket out the back of the ground, I very nearly took my first wicket of the tour . . . Bruce Laird snicked one, but in the end I had to agree it wouldn't have carried to the slips. 'Oh well,' I said, 'perhaps Monday!' That's when we were due to bowl after the rest day.

On the Monday we batted right through our innings and made 617. Greg Chappell had ground out 235 and Graham Yallop 172. I made a 'duck' and there's nothing unusual about that, except that

I'd set out to make the longest duck on record: I reckoned I sure wasn't going to break any bowling record in that game, so why not one for batting! I managed to last about 35 minutes. We were in the field just after lunch and I just didn't look like getting a wicket, hence my diary note, 'I don't think I'll get a wicket for the 3 Tests!' That gives you a slight idea about my state of mind at that stage. Geoff Dymock broke his 'duck' with the ball when he trapped Haroon Rashid leg before. There just wasn't even a glimmer of hope for any bowler on that dustheap.

We started the final day's play earlier than usual at 9.30. Perhaps that was why I wasn't taking wickets—my system doesn't even start thinking about working until well after that time! Once again I didn't look like taking a wicket, so 2 Tests in a row and no wickets for me. It was quite depressing. In the end the game was drawn, with Taslim Arif making a double century and Javed Miandad a century, but what a boring game it had been on a wicket that gave the game absolutely no hope. In that innings every Australian player had at least 2 overs. Greg Chappell kept wicket to allow Rod Marsh to have 10 overs. I'm not quite sure what was worse, Greg's wicket-keeping or Rod's bowling!

The following day a few of us decided to go partridge shooting and were up bright and early ... by now I was getting used to the early rising. We got 15 or 20 partridge and an eagle, which Mick Malone shot, and it was a very entertaining morning. From there the team went to Multan to play a 3-day game, while Greg Chappell and I decided to go straight to Lahore, where the third Test was to be played. The guys voted Multan as a worse place than Faisalabad, but reported that the wicket had been grassy and quick ... just my luck! The accommodation in Lahore was very good, though once again there was no water in the swimming pool. There was a tennis court and little golf course, so at least it looked as though we were in for a pleasant stay.

We ran into Majid Khan at Lahore. He took us to a carpet manu-facturer, where we watched the carpets being made and learnt that a particular ten by twelve carpet took a year to weave. Later that day I played in a practice game at Majid's club ground, where the wicket was as fast and even as the WACA Ground in Perth. My diary note that night, 'They *can* make fast wickets here if they want them!' The following day Greg and I had a look at the wicket square at the Qaddafi Stadium, where the early preparations were under way for the Test. It was immediately obvious to us that the ground staff were preparing two wickets ... one like Faisalabad strip, cut down past the roots, and next to it one of the grassiest tracks you could imagine.

Greg and I looked at each other and agreed, 'They're not playing it fair and haven't really played it fair right through.' It was then that we hatched a plot of demoniacal proportions that snowballed and snowballed and was very nearly swallowed by the local authorities. It was decided that I should fake a breakdown and in that way try to force their hand on which wicket they were going to use. Perhaps if they thought I wasn't playing they'd opt for the grassy track and we'd all have a good game of cricket. We said I'd suffered a serious injury to the side (actually I did have some pain there, but nothing bad enough to prevent me playing in a Test match) and would be doubtful for the game. The local Press picked up the story.

I spent a whole day closetted in my hotel room as the story gained momentum. The following night I went out on a pig-shooting expedition with Majid. We drove some 80 kilometres out to a place near the India-Pakistan border, didn't see any pigs, but shot 5 rabbits and a fox. Out near the border we were driving along in our open jeep and I was on the passenger side holding a gun when we pulled up at an outpost station. Just at that moment a fellow screamed out at us and pointed his gun right at me. I thought, 'Hell, this is the end ... I'm going to cop the lot.' He came forward at us and I panicked. He was obviously worried about my gun ... he could have it gladly, as far as I was concerned. Finally he cooled down and we were allowed to go. Apart from that rather tense little incident we had great fun and I even ended up swapping my tracksuit with a Pakistani Army major for his jumper and jacket. The day is one of my best memories of Pakistan.

Naturally during the day Majid asked me how my side was and I said it wasn't too bad and that I had it strapped up. I don't know whether he believed me or not ... in fact, I don't think he even cared. Greg and I had kept the Press bubbling on my injury by hinting that off-spinner Ashley Mallett was to come over to replace me and make use of the spinner's wicket that was certain to be made for the third Test. And at practice the following day we kept up the momentum. I bowled about an over of very slow deliveries, then clutched my side and walked away to have a rest before giving it up altogether. I think the Pakistanis had almost fallen for the trick, but still they wouldn't give us any official indication as to which wicket would be used for the Test.

The greatest Pakistani Test batsman of all time, Hanif Mohammad, was in charge of the preparation of wickets and he was assisted
by his brother Mushtaq, who was also manager of the Pakistan team.
Finally late on the day before the game was due to start they admit-
ted they were going to use the 'dead' wicket. The following morning
I made a 'miraculous recovery' and took my place in the side. Going
into the game I was totally convinced that I would end up playing
a full Test series without taking a single wicket. To confirm my feelings Imran Khan, who had pulled out of the second Test, came up
and saw me before play.

'I wouldn't play in this Test if I didn't need the money,' he said.
'It's an absolute mockery of the game. I don't know why you're playing. It's not going to be any good for you or me . . . why be a fool?'

I smiled resignedly and said, 'I feel I have to play because I'm fit
to play.' He replied, 'I think it's silly and I'm going to say something
about it at the end of the tour.' And he did. He made a Press statement about the wickets and what a waste of time the series had been
for him. As we'd all predicted, the Test wicket was just a lifeless
length of rolled out clay. We batted first and worked our way along
to 407, with Allan Border making a fine 150 not out. In fact, we batted on the first two days, then had a rest day and on the third day
my diary note read, 'I broke the ice today as I actually got a wicket.
In fact, it doesn't rain but it pours—I got two!' Indeed I ended up
with the grand figures of 3 for 114 from 47 overs.

Pakistan led by 13 on the first innings and we just strolled along
to the draw in our second, with Border making 153 to record a
unique Test match double. In fact those runs in the third Test sent
Border home with an average of 131.66 for the three Test clashes
and 112.33 for the whole tour. He really was emerging as a player
of great class, a pugnacious left-hander who quietly goes about his
work and is a very effective runmaker. But it was another boring
game. And as we packed to go home I reflected on the fact that
against my better judgement I'd toured Pakistan . . . and declared
that I would never go back. To actually admit that you are preparing
wickets to counter your opponents and suit yourself as several
people 'in the know' reluctantly did admit to me, just isn't on and
I don't want to be any part of it.

15. New Zealand and India in Australia, 1980-81

We arrived back in Australia after the tour of Pakistan before the 1979-80 domestic season had ended. Just in time, in fact, for the club cricket finals in Perth. That is significant, because it relates directly to what I consider to have been the rather unsavoury dumping of Rod Marsh as captain of the West Australian side. You will recall that Marshy got the job at the beginning of the season, after the compromise had been negotiated. In fact, during that season WA had two other captains in Ric Charlesworth and Tony Mann because of the general unavailability of the more senior players because of the international programme. So, the fact that the State team didn't perform too well that summer could barely be blamed on Marshy . . . and I for one expected him to be named captain again for the following season.

However, an incident in the hot and dusty Pakistani city of Faisalabad sowed the seeds of doubt in my mind about his prospects of holding the job. Remember we're talking about a captain for the 1980-81 season, while the 1979-80 Australian season still has a month or so to run.

A few of the Australian players, coincidentally all from Western Australia, were playing cards and having quite a few beers in our guest house before going across for dinner. I happened to be sitting opposite Kim Hughes who, having played a hand, looked up at me and said, like a bolt out of the blue, 'What are your plans for next year?' I was rather taken aback. 'What do you mean?' I replied. 'I mean, are you going to play or not?' Still not quite certain what he was driving at, I told him that I didn't know at that stage and that I'd wait to see how I felt during the winter months back home.

His next comment was very interesting. 'Well, you're very important in my plans.' Again I asked him what he meant. 'Well, I'm captain of Western Australia next season,' he replied stoutly. The other players present just couldn't believe it and Marshy just shrugged his shoulders in disbelief. I was dumb-founded. Firstly, I couldn't comprehend that the season wasn't even over and here was Hughes telling us in his own cute way that he had the job already for the next season. It seemed to me patently obvious that Rod had been given the job in the first season of the compromise, just to smooth things over, then Kim would take over the following season. Secondly, I believe Hughes was irresponsible in coming out with something like that at that stage.

It was certain that if Hughes had been told before the Pakistan tour of a decision to appoint him captain of WA the following season, then he'd been told in confidence. To his credit, Marshy's attitude was, 'Oh forget it, it's not worth worrying about.'

The rest of us didn't talk too much about it, because I guess there wasn't much to say. It seemed like a *fait accompli*, well and truly. Hughes was right, he did get the job, but the way it was announced left me stone cold. Whether it was by design or not, the cricket authorities chose the moment when Marshy, Bruce Laird and I were in Singapore doing a bit of coaching and having a holiday with our wives.

I thought it was absolutely diabolicial that the matter had been handled in this way and when we returned to Perth I fronted those who were involved. I went to the chairman of selectors, Allan Edwards, and told him I thought he had no guts. I referred back to what had happened in Faisalabad and told him it was beyond my comprehension that they'd found it necessary to wait until Rod was out of the country before making the announcement. I had been named as Hughes' vice-captain, but I withdrew immediately, giving my reason officially that I wanted to concentrate on my own game. That wasn't the full story of course . . . in simple truth, I couldn't take the way they'd dealt with the removal of Marshy and the appointment of Hughes.

So the 1980-81 season, which promised another hard slog through twin series against India and New Zealand, the World Series Cup international one-day competition and expanded involvement for Test players in the Sheffield Shield and McDonald's Cup competition, got off on the wrong foot for a couple of us. As it turned out we soon got into stride and made a good fist of it . . . Australia defeated New Zealand two-nil in the Test series, drew one-all with India in that series and beat the Kiwis in the World Series Cup, while Western Australia had a great year, winning the Sheffield Shield and being beaten in the final of the McDonald's Cup. And Kim Hughes and I both had good seasons: Hughes making his first Test double-century and the season producing 37 wickets in 6 Tests *and*

Richie Benaud's Australian Test wicket-taking record for me.

However, approaching this new season I wasn't all that confident about how things would go for me. Perhaps it's just the fact that you're getting older that makes you wonder how you're going to fare over the next five or six months of a season. I think I realised before this season began that I had moved into a new phase of life, so to speak, and that I'd have to atune myself to it or perish. In fact, I'd been battling with the thought of the ageing process for some four or five years—I think mainly because everybody tries to tell you that fast bowlers are over the hill at thirty. To a degree that's a totally false premise, because if you keep yourself pretty fit and you have a good injury-free run and your enthusiasm stays up, you can still bowl fairly fast into the early thirties.

And, as proof of that theory, in the 1980-81 season during Tests against New Zealand and India there were a couple of occasions when I thought I bowled as fast as I had at any time over the previous four or five seasons. At times you just get it all together. The big difference is that you can't sustain it ... and that's the ageing process in a nutshell. You can hold it together for, say, five overs in an opening spell, whereas in your youth you might have been able to keep it up for seven or eight. Again when you come back a second time it's just the three quickish overs and in your final spell for the day perhaps two. At your peak you'd have prided yourself with the fact that you'd be able to keep firing away for six or seven in the second spell and five or six in your third. Your body was that much more resilient and could fire up that much longer.

Of course, when you stop to think about the ageing process—as I did because I wanted to get the most out of my career and didn't want to just wake up one day and find that I was no longer an express bowler and, as such, no longer worthy of a game—the big question is 'timing'. If you are going to change to become virtually a fast-medium bowler who tries to do a lot more with the ball and think the batsman out, when do you do it?

Do you say to yourself one day, 'Okay, from now on instead of running from thirty paces I'll run from twenty and bowl within myself.' Or do you say, 'I'll do all of that, but if the conditions suit I'll revert to the longer run and I'll fly once more.' When I was young I didn't think I could ever come to either of those decisions, but going into the 1980-81 season at the age of thirty-one I think I'd come to terms with what both of those thoughts meant to me. You've got to convince yourself that it's for your own good and the good of the team, that you are making the change, but of course half of your mind doesn't accept this readily. It remembers that fact that you'd taken all your major wicket hauls thundering in from your long run-up.

Common sense tells you that it's so much easier on your body working off a shortened run and that raises the question of your longevity in the game. If you continue to work hard at your fitness and, in particular, your flexibility and suppleness, because in the end that's what brings most fast bowlers down, you can put off the decline of your physical capabilities and get several more seasons out of yourself.

Well, that was the decision I reached and since I've come to terms with the whole philosophy of it, life's been a breeze relatively. Part of your success lies in coming to an agreement with yourself on your approach to training. There's a certain amount of personal pride involved in competing out in the middle and that pride also comes out when you're training or doing physical work with the squads. I was always competing with the rest of the squad members . . . even at the age of thirty I used to say to myself, 'I've got to show them I'm still there,' and I'd push myself to the very limit to prove that to myself as much as to others.

But that had to change. I finally realised the folly of a thirty-year-old trying to stay up with a nineteen-year-old and I thought to myself, 'What's the point? . . . you're giving most of them eight to ten years . . . let them win the sprints and the long-distance runs . . . just do what you think you must do to be able to perform at your best out in the middle.' So I learnt to back off and spend the time instead on keeping up the skills side of my bowling, which was more important than ever, while always maintaining a good level of fitness at my own pace.

For once, in the long-distance runs I was just as happy to run second as I was to run second last, as long as I was doing what was needed. It was awfully hard accepting that. I found that perhaps the best thing for me was to change from doing a lot of work in a few workouts to doing less work in more workouts. That way I didn't run myself into the ground at any stage and that was important.

One side effect of slowing down of course is the change of the batsman's attitude toward you. When you are bowling at speeds around the ninety miles an hour mark you command a lot of respect, even from the very best batsmen . . . but as soon as you slow down it's a different ball game. From seeing batsmen jabbing apprehensively at maybe three or four balls an over, it becomes more like one or two balls an over. You also see more players tending to come on to the front foot and a few of them more confident than they'd ever been before. That can get to you, because you remember how things used to be, but you've got to keep your head and press on with your overall plan. Perhaps occasionally you really slip one in just to remind the batsman that you've still got it there, but don't want to abuse it.

Of course, a major part of my weaponry when I reached the point where I had to make concessions to my age was the experience gained in the very years which had put me where I was. I had learnt so much about the delicate machinery of bowling over all those previous years. If I couldn't put that knowledge and those acquired skills to use now, I might as well pack it in. And the many years of looking, listening and honing the skills began to show, because I found that I was able to bowl a string of different deliveries at fast-medium pace which in reasonable conditions could put most batsmen on the rack. And I really looked back to the summer of 1973-74, when I had to stand out of interstate and international cricket because of my back injury, the time when I really started thinking about bowling and getting batsmen out with subtlety, rather than brute force.

And I also remembered the 1975 series in England and a chat I had with John Snow, the greatest England fast bowler of my era. I seized the opportunity during one of the traditional periods in the dressing-room after play in a Test match, when the players of both sides get together for a few drinks and a good yarn, to have a word with 'Snowy'. I went up to him and said, 'Can I have half an hour of your time?' He said, 'Of course,' and away we went together. 'I want you to show me how to bowl the leg-cutter,' I told him. He simply took hold of an old ball and showed me exactly how it was done. I was twenty-five at the time, but I knew I'd need that ball one day. I'm eternally grateful to Snowy for readily passing the technique on to me, because the leg-cutter has been a vital cog in my wheel since I've gone through the slowing down process.

With the leg-cutter up my sleeve, I can turn to my advantage the fact that more batsmen these days are coming to me on the front foot. You see, I'm trying to take the outside edge with that delivery as it moves off the wicket and if they're pushing forward, that's great as long as I've got the ability to make it shift off the wicket fairly quickly. It's great that I've been able to change with some degree of success, but I must admit that I don't really like the new Dennis Lillee. There's no substitute for bowling fast and being able to make the good players jump. I don't enjoy my bowling now as much as I used to when I was steaming in and letting them fly, getting that exhilarating feeling of beating a player completely and just standing there and smiling with some sort of self-satisfaction. It's nowhere near the same feeling when you beat a guy with a good out-swinger or a sharply moving leg-cutter.

Down to the cricket . . . the season began with three Tests against New Zealand, thankfully the Australian Cricket Board had decided not to mingle the two Test series and the Indian series followed. My first impressions of the New Zealanders were not good ones, because they'd changed as blokes. They seemed to have quite a strut about them and they carried on as though they expected to wipe the floor with Australia.

Perhaps that was because of their surprise victory over a jaded West Indies side in New Zealand at the end of the previous summer. Whatever it was, it wasn't too pleasant to see the way they carried on both on the field and off. It was a stark change from previous meetings with New Zealand, when I'd found them a good bunch of guys who mixed well and got on with our players much in the same way as we enjoy relationships in Sheffield Shield games.

They didn't want to mix at all, particularly early in the piece. They didn't come into our dressing-room after play as is traditional, and weren't in when we went to theirs. It was a shame. Obviously they thought they'd play it hard the whole time, on the field and off. For instance, after stumps on the first day of the first Test in Brisbane, when we'd been in the field and it was their turn to come to our room, none of them bothered.

At the end of the second day I said to a couple of our players, 'Are you coming in for a drink?' They said, 'No way, why should we?' So I went into the New Zealand room on my own about fifteen to twenty minutes after play, to find just three of them left. Having started to talk to a couple of them I found five to ten minutes later that I was the last man in the room! Fortunately as the tour progressed things improved in this regard. You don't have to play it hard off the field to do well on the field. After all's said and done, comradeship is a most important part of cricket.

Anyway, Australia showed them how to go on the field because we won that first Test in three days. I have fond memories of this game, firstly because of the return to the Test cricket scene of Doug

Walters and secondly because after bowling poorly in beautiful conditions in the first innings I was able to really lift myself and bag 6 wickets in the second. It was a most frustrating experience when New Zealand batted first and none of our pace bowlers could get on a line to make use of the favourable conditions. In fact, they reached 190 for the loss of just 4 wickets, before leg-spinner Jim Higgs came into the attack and they were soon all out for 225. Higgs bowled beautifully. He got Geoff Howarth, then cleaned up the tail. Graeme Wood then batted very well for 111, almost a lone hand as we struggled along to 305. Wood is a player with a lot of ability, who has learnt to control himself in tight situations. We bowled them out for just 142 in their second innings and ended up winning by 10 wickets.

Dougie Walters made just 17 in his only innings for the match, but it was the springboard for a remarkable comeback season. Dougie is one of the best batsmen I've had the pleasure to play with or against. Only too rarely in cricket do we see a man who has the ability to win a game off his own bat, but certainly he has shown that capacity. He had a marvellous career leading up to the formation of World Series Cricket and we were thrilled to have him in our camp for the battles ahead of us in WSC. However, all of a sudden the faster bowlers seemed to sort him out. They bowled shortish to him all the time, directed their attack at his body and he couldn't cope. Sadly we all thought Dougie had lost it and was gone for ever.

It was very much to his credit that a couple of years later he was able to knuckle down and have another real crack at Test cricket ... and succeed! He put in a heap of work in the nets, straightening out the technical problems that had plagued him, that backlift towards point and the consequent tendency to play across the line, which resulted in so many catches behind the wicket on the off side. Of course he wasn't facing extreme fast bowling in the Tests against New Zealand and India, but those improvements in technique stood him in good stead. Dougie is an incredible man, he's so cool the whole time and such a nice guy ... I've never heard him say a bad word about another cricketer or anybody. He's also a very comical fellow, who has the ability to see the funny side of things and has perfect timing in telling his stories. He was a great fellow to have on a tour ... if things ever got tough Dougie would find a way to break the tension. When he retired before the start of the 1981-82 season, Dougie certainly went out on top and with lots of friends all over the world.

Australia won the second Test in Perth, again in three days, but New Zealand could consider themselves unlucky in that they lost captain Geoff Howarth before the start of the game with a hand injury. The Kiwis again batted first and I picked up 5 as they were soon out for 196. But we were in all sorts of trouble at 5 for 68, before Doug Walters and Rod Marsh took charge of the situation with a match-saving stand. It was Dougie's first major innings (he made 55) and Rod's 91 was his best in Tests for some time. We took a respectable lead and in the second innings once again it was Jim Higgs' spin which broke the back of the New Zealand innings.

Victory by 8 wickets cemented the series for Australia and we were quite happy about that, but there had been times in those two Tests when I thought we weren't completely in control of the situation. To Melbourne on Boxing Day for the third and final Test and on the opening day a huge banner hung from a tier above the dressing-rooms, 'All we want for Xmas is a five-day Test!' It could have been put there by the Australian Cricket Board, which must have lost much revenue with two three-day encounters at the start of the series. Well, they got their five-day Test, despite the fact that the MCG wicket had deteriorated to an unacceptable standard and made batting a nightmare. I just couldn't believe the arguments being put up in Melbourne (by interested parties, of course) that the wicket was level and was playing as well as it had done in their day.

The wicket was a disgrace, and towards the end of the season so, too, was the outfield. I was embarrassed as an Australian who had always supported the theory that the MCG was a top Test arena. A big effort had been made to get it right, with thousands of plugs of grass and runners planted on the pitch and in the outfield, but the damage had been done and it just wasn't good enough. To make matters worse when we played India there later in the season, there was a noticeable ridge, which made batting downright dangerous when the ball flew. I remember a few of our boys saying during that India game, 'Thank goodness we're not playing the West Indies attack on this track; somebody would be killed for sure.' The real fact of the matter was, we all knew the Windies were coming the following summer and then we *would* have to play them on that ground. Nobody relished the thought.

We found ourselves in some danger of losing the game against New Zealand after really controlling things until our second innings, which was the third of the match. Doug Walters got us out of a hole when we batted the first time when he made a great 'ton', thanks

150

to some unbelievable sticking by our number eleven Jim Higgs. For a man who has made more noughts than any other score in his long first-class career, Jim stuck around like a veteran for about 90 minutes to help Dougie score his century.

Actually, he was very lucky to have been able to do so, because he was dismissed early on when he edged a Lance Cairns bouncer to the wicketkeeper and was caught. Umpire Robin Bailhache ruled it was a dangerous delivery to a tailender and called 'no ball'. I felt that a Cairns bouncer was not all that dangerous because he is only a medium-pacer, but rules have to be adhered to and it was a bouncer, no matter how slowly it was delivered.

The Kiwis trailed by just 4 runs on the first innings and then we ran into real hot water as Richard Hadlee made full use of the wicket keeping low to take 6 wickets as we were all out for 188. So New Zealand went out in the final innings chasing 193 for victory and began very positively. With still only 1 wicket down and the score just 1 run off the halfway mark, we were staring to look a bit shaky. Then Greg Chappell came on to take a couple of quick wickets and put the stopper on the New Zealand charge. From that point they held on grimly for a draw. It was a pretty blank game for me, with no wicket in the first innings and just one in the second. On reflection, perhaps the wicket was so bad that I was guilty of thinking things were going to happen for me, rather than getting out there and making them happen. That's a trap you can fall into when operating on a bad wicket.

So it was a two-nil victory to Australia in the series, but the win was by no means convincing and I was a little worried at the prospect of going into the second part of the summer against the Indians with all their good batsmen and a fairly good attack. My fears weren't to be immediately justified, because we thrashed them in the first Test in Sydney the following week. As a result of some good bowling and batting by Australia, but some awful batting by India, we were able to finish them off in three days—the third time in the summer we'd won a Test in that space of time. It seemed the Indian batsmen were just out to belt the bowling around, an aim they achieved while losing wickets in a rapid fire as we defeated them by an innings.

The highlight of the game was a superb double century by Greg Chappell. His score of 204 was a record for Tests between the two countries and it was an even better performance for the fact that he was quite ill yet stuck at it throughout a long and hot day. It certainly was a masterpiece of concentration. Several times I've seen Greg

151

having to battle against illness and yet still make runs. Not many people would realise that he was having problems out there. It reflects the character of the man as he quietly goes about his work. He is not a robust person, but what a player and what a family—to produce one great player is one thing, but to put an Ian Chappell and a Greg Chappell from the one family on the international cricket arena is almost unbelievable. Both men are champions in any company. And not all that far behind them, but well and truly in their shadows, is their younger brother, Trevor.

This game gave us our first look at Kapil Dev, the Indian opening bowler who had come to Australia with a huge reputation. From first sight there was no doubting he was a tremendous bowler. He bowls beautiful outswingers and good off-cutters at a pace that really makes it awkward for even the best batsmen. He's always at you, very accurate—like Richard Hadlee in a lot of ways. I could see he was going to be a matchwinner many times during his career for India. After the game, which India had thrown away really by batting like millionaires, their captain Sunil Gavaskar made a classic statement. Bearing in mind that the game had been played only a few days after Christmas, you can imagine Sunny got a few laughs when he said, 'We gave our wickets away like Christmas presents . . . only trouble is, we Indians don't celebrate Christmas!'

The second Test was played in Adelaide in five scorching hot days, yet there were two memorable big innings to mark the game. In the first innings of the match Kim Hughes compiled a superb 213 to upstage Greg Chappell's record performance in the previous game. He capitalised on an extremely good start and a beautiful batting wicket to celebrate the birth a day or so before of twin sons. There was something almost symbolic in that innings, which helped us to 528 and what I thought would be plenty for yet another victory. But young Sandeep Patil had different ideas. He came in with India on 4 for 130 and played a most magnificent innings of 174, which also was a record, for an Indian against Australia. Patil used a very heavy blade and took a high backlift, so that when he made contact with the ball it really stayed hit. His innings was every bit as good as that of Hughes.

So we took a handy lead on the first innings and pushed on for the outright. However, on the flat wicket at Adelaide we just couldn't force it home. Lenny Pascoe gave us a chance with some very fiery work at the start of the innings, but in the end the extreme heat and the wicket won and India held on for a tense draw. Perhaps we would have won that one if we had taken Jim Higgs into the game. Actually I couldn't believe it when I learnt he was to be twelfth man. He'd been such a good contributor throughout the season and you didn't have to be a Rhodes Scholar to work out that an extra spinner would be required in those conditions. In my opinion, the Australian selectors then compounded their error by changing tack and leaving a 'quickie' (Rod Hogg) out of the side for the final Test in Melbourne and playing the two spinners. It just didn't make sense. The Melbourne wicket at that time was tailormade for fast bowlers because of the variable bounce.

And we did pay the price for not having an extra 'quick' on a track that certainly favoured fast and straight bowling. India won the toss and batted first and Gundappa Viswanath made a very good century in the circumstances to give his side a total of 237. Once more our batsmen fired and with our first innings score of 419 we were all set to cruise to victory. Batting a second time, at last Gavaskar got amongst the runs . . . and how his team needed him. He is without question one of the finest batsmen in the world, but he'd had a horror run up to that innings. He and Chethan Chauhan gave India a great start, reaching 165 before the first wicket fell. I had Gavaskar before for 70, but as the umpire raised his finger the Indian pointed to his bat and stood his ground.

I went up to him and pointed to the umpire and gave him a little advice about what he should do, whereupon he walked off—taking a rather reluctant Chauhan with him. It was a very tense moment indeed, as the two players walked slowly towards the boundary, Gavaskar actually pushing Chauhan ahead of him. A disaster was avoided when the Indian team manager, Wing-Commander Shahid Durrani, met the players at the gate and ushered Gavaskar off then Dilip Vengsarkar and Chauhan back out into the middle. I was glad to see it all tidied up and the game continue. As it turned out, Chauhan was upset by the incident and only a few minutes later slashed at one wide of the off stump for Bruce Yardley to take the catch. And I'd passed Richie Benaud's Australian Test wicket-taking record of 248. I turned to the Channel Nine broadcast position, where I knew Richie would be sitting, and signalled to him with a smile that I was now number one!

I felt proud and happy to have broken Richie's record. Proud because he was such a great player and happy because it took a load off my mind not to have people forever talking about the possibility of the record coming my way.

India played very well indeed to go on and total 324, though they did fall to pieces after losing their third wicket at 243. That left us with just 143 runs to make in the final innings, with plenty of time to spare and with Kapil Dev on the injured list and off-spinner Shivlal Yadav definitely out of the firing line with a broken bone in a foot. I thought we'd struggle to get those runs, because the wicket had deteriorated to such a degree, but I felt sure we'd win the game and in no way did I expect the ending that ensued. We played in a tired fashion, but let's not take anything away from Kapil. He made a remarkable recovery from his injury to take 5 wickets for 28 runs and lead his side to a wonderful victory. Only 3 Australian batsmen reached double figures as we were dismissed for just 83. So the Indians levelled the series at one-all.

In between the second and third Tests against India we had played the finals of the World Series Cup one-day competition and this time we emerged victors after a tight and sensational series against the New Zealanders. We lost the first one in Sydney, picked up two in Melbourne the following weekend and then won the next in Sydney to clinch the trophy. Sounds awfully straight forward, but it wasn't. The second of the Melbourne games produced one of the great controversies in my cricket career—and to my way of thinking it was not much more than a storm in a teacup. I suppose you could say the scene was set early in the game when Greg Chappell was given not out, much to the amazement and horror of the New Zealanders, after Martin Snedden had made a magnificent, running, diving attempt at a catch way out in the deeps at mid-wicket.

Snedden held the ball up and Mark Burgess, who was nearby supported the appeal, but Greg stood his ground and the umpires, after consultation, ruled in the negative. The Kiwis argued loud and long with the umpires and even with Greg, but to no avail and they were obviously extremely angry. I don't blame Greg for standing his ground . . . after all, it wasn't up to him to give himself out. I don't blame the umpires for not giving him out. Obviously they weren't sure that Snedden had taken the ball cleanly (his fingers were very close to the ground and the television replay wasn't at all conclusive). Snedden himself could have been wrong. I've seen many examples of players throwing themselves forward to a catch, taking it on the half-volley and swearing that they've taken it cleanly. It was unfortunate, but I could only support the actions of Greg Chappell and the two umpires.

Then Greg was involved in a major incident which did little to cement relationships between Australia and New Zealand. Going into the last over of the game, to be bowled by Trevor Chappell, New Zealand needed 11 runs to win the match. They'd scored 5 off the first 5 balls, so (barring a wide or a no-ball) they had to score a six off the final delivery. I remember thinking, 'Oh well, set them as far and wide as you can, bowl him a yorker and let him try.'

On the wide expanses of the MCG and with a new batsman, tail-ender Brian McKechnie, the odds were thousands to one to win. Then I saw Greg and Trevor talking and I thought, 'That's what he'll be telling his brother to do ... throw it right up in the slot, close to his legs, or something like that.' But next I saw Greg talking to the umpire, then the umpire talking to McKechnie and I wondered what was going on.

All of a sudden I realised as I saw Trevor walk up to the crease that he was going to bowl the final ball underarm. I thought, 'Heck, there's going to be a bit of an uproar about this.' But it was within the rules and I could see why Greg was doing it ... we were very tired and here was a chance to guarantee that the end of the one-day series was one game closer for Australia. If the Kiwis had won that game it would have meant having to go one extra game to win the series before dashing back to Melbourne for the final Test against India. Greg had given so much to the side that summer; batting, bowling and leading the team superbly. I could see what was going through his mind and I felt for him, I really did.

On reflection Greg realised that what he'd done was morally wrong and he took steps to put the matter right. I backed his decision at the time and if he'd asked me to be the one to bowl the ball I would have. Mind you, I would have tried awfully hard to convince him that I could have bowled a ball that couldn't have been hit for six. If he'd still instructed me to bowl underarm, then I would have. Straight after the game there was a real stir brewing and Greg and I decided to slip off up to Sydney that night, rather than wait and go up with the other guys the following day.

Greg said to me, 'Could be a good idea to get out of that hotel ... could be a few bombings tonight!' So off we went with the Sydney-based players, who wanted to have the night at home. One of them was Doug Walters, who was overheard saying to another (just loud enough for Greg to hear), 'You know, pal, there's only one thing that worries me about that game.' Came the reply, 'Yes, what's that?' Said Doug with a smirk, 'When I was a kid I was always told the game's not over until the last ball's *bowled*!'

The media really went to town, calling for Greg's blood, and even the two countries' Prime Ministers had their crack. But it gradually simmered down and by the time the next final game began two days later the crowd were back on Greg's side and there were no real problems. I thought the New Zealand players did their bit in playing it down, too. There were a few banners at the ground—one saying 'Greg . . . your underarm stinks!' perhaps summed it all up best—and the game was uneventful as we strolled to victory and won the trophy for the first time. I suppose when it's all boiled down, the rules were to blame for what happened. Now the rules have been changed and there can be no repeat performance of an underarm delivery in an international one-day game.

At the end of that long and testing international season it was not a case of going home and putting my feet up for a while. Rather it was back into harness for Western Australia as we made a last-ditch effort to win the Sheffield Shield. We had to do very well in our last two games to clinch the Shield and I really had to make a gargantuan effort to lift myself. We had to take on New South Wales and Queensland in Perth and do well against both, because they were strong contenders. I was very tired after all the bowling I'd done that summer, so, like it or not, I took every opportunity I could to sit down on the grass for a breather when a wicket fell or the drinks came out.

We had New South Wales all but defeated in the first game and as their last bastman walked out I was lying down having a rest on the fine leg boundary, when Kim Hughes (the WA captain) started yelling over to me, 'Come on, up you get . . . let's go.' I was very upset about this and went across to him, and said, 'Look, I've had a pretty hard summer. If some of you guys as batsmen had stayed out there a little longer a few times perhaps it wouldn't have been so hard and I wouldn't be needing a rest now.'

It was said on the spur of the moment, but I felt I had to let him know how I felt. It was my way of saying, 'I'll play it my way . . . I've done my job and I need a rest.' So the season which began with the two of us somewhat at loggerheads, ended in a similar fashion.

16. To England, 1981

It seems that I have a definite penchant for getting myself into major bother healthwise more times than not when I embark on a full tour of England. In 1972 I had an agonising beginning to my first Test tour to the mecca of cricket because of troubles with my back. For quite a few weeks it looked as though I might not even bowl a ball in a Test on that tour—and I must admit the prognosis was something similar for a week or so early in the 1981 tour of the same country. There I was isolated in a hospital bed just out of London, stricken with viral pneumonia and wondering whether I'd ever get out of those confines, let alone if I'd recover enough to play a significant part in what proved to be one of the most intriguing series imaginable.

Lying in the sterile confines of the Coppett's Wood Hospital isolation ward trying to shake the bug that had overcome me and endeavouring to keep my spirits up, I just couldn't believe what was happening to me. Before leaving Australia I'd done absolutely everything right to prepare myself for a marvellous tour of England, more than likely my farewell appearance in that country. Immediately the season ended back home I'd had an operation to clear up my sinuses and overcome a problem I'd been suffering with my breathing for quite some time. Then I'd gone through a steady, but searching, build-up with the other West Australians in the party before they left on the Sri Lanka leg of the tour.

I'd made a special plea to the Australian Cricket Board to be released from the Sri Lanka part because I didn't want to pick up any infections or problems after my recent operation. Rod Marsh had also been given permission to miss Sri Lanka because of problems he'd been suffering with his knees. When the others left, the pair of us then poured on the pressure in training—we called it our 'spartan routine'. So I left for London as fit as I'd ever been *and* my breathing was better than I could ever remember. Rod's knees seemed to be bearing up well and we both felt great and were eagerly looking forward to the tour ahead. Actually, although we left Australia after the main touring party, we actually arrived in London a couple of days before the others.

The weather was consistently overcast and very cold and wet, but Rod and I kept up our own training routine till the rest got in, then we fell in with team programmes. Unfortunately Rod and I also fell in for the heavy load in dealing with the media people who seem to flock around in hordes after the arrival of an Australian team. We handled interviews while we were practising, eating meals, walking down the street . . . you name it.

It was just too much; I think once you've done a Press conference, that should cut out a lot of the nagging of the senior players. It's just not right to feel you've got to fit in interviews during practice sessions. That means sitting down for half an hour or so when perhaps you're hot and perspiring, and then gradually getting cold.

Sadly you always learn your lessons too late, because before I'd even got my feet firmly on the ground in England I was struck down by this pneumonia virus and was fired off to hospital. At the hospital I had all the routine examinations and was told that I could expect to be out of action for quite some time, but initially nobody would be specific and that only added to my woes. Suffice it to say that in the hospital I was given the real kid gloves treatment. I wasn't allowed to get out of bed and have a shower, that was all done by hand in bed. I did a fair bit of coughing, but the main thing seemed to be the fevers and at the height of them I'd have to change my clothing three or four times a night because I was wet through with perspiration.

There was nothing whatsoever romantic about my situation. The isolation ward was set some fifty metres away from the main hospital, flanked by parkland and really remote from the world. You had a room on your own, because of the contagious nature of the diseases, and great care was taken to maintain a sterile atmosphere. For example, using the phone was quite a routine . . . you couldn't just reach over and grab a phone by your bed, or even walk out into the corridor to use a public phone. The staff would bring in a large coin-operated machine on a trolley, having dialled the number for you out in the corridor. They would then hand you the receiver and you would have to hold it inside a plastic bag. After you'd finished they would wipe the phone down carefully with a special cloth and remove it from the room.

After a few days I started to get some opinions from the doctors, but they were varied and quite depressing. They all seemed to feel

I'd have to miss the one-day internationals at the start of the conflict with England and that to be safe I should leave it six or seven weeks before bowling again. I wasn't at all happy with that and decided that if that was the case I might as well make arrangements to go home. I just wasn't prepared to sit around and miss that much of the tour and then try to do my best in the last three or four Tests. I could see that being fruitless and certainly not in the best interests of the team. Better for a replacement to be sent.

Helen was on the phone constantly and more than once she was all geared up to come over, but we realised there was little she could achieve and she had the kids to look after. A few of the team came and visited me, but they had to wear special clothing and weren't allowed to stay too long and definitely were not to stay around the corridors of the ward, for fear of picking up some disease. Jeff Thomson, who was in England playing for Middlesex, came and saw me a few times and it was great to see his face.

After a week or so I was allowed to leave the room and have a shower, but I felt so weak when standing up that if I closed my eyes I could feel myself keeling over. I must admit I was feeling very down in the dumps—the only saving grace was that it was raining almost incessantly outside and that meant I wasn't missing much training or match practice. The thought kept me going. That was silly really, because I suppose I was so sick that playing cricket should have been the last thing on my mind.

I must say that I was looked after very well by the staff. They did all they could to make a tough time for me a little better. The doctor in charge of my case was a very nice fellow who gave me a lot of encouragement, even though his superior wasn't all that optimistic. He was a man with some thirty years' experience with this type of disease. He was aware of the complications of my illness and finally only reluctantly agreed to let me be discharged from the hospital after ten days, on the understanding that I wouldn't attempt to play in the one-day international games and would just have a look at the outside chance of playing in the first Test. So, having arrived in England as fit as a trout about a fortnight before, I walked out of that hospital very weak indeed. I'd lost over a stone in weight and had no strength or stamina at all . . . just walking was an effort.

Fortunately I had no congestion on my chest, so after a couple of days successfully convalescing and gradually getting into action I decided that I felt just about good enough to have a crack at getting right for the three one-day games. I began my build-up with some jogging—or should I say plodding—my first effort being from the Waldorf Hotel in the heart of London, down Fleet Street and back again. It was about a mile in ten minutes, but I was totally exhausted at the end of it. I repeated that same run for the next couple of days and then went down to practice at Lord's all rugged up and warm. I bowled a little, then did a bit of stretching and exercising, but after about half an hour I felt myself dropping off sharply.

I stopped for a rest, but when I tried to come back for a second stint there was nothing there. I recognised then that I'd have that problem for quite a while and in fact it plagued me throughout the tour. I was to find that in my initial spell I'd feel really good for three or four overs, but then all of a sudden I'd run out of gas. To overcome this I'd go a little easier in the first spell and this would enable me to carry through at a fairly steady work rate for the whole Test.

The other problem I had was that I'd pick up all the sniffles and niggling things that were going through the team. I was forever on antibiotics or some form of medication. At the end of a Test match I'd be so low that for three or four days I'd do virtually nothing but try to recover my strength. Then I'd train back up again for the next Test, and so on. It wasn't a thrilling or interesting tour at all as much of my time was spent lying around hotel rooms.

Just twice in the tour I felt really good. The first was in my initial spell in the fifth Test at Old Trafford in Manchester, when I felt something like my old self. Then in the final Test at The Oval I felt good for the whole game. Actually, I'd put it at 70 or 80 per cent, but before that I'm sure I was only 50 to 60 per cent. So, personally, I had a disappointing tour . . . I am sure that if I'd been 100 per cent fit I'd have done a lot better in the conditions and perhaps Australia would have fared that little bit better. In the final analysis there was only a whisker between the two sides. The figures might have indicated that I had a good tour, but for the most part I was only bowling from memory. I knew I had problems with my action, but I simply didn't have the energy to sort them out.

I was just surviving for most of the time. Certainly in the one-day games before the Tests I made it through on no more than adrenalin. I got through the first one bowling medium pace and no more. In the second I bowled a little quicker, but I remember in my last spell, when it was desperate for us to get wickets to win the game, I was absolutely gone after bowling five or six balls—trouble was, I had four more overs to go! I didn't know how I'd make it, but each time I looked like faltering I'd be lifted by a wicket or something happening. In the third one-dayer I just wasn't there. I had nothing left. Three games in five days with travel in between and I was a goner. I knew then that I'd have real problems when we got into the Tests.

The doctor who was looking after the Australian team told me I'd have to take great care not to get a chill during practice or in games. This meant not staying out on the ground with a shirt wet with perspiration, especially in cold conditions. So I got into the habit of changing my shirt in the dressing-room after each spell and I continued that practice throughout the series.

I seemed to be perspiring more than ever and was forever having to leave the ground and before long the subject became a matter of controversy. The media began suggesting that while I was in the dressing-room I was having a shower, a drink and a general revival course. I was really upset at those allegations. They just didn't understand that I was lucky to be able to play, without having to endure accusations of cheating. The media really got into the subject when Ian Botham was replaced by Mike Brearley after the second Test and it was rumoured that Brearley wouldn't allow me to continue the habit. To my knowledge Brearley said nothing.

Once again the British Press gave us some needle about one-day cricket as we approached the three-game series. They carried on as though it was a matter of course that England would win them all without even trying. After all, some had written us off as the weakest Australian team ever to tour England. But we were confident we could give them a real shake, even though our captain and master one-day player Greg Chappell had been unable to make the tour and his absence would leave a hole very hard to plug. We realised that England had just returned from a very demoralising tour of the West Indies and because of the weather had had very little chance to get into form back home. Even after England won the first one-dayer at Lord's I thought we still had their measure.

They hadn't been convincing and we felt we'd learnt from that loss. We left spinner Ray Bright out for the second at Edgbaston and brought in Terry Alderman. It turned out to be a real close go—in fact, one of the best one-day games I've ever played in—and we won by taking the last wicket with the second last ball and with England just two runs short. We then won the third at Headingley quite easily, thanks to a fine century by Graeme Wood, and were delighted to have won a one-day series in England. Alderman bowled well enough in these games to gain a place in the Test team. He'd come from nowhere and was destined for instant stardom.

After the one-day series we had County games against Derbyshire (in which I bowled 24 and 19 overs) and then Middlesex (when I bowled 11 overs in the first innings for a return of 5 for 41 and 12 in the second). I felt I had to play in these two games to try to make up for lost time in terms of form. However, in doing that I was using up a lot of my reserves of strength and stamina. I really struggled in those two games and it was all I could do to get through a day's play. I had no energy at all left in me to do any running or exercising and this was right out of my normal routine in the weeks leading up to a Test and the series.

The conditions at the Racecourse Ground in Derby for the game against Derbyshire were quite the most archaic I've ever come across in first-class cricket anywhere. The toilets and shower room—actually there were no showers, just the piping—had to be seen to be believed. There was a great big team bath and two smaller individual baths, if you cared to fill them up. You can imagine that with thirteen Australians and twelve Derbyshire players all trying to wash after a day's play there was minor havoc. Then trying to dry oneself was an interesting exercise . . . we were offered the same towels every day. On the second day I was offered a towel with dirt marks all over it from being left on the floor the day before. That was too much for me and I complained.

I started on the team physiotherapist, who in turn saw the woman who cleaned the room overnight. She got upset and carried on about the state of our rooms, saying we had a hide to expect clean towels. I fired back. 'How could anybody respect anything like that?' I said, pointing in the direction of the dilapidated room. She really got upset and I was asked for an apology by the Derbyshire captain, Geoff Miller. I apologised for some of the language I'd used, but told Miller that if the club didn't turn on clean towels immediately we'd get some ourselves and charge them up to the club. The club secretary later apologised and said the matter had been taken care of. About the only happy thing I recall about the Derbyshire game was the fact that during the match it was announced that I was to receive the MBE. It was a thrill . . . an honour for cricket as much as for me personally.

In the Middlesex game the lads celebrated the first sunny day they'd experienced on the tour so far. That date was Sunday, 14 June—a date we'll not forget in a hurry. It had been a long wait to see the sun. In this match Jeff Thomson came up against his country and it was a bit of a grudge match for him, because he'd been upset

162

at not being chosen for the tour and in fact had written a few stinging articles in a London newspaper about the Australian side. He bowled like a man possessed, very fast indeed, and as I looked at him I thought, 'Wouldn't it be great to have him in our side for the coming weeks?' In the first innings he clipped Graeme Wood with a short-pitched ball and Woody was very lucky not to have been seriously hurt, because the ball struck the side flap of his helmet.

The Middlesex game was drawn and so we went to Nottingham for the first Test at Trent Bridge in not the best of form. To make matters worse for me, the day before the Test was due to start was overcast and windy—and very cold. When we went to the ground to practise I rugged right up and didn't risk taking too much part in the session. We had the usual team meeting that night and Kim Hughes, captaining a full-strength Australian side in a Test for the first time, gave a long speech outlining what lay ahead and what he expected of the team. I was given the chance to speak and my main theme was that there's not a lot of value in talk, it's what you do out in the middle that counts. I've always believed cricketers generally base too much on talk and not enough on action.

It turned out to be an amazing Test, mainly because of the nature of the wicket. It was hard, but it had a really good cover of grass and was reasonably fast. We knew that it would favour the bowlers and when the game began in overcast conditions I thought it would swing and seam for a couple of days. As it turned out, there was movement through the air and off the pitch throughout the game and it was one of the most difficult batting wickets I'd played on in Tests for many a year. In fact, only two players scored more than 50—England's Mike Gatting made 52 in their first innings and Allan Border made a streaky, but gutsy, 63 in our first innings. I remember reflecting on the Trent Bridge wicket in 1972, when that ground was referred to as the 'bowler's graveyard'. How things had changed!

We ended up winning the 1981 Test, simply because we held our catches and England dropped theirs. We didn't bowl any better, we didn't bat any better, we just held those vital catches. Of course, the highlight of the game was the dream Test debut of my West Australian team-mate Terry Alderman. He bowled magnificently to take 4 wickets in the first innings and 5 in the second. He bowled 24 overs on the trot in the first innings and was able to maintain pressure throughout. This long stint was the pattern of things to come for Terry in the series and I must admit I didn't agree with the tactics in flattening a front-line bowler with spells like that. At times we paid dearly because we were unable to clean out the bottom half of the England batting. Because of my illness I had little to give late in an innings and Terry was invariably a spent force.

We needed only 132 to win the match, but we really had to work for them. We were cruising at 2 for 77, but then Graham Dilley chimed in with 4 wickets to really put us under the hammer. That batting lapse was a sign of things to come. In the closing stages England were bowling really well. They beat the bat several times and even dropped a couple of catches. With 6 wickets down and 10 runs to get I still wasn't sure we'd win. It was real nail-biting stuff. Finally Trevor Chappell and Geoff Lawson saw us over the line by 4 wickets. Having won the one-day series and gone one-up in the Test series, you can imagine we were very happy lads . . . but in the back of my mind was a little reserve, as I'd felt we hadn't outplayed England at any stage in the Test.

After that game I had a long rest—and I really needed it. I went down to London and spent a couple of days lolling around the tennis at Wimbledon and had a couple of relaxing days, which really fired the engines up again. In the meantime the team had played Kent at Canterbury and, unfortunately, Rod Hogg broke down while bowling there. But on the positive side of the ledger, Lawson bowled very well. So we went into the second Test at Lord's without Hogg, taking instead left-hand spinner Ray Bright. We were quite confident going into that game, but we didn't have everything at our fingertips. We were told that the Test was going to start at eleven o'clock and were all keyed up for that time. We went to the ground bright and early, only to be told at half past ten that play wouldn't start until half past eleven.

I just couldn't believe something like that could happen at Lord's. Sitting around the dressing-room for that extra half-hour really took the sting out of us and perhaps it showed in our opening stint after we'd won the toss and put them in. It was an easy-paced strip, but there was a bit of a ridge just short of a length at one end.

Lawson bowled beautifully into that ridge in the first innings. It seemed to be just the right length for a bowler as tall as Lawson and he hit the spot enough times to give the England batsmen big troubles, finishing with 7 for 81. After a solid middle-order contribution, England lost their last 6 wickets for just 27 runs. I felt languid throughout the innings and just lacked the strength to fire the quicker one through, something I've always been able to do on a dead slow track.

We led by 34 on the first innings, Border top-scoring again and Lillee 40 not out—another century nipped in the bud! I picked up a little in the second innings to grab 3 wickets and Bright bowled very well to also claim 3. England made a declaration, but the game was always going to be a draw on such a good batting wicket. In this game England captain Ian Botham made a pair of 'ducks', following on scores of 1 and 33 in the first Test. He had taken just 6 wickets in the 2 Tests *and* England were one down in the series. The inevitable occurred when the England selectors removed him from the captaincy. It would have been no surprise to Botham, because he'd told me after the first Test that he had a feeling he'd be dropped then, not only as captain but also as a player.

As luck would have it, the England selectors chose to retain him in the side and give him another chance to prove his worth as a player without the pressures of captaincy. The remainder of the tour was to prove a point or two in that regard. There was considerable conjecture about who would be appointed to replace Botham as captain and I was surprised when England went back in time and plucked Mike Brearley out of retirement. After the Test I remained in London, hopeful of another good rest to re-charge the batteries. But I was a bit of a mess. I just couldn't sleep and in the end was so desperate for some sleep that I had to use some strong sleeping tablets. They worked, thank goodness, and I had three nights of at least twelve hours' sleep before leaving for Headingley, Leeds, for the third Test.

During this period of considerable personal tension I ran into troubles at Lord's. I was desperate to get in some net practice with Allan Border and John Dyson, who had stayed down while the team went to play Northamptonshire. But I'd found in the past it was no easy matter getting facilities for practice at Lord's. Several times before I'd been thwarted when I'd telephoned the ground and asked to use the nets. I'd been told by some official that nets were not available, only to find out myself later that I could have been fitted in quite easily. When I phoned this time I was put through to the room attendant, who said there was a game in progress between Eton and Harrow. He said we wouldn't be able to use the change-rooms, but that we could change somewhere else at the ground. He also said there'd be a bit of activity near the nets area, but I said we only wanted to use the nets and shouldn't get in the way. He said he couldn't okay that, but it should be all right, so the three of us went to the ground.

We'd contacted Jeff Thomson to make arrangements to borrow some of his gear (ours was with the team in Northampton) and he agreed we could get some of his gear out of the Middlesex dressing-room (the home team room at Lord's). We got some balls from the room attendant and some towels for a shower afterwards and when we went to get Thommo's gear the boys using the room told us they were quite happy for us to change there, which we did. We duly had our net practice and by the time we'd finished the Eton-Harrow game was all over, so Allan and I ran a few laps of the ground—to the accompaniment of some terrible jeering from the Eton and Harrow supporters still drinking and eating away up in the private boxes and in the grandstands.

When Allan and I arrived back at the dressing-room we were confronted by Jack Bailey, the secretary of the MCC (which controls Lord's). He'd kicked John Dyson out of the room and when he saw me said rather venomously, 'What are you doing here?' 'We've been practising,' I replied quietly. 'Who said you could practise?' was the sharp retort. 'Surely we're allowed to practise and determine ourselves when we do that?' I said. Bailey's voice rose each time he opened his mouth. This time, 'But who said you could practise here?' I shrugged. 'Nobody said we could practise, but we thought we'd come down here and if we found we couldn't practise we'd just have a run around and do some exercises.' His reply brought my blood to the boil, saying, 'But you can't do that without official consent.'

'I've got a few things to say to you,' I said through clenched teeth. 'In the past I've rung here on four or five occasions and have been told there were no practice facilities, have then come down here for a run and there have been practice facilities every time. I'm sick and tired of going through those channels only to be told one thing and find out another. We thought we'd take the chance and come down here today ... if there were no facilities we'd have had a run and gone back to the hotel.' By now I was nicely warming to the occasion. 'We've got to practise somewhere,' I added, upon which he repeated his edict about requiring official permission. 'That's so much like you people,' I said, 'you sit at your desk with your suit and tie on and try to control guys like us who are just trying to get out and do something. In Australia, if your players wanted to practise before a Test they'd be treated like kings. Look at it from my point of view ... I'm a professional cricketer wanting to get some practice and at this ground we can't get facilities at any particular stage. Don't you think that's a bit silly?'

Then followed a tirade of abuse. Bailey tried to blame the room attendant, but I cut in and put him right on that one and then he tried another tack. 'What are you doing in that dressing-room?' he said, to which I replied, 'We wanted to get some of Jeff Thomson's gear from in there and were then invited to change there.' 'But don't you know that's the England dressing-room?' came the retort. I replied that, of course, I knew that, but so what! 'You can't change in the England dressing-room,' he said.

'But the England team isn't in there,' was my rejoinder. 'But it's still the England dressing-room and you must have permission to go in there.' My reply, 'Don't give me a load of rubbish,' really got him going. 'You can get out of here,' he shouted, 'get all your gear out of here and take Thomson's gear, too.' I replied that I wasn't moving Thommo's gear and that he'd have to ring Thommo himself.

More abuse followed ... 'you people are all the same' ... 'arrogant' ... and 'there'll be something official done about this. Fred Bennett will learn about this and then you'll be in real trouble.'

I said, 'I hope you do speak to him about it, because I'll be putting in a full report myself. I think it's such a normal carry-on from you guys that I'm not at all surprised—but I am disappointed.' And that was that. There was a furore about the incident, but again it was a storm in a teacup *and* I don't regret one bit of what we did or what I said there. When it was all boiled down, it was no more than three cricketers desperately trying to get some practice. We weren't interfering and one of the groundsmen had said we could use the nets. The only reason I'd stuck at it with Bailey was to try and take the heat off the room attendant, who it seemed was getting all the blame.

While all this was happening the boys had played their game against Northamptonshire. During the game Rod Hogg had proved his fitness and Dirk Wellham, the promising youngster in the party, had scored 135 in the first innings. There was talk of Wellham displacing Trevor Chappell in the line-up. In fact, I'd discussed Wellham's case with the playing manager, Peter Philpott, with a view to him going into the side, but I wasn't quite sure whom I'd have left out. There were a couple of candidates, in my opinion. Dirk had the weight of runs in his favour, but was to wait until the final Test before getting his chance. Rod Hogg, too, was overlooked for the Leeds Test.

I still can't believe we lost that Test ... I guess I never will come to terms with it. We batted so very well to declare at 9 for 401, with Graeme Wood a century-maker and Kim Hughes making 89. The track had been seaming about all over the place and it was playing two heights. It was a really gutsy effort. After that we bowled extremely well to knock them over for 174. When it was decided to make England follow-on, I immediately had my doubts, because I felt it would be very hard to bat on that wicket on the last day as wear and tear set in. Also I didn't think England would bat as badly again, but they did and when they were 7 for 135 we all thought we were home and hosed. They still needed 93 runs to make us bat again and we were long odds-on to go two-up in the series.

However, once again we had trouble knocking over the tail and how we paid for it this time! Botham was at his irrepressible best. No matter where we bowled to him he seemed to have the answer and he literally raced to a most memorable century. He received grand support from Graham Dilley, who made a half-century, and Chris Old, who chimed in with 29. Perhaps we gave Dilley too much room to play his strokes, perhaps this, perhaps that; whichever way you looked at it, it was an incredible fact that England added 221 runs for those final 3 wickets. It's true we were dead unlucky in that, having made England follow-on, we had to struggle on with one of our bowlers, in Geoff Lawson, sick. And there was criticism, perhaps justified, that Hughes only gave Bright 4 overs during that avalanche of runs.

Still we had our chance to win the game. We only needed 130 to do it and at one stage were 1 for 56. Then big Bob Willis gave an inspired performance with the ball, helped no little by the great vocal support of the crowd and the fact that our batsmen perhaps went too much on the defensive. In doing so we lost 5 wickets for just 19 runs and finally we were out for 111. England had recorded one of the most remarkable victories in the history of Test cricket. I was terribly despondent after it was all over. It was a game that might have been drawn, but never should have been lost by Australia. I remember thinking it was just a dream, one of those fairy tales . . . but the following morning, there it was all over the newspapers and it was for real.

There was quite some controversy surrounding this game as far as Rod Marsh and I were concerned. It hinged on the fact that we had a bet on the outcome. Not that having a bet on a cricket match is anything out of the ordinary. The trouble was, Rod and I backed England to win. That sounds unbelievable, but so were the odds that flashed on the new scoreboard at Headingley on the fourth day. England were set at 500 to 1! We were in the dressing-room during lunch at the time and I said to the guys, 'Have a look at that. Five hundred to one! In a two-horse race there's just no way those odds can be right. I'm going to put fifty quid on that, because I can't believe anybody would offer odds of that nature. I'm prepared to risk fifty on the off-chance that I might get twenty-five thousand.'

The others said not to be stupid, there just wasn't a bet at that stage because England were so far gone. I said, 'You're right, there's no bet, but it's a chance of a lifetime with such stupid odds.' At no stage did any of us think there was anything wrong with taking the odds and betting against Australia, just that it would be stupid to throw the money away. The boys talked me out of wasting fifty pounds, but I decided I'd still throw ten pounds at the bookies. I went round the others, asking if any of them wanted to have a bit, but there were no takers. I got to Marshy and said, 'Look, you're silly if you don't . . . put ten on.' He said he wouldn't, so I suggested five, 'just to be with me'. However, I just couldn't talk him into it because he was convinced, like the others, that there was no way England could win.

So I decided to go it alone and asked our bus driver, Peter, to go and put the ten on for me. As we were walking down the stairs to go out on the field Marshy saw Peter going round to the betting tent and yelled out 'Pete!' When Peter turned round Marshy showed him five fingers, indicating a five-pound bet. When we got out to the middle we forgot all about the bet and got on with the game. Peter later told us that when he got half-way round to the tent he'd decided it was ridiculous to waste the money. He had stopped and turned back to the dressing-room, saying to himself that he'd give us our money back at afternoon tea time. But he had stopped again, thinking, 'I've heard of these things happening and I'd better not take the risk.' So he put the money on for the two of us.

That meant that when Australia were losers in the Test, Marshy and I were winners. Even though we weren't all that happy about being winners in those circumstances, we reasoned that there have been many instances when teams have bet against themselves or against a number of runs being scored or the like. Nobody could claim that because of the bet either Rod or I weren't trying as hard as we possibly could. At the time we realised we'd won the money we felt a bit bad about it, but what could you do . . . the odds were ridiculous and it was just one of those stupid bets. But after we'd collected our 'ill-gotten gains' Marshy and I did spend a little of it buying the lads a few drinks.

There was another reason why this particular Test will always remain in the forefront of my cricket memories. It all revolved around the scoreline in the first innings: 'Botham . . . caught Marsh, bowled Lillee . . . 50'. That dismissal, the umpteenth time that Rod and I had figured together in a Test match dismissal, had special significance because it gave my mate the world record for the number of Test victims for a wicketkeeper. And I can tell you it gave me great pleasure to be the bowler to provide Rod with the chance. We'd worked in tandem for a long, long time and a great friendship had developed over and above the 'professional relationship'. There's no doubt Rod has had his knockers over the years, but I've always been a great believer in his ability.

For mine, there's nobody safer behind the stumps . . . certainly over a long period of time. There were times when it seemed to be a toss-up between him and Alan Knott, whose record he eclipsed with that dismissal. However, over all Marsh has been the better and the records show that. The only thing I could possibly say against Rod is that he has proven he has tons of ability with the bat and at times hasn't fulfilled that promise. But then again, it must be very hard for a guy to be Mr Perfection behind the stumps for all those hours and then go out and score one century after another. He passed Knotty's record with plenty of Tests in hand, having earlier in the series passed the Englishman's mark for the most dismissals in Australia-England matches.

Perhaps the best tribute I could pay Rod is to say that out of the hundreds of days we have spent playing cricket together I can recall him having only one really bad day. That was in 1979 in Antigua when we were playing a World Series Cricket Supertest. Rod started off by missing a stumping chance offered by the West Indies' Lawrence Rowe. Then followed an unbelievable run of 3 dropped catches as Rowe went on to score 135! The missed chances have been few and far between for Rod and, of course, he makes so many catches that others wouldn't even attempt, because of his magnificent technique and his acrobatic diving. Apart from all his skills, Marshy really knows the game and has been of great assistance to me over the years with little hints and bits of advice both out in the middle and back in the dressing-room when we're planning a day's play or having a post mortem on a day in the field. At the time of writing this book Rod is keeping better than at any other time in his career.

The loss at Headingley made it one-all for the series and I must admit that we were all down in spirits after that. We were down, but not out, because we thought that result had been a 'oncer' and that we had outplayed England for most of the game. Straight after that Test Rod Marsh proved that his luck was still in when he captained the side in a one-day game against Scotland in Glasgow and actually won the game with his bowling. He had figures of 1 over, 3 wickets for no runs to win a tight match—and he never let us forget that solitary over! Actually, when he puts his mind to it Marshy can be a darned good bowler, either at medium-pace or sending down his mixture of spinners.

There has been a standing tradition among recent touring Australian sides to visit the Red Hart Inn, owned by Dick and Nan Thomas, during the Australians' game against Worcestershire. It's a very relaxing night with a beautiful meal, way out in the middle of nowhere on a winding road some 28 kilometres out of the city. Once again this year we had a terrific meal and then a few drinks with the locals and the experience put us all in a good frame of mind. At this stage, going towards the fourth Test at Edgbaston, Birmingham, both Rod Hogg and Geoff Lawson were under a cloud with back injuries and there was talk of a replacement, possibly even Greg Chappell, being brought into the side. As it was Hoggy bowled pretty well at Worcester and he took Lawson's place in the side for Edgbaston.

However, he wasn't completely fit, which gave Ray Bright the chance to do a fair bit of bowling and he came out absolute trumps. England batted first and we had a few close ones turned down early on, but still had them out for only 189. At stumps we were 2 for not many and things deteriorated the next day when Graeme Wood was adjudged run out in controversial circumstances. Still we battled back to lead by 69, despite an embarrassing period of play when Kim Hughes was actively shielding Graham Yallop from the strike when Bob Willis was bowlig.

That wasn't the only part Willis had to play in that innings, because he and I had a little run-in later in the piece. When I went in I smashed him for a four and the very next ball he ran right through the crease and bowled another bouncer at me. Despite the fact that the delivery came at me from a couple of yards short of the pitch length, I got it away and as I ran down the wicket I clipped Willis pretty hard and said something along the lines of, 'If you've got to resort to that sort of stuff you should give up bowling.' It's a gutless thing to try and pin a tail-ender from a position a few yards down the wicket. I did the same thing once as a very young player (bowling at an opening batsman) and I was very upset about it afterwards . . . somehow I don't think Willis cared a scrap about his act.

Again we bowled pretty well in the second innings, with Alderman grabbing 3 (for a total of 8) and Bright picking up 5 from 34 overs. We were left a target of 151 to win with plenty of time to spare, but were 1 for not many overnight and again I had the terrible feeling that we were going to make a mess of it. We lost a couple of quick wickets early the next day and for the second game in a row capitulated, to be all out for 121. Admittedly we thought we were on the receiving end of a couple of 'rough' decisions, but as Ian Botham cleaned us out at the end of the innings I had the feeling that we didn't bat all that well, either. So we endured the bitter disappointment and frustration of seeing another game slip out of our grasp. England took a two-one lead, which so easily could have been three-nil in our favour.

There was a nice old to-do after the Edgbaston game when a story hit the London newspapers about Rod Marsh having allegedly struck the Bishop of Birmingham's secretary. There was an incident, it's true, but the newspaper report was a long way from the truth. As we waited in the team coach to leave the ground a fellow stood on the other side of a fence shouting abuse at us. After a while Marshy got out of the coach to tell the rude chap where to get off. The debate hotted up somewhat and Marshy tried to grab the fellow, but he had to reach almost a metre up and through the fence to where the man was standing on a higher level of ground and got nowhere near him. The bloke then claimed Rod was taking a swing at him and it was really blown up in the Press. However, only half the story was ever told.

Back in London the following day we all decided to let our hair down. We held an impromptu meeting in our local pub, the Gilbert. After the lunch session had ended and the pub was shut to the public, we stayed on and had a few more beers and sang a few songs. At the end of it there was a mess-around all-in wrestle with the guys all letting of a heap of steam. It really was a funny day, with ripped shirts and all sorts of things happening . . . and the sight of the fellows making their way back to the Waldorf Hotel in different stages of undress must have been quite humorous. Heading the list of the best dressed on that journey was the captain, who had to walk through the streets of London clad only in a pair of briefs.

A day or so after the Birmingham Test another major story hit the Press. South African interests were trying to get together a team to tour their country and there was an immediate reaction from the cricket hierarchy, who obviously still had World Series Cricket fresh in their minds and were aware of the tricky South African politics. Our manager, Fred Bennett, very smartly informed all of us of the Australian Cricket Board's viewpoint, which was a strict 'no-no'. It was quite funny actually, because though some of us had been approached (myself included) none of us was interested in going. There was Fred trying to get all serious about it and lecturing us, while we could barely keep a straight face. I can say there was a lot of money involved, but I knew there was no way we could accept because of all the political implications.

As the pot boiled on that subject I went across to the Isle of Man with Kim Hughes and very good friends of mine in London, Charles and Caroline Benson. We were house guests of Robert and Susan Sangster and we had a great time, about the only occasion on the whole tour that I was able to relax and really enjoy myself. It was a hectic programme, flitting off to race meetings and casino nights here and there, but I still managed to get in plenty of sleep and go for a good run every day. Above all else, it was interesting to see how the other half live. The Sangsters are obviously extremely wealthy, but, more than that, they are really down-to-earth people and especially good hosts. The weather was turned on just right for us and it was a marvellous break.

Then it was back to the realities with the fifth Test at Old Trafford in Manchester—and we faced this vital game with two of our fast bowling staff unavailable because of injury. Both Rod Hogg and Geoff Lawson sat on the sidelines with back problems as young Mike Whitney, a lively left-hander from New South Wales, took a dream ride into Test cricket. He had played just a handful of first-class games back in Australia and for an English County side in between playing as a professional in one of the Lancashire leagues. He just happened to be on the spot when a fast bowler was desperately needed. I was put down to room with him in Manchester and I was immediately struck by the nonchalance of the chap. He fitted in very well and went into the Test with all the confidence and composure of a veteran.

We lost the toss and bowled and again I thought we were on the wrong end of some pretty ordinary decisions. On top of having a few 'plumb' leg before wicket decisions go against me in the first 2 or 3 overs, I was warned for running down the wicket. That had never happened to me before when operating over the wicket in any grade of cricket and at the end of my opening spell I was very upset at what had appeared to be a 'get Dennis Lillee' session. However, we still managed to have England 8 down for 137 and at that stage we gave ourselves a good chance of fighting our way back into the series. Then the England tail wagged again and we finally had them out for 231, with the last pair, Paul Allott and Bob Willis, putting on a frustrating 56.

It should never have happened, but once again it did ... we'd battled so hard for an advantage and then been unable to capitalise. Things soon deteriorated even further. We lost our first wicket at 20 and then 3 with the score on 24. Playing only his third Test innings, Martin Kent batted beautifully for 52, but we were dismissed for 130, a deficit of 101. And we'd lasted only 30 overs and 2 balls—it was just disgusting. Again I was left wondering if it had actually happened that an Australian side had folded up so hopelessly for the third time in successive Tests. It was irresponsible batting, there's no other way to describe it. Okay, the ball was doing a lot, but it wasn't an impossible wicket by any stretch of the imagination.

If anything the wicket was getting better for batting as the game wore on and when England batted a second time they just ground us into the Old Trafford earth. In the first session Geoff Boycott and the recalled Chris Tavare (69 in the first innings) put on 29 in 28 overs. To be fair to him though, I thought Tavare batted very well indeed, adding 78 to his first innings knock. He was quite boring to watch, I'm sure, but without his devotion to the cause England could have been in all sorts of trouble. Ian Botham completed his domination over the scene with another century and when we finally dismissed England after agonising half-centuries to Alan Knott and John Emburey, we faced the daunting task of scoring 506 runs to win the match.

Once again Australia made a poor start, but then a spirited 43 from Hughes (out leg before for the sixth time in the series so far) and centuries from Allan Border and Graham Yallop put us in with a whisper of a chance of winning. It was a great performance by Border, who batted with the discomfort of a broken bone in a hand— what a brave player this fellow is! So quiet and efficient about everything he does in cricket, so determined to succeed and so professional. Marshy picked up 47 and myself 28, but we just ran out of batsmen and were dismissed for the most creditable total of

174

402. That innings was a more heartening performance, but the victory had given England an unassailable three-one lead in the series. Then it was off to The Oval in London, my favourite hunting ground in England. As I threw my gear bag down in the dressing-room I remembered my first Test match at the ground in 1972, when we won the fifth Test and I took a total of 10 wickets for the game. In 1981 we didn't win, though I think it's fair to say we had the better part of a draw, and I went one better in taking 11 of the 17 England wickets to fall. It was a rather satisfying personal result in what was probably my last Test in England. In fact, all but one of the remaining England wickets to fall were taken by Terry Alderman, who finished the six-Test series with a phenomenal tally of 42 wickets. That meant he and I had 81 victims between us for the series.

Terry's performance in England was all the more remarkable when you take into account the fact that the first Test of the series was his debut Test. He galloped past my record of 31 victims in a series (in 5 Tests in 1972) and took 5 or more wickets in an innings no fewer than 4 times. He simply bamboozled the England batsmen, in a manner somewhat similar to the way my old pal Bob Massie did in 1972. He made full use of the conditions, which more often than not favoured fast-medium swing and seam bowling. He bowled a couple of yards faster than usual and, above all I think, he bowled a consistently good line and length. So much for the theory of all the so-called pundits back home that Terry couldn't and wouldn't take wickets away from his home ground in Perth! And it couldn't have happened to a nicer guy . . . in a lot of ways he reminded me of another West Australian fast bowler, Graham McKenzie, with his similar muscular build and pleasant nature.

Young Dirk Wellham got his chance in this final Test, with John Dyson making way and Kent being advanced to the opening role. We batted first and a solid start paved the way for another century by Border. All the batsmen got a few and we were dismissed for 352, with Botham picking up 6 wickets. Then Geoff Boycott arrived at last with a long and hard-fought century, but just for once we were able to clean out the bottom half of the England batting and lead by 38 on the first innings. My own figures for this innings, 7 for 89 from 31.4 overs, represented my best performance in a Test match innings.

At long last I was feeling I was at something like my normal health and fitness . . . and at the start of the innings I was able to sort out a couple of problems with my technique. I had been falling away badly at the delivery point, resulting in loss of pace and control, as well as my away-swinger to the right-handers. I had known about this problem, but had been too jaded to do anything about it in the nets.

We pushed on positively in our second innings, which was marked by a century by Wellham in his first Test. He certainly is a promising player, obviously made of the right stuff in terms of his ability to make three-figure scores. Border again was in the runs with 84 . . . what a grand series he'd had! So we declared with an overall lead of 382 and threw down the gauntlet to England. We made a great start when I had Boycott leg before without scoring. It was quite likely the last time I'd bowl against Boyks in a Test and I suppose it gave me some satisfaction to get him for a duck. It was like a random knockout punch at the end of a long and even bout.

Boycott has been a very successful collector of runs over his long career for England, but I have always thought he had too many limitations. He is a great player against medium and fast-medium bowlers. They're his bread and butter, but somebody who is really fast has always been a worry to him and a threat to his average and career. Since the development of more sophisticated protective gear Geoff has been more at home against the quicks. He wears everything from head to chest to arm to thigh protection and surely can't feel vulnerable. Then the only problem is technique and there's no doubting his technical mechanisms.

Trying to make a comparison between Boycott of 1972 to the player we saw in 1981 is difficult, because in those days I was a very fast bowler. I believe I was able to worry him a lot in 1972 and even in the Lord's Centenary Test in 1980 our fast bowlers shook him when we were fresh and the ball was new. I have always fancied getting him with a short-pitched ball directed to his body, or the shortish ball outside off, which he tries to parry and push away square. He gets out a lot on that shot. But keep the ball up to him on leg stump and he'll always look a champion. He's not exciting to play against or to watch and from that aspect he hasn't been a great advantage to cricket. In fact, I think he may have turned a lot of people away.

Would I have him in my side, bearing in mind that he has been such a prolific run getter? No, for two reasons. One, he's not a great mixer and, two, he seems to be only interested in scoring runs for himself and in that regard has been a disadvantage to a lot of teams in which he has played. I have always believed that Geoff has placed too many limitations on the number of strokes he is prepared to play ... in the interests of safety. That's admirable to a certain degree, but in the act of eliminating errors he went too far and eliminated almost all his avenues of scoring. The end result is that he scores his runs so slowly and keeps the strike so regularly that his innings sometimes becomes a liability, rather than an asset, to the overall picture of team performance.

Having dismissed Boycott, we continued our charge towards victory with considerable purpose, until we came face to face with Alan Knott at the fall of the sixth wicket with the score at 144. The determined little wicketkeeper, the third glove man used by England in the series, came to England's rescue yet again in a Test against Australia. He just stuck at the job of keeping our attack at bay and no matter what we threw at him, he had the answer. Knott made a typically gritty 70 and enabled his team to hold out for the draw. So we lost the series three-one, which was a bitter pill to swallow, because I thought if anything we'd been the better of the two sides. Our bowlers had done everything that was asked of them, nobody could question that, despite a series of injuries. Our failure to win the Ashes was the direct result of one batting failure after another— perhaps we missed Greg Chappell more than anybody imagined.

On the positive side, the most significant factor was the emergence of Terry Alderman as a front-line bowler. Then there was the arrival of young Dirk Wellham as a possible batting star of the future, the promise of further development by Geoff Lawson and Martin Kent and a confirmation of the great tenacity and ability of Allan Border with the bat. Despite the disappointing result, we could look to the future with some confidence. From a personal point of view, a series that might never have been because of my illness at its outset produced great satisfactions. I was thrilled to have bagged as many as 39 wickets in the 6 Tests—indeed had I been fitter throughout I would have expected a figure more like 50 in the most favourable conditions. And I passed a milestone in Australia-England Test matches when I claimed Peter Willey's wicket in the second innings of the third Test, eclipsing Hugh Trumble's record of 141 victims.

17. Pakistan and the West Indies in Australia, 1981-82

I just knew that the summer of 1981-82 was going to be a tough grind for me in many different ways. First of all physically, because the programme showed a total of nine Tests: three each against Pakistan and the West Indies in Australia, then three against New Zealand in their country. And remember this was hard on the heels of a solid twelve months' commitment with six Tests in Australia and then half a dozen more in England. I was well aware that I'd have a battle to hold myself together without some problem or another for that eighteen months duration, with twenty-one Tests and volumes of one-day and other games in between.

Being a bowler who gives a lot of physical effort to his work, I was probably more aware than most that such a packed programme could take its toll. So, I guess I wasn't all that surprised when I suffered a setback in the final Test of the Australian summer, against the West Indies in Adelaide. Early in the first innings of that game I suffered a strained groin when trying to stretch out for a quicker one and I can tell you that injury really slowed me down. More than that, it left the team a bowler light—and that cost us the match.

But it was to be expected that something would give in the end. And perhaps this raises the argument that during a long and intensive campaign such as the one we went through, the Australian selectors should carefully programme the use of their fast bowlers, much in the same way as a baseball team manager does with his pitching staff. At the peak of a season such as 1981-82, there should be a travelling bowling squad. Even if it means picking the odd game when your top quickies are rested, it may be better for the team in the long run. And I'm sure it would be better for the individual to have the occasional game off.

Apart from the task of trying to keep myself intact physically, I faced two other rather substantial mental distractions, if I could call them that, during 1981-82. First, was the fact that I had been granted a testimonial and, having seen the demands on others in the past, I was fully aware of what that would cost me in terms of time and emotional energy. There would be much work to be done and many functions to attend, where I would be under a different sort of spotlight and I was sure the pressures would tell. Of course they did, but it could have been much, much worse if it hadn't been for the efforts of a marvellous committee and band of workers all round Australia.

It would be folly to try to mention them all, but I must single out the Melville Cricket Club, who had the original initiative for the testimonial and then saw it all through with magnificent commitment. And I must also mention my wife Helen and my manager and friend Austin Robertson, both of whom did so much to shield me from the brunt of it. But to everybody involved and to all those who supported the fund, my most sincere thanks for a fantastic effort. I'll never forget you all, your generosity and kindnesses have left a deep impression on me.

Of course, the other matter weighing on my mind when the new season began was the fact that just around the corner was Lance Gibbs's world record for the number of wickets taken in Test cricket. I needed just 20 wickets to break the record and it was very hard to escape that fact. Enthusiastic friends and supporters kept on reminding me and reminding me until the darned figure of 310 wickets began to haunt me. In the end I just couldn't wait for it all to pass, so that I could settle down to my regular routine of trying to dismiss some of the world's best batsmen for no reason other than the advancement of the Australian team's cause. And when the record finally came my way in the fourth Test of the summer, I felt a great weight lift off my shoulders.

As it turned out, circumstances also contrived to add to my burdens for the season. In the very first Test in Perth I was involved in an incident with the Pakistani captain, Javed Miandad, which brought the wrath of the cricketing world down upon my shoulders. It occurred during Pakistan's second innings, on the fourth day of the game, with Australia well on the way to victory. On the opening day we had struggled manfully to hold our innings together, having been sent in on a wicket that was very helpful for the fast bowlers. At stumps we had battled our way along to 159 for the loss of 7 wickets in the face of a woeful over rate by the Pakistanis.

In fact, when I continued my innings the following morning I was so disgusted by the slowness of the Pakistanis' movements in the field and their bowlers' slow march back to their marks that I made my own protest. I sat on the wicket while Imran Khan trudged back to his mark and, of course, the Pakistanis weren't too impressed. I suppose I could have chosen another bowler, because Imran could well have picked me off with his next delivery, but I was so angry that they just wouldn't get on with the job that I didn't care. In the end we were all out for 180 and, looking at the Pakistani batting line-up, I fancy most people thought we were in deep trouble with that score.

However, I felt the wicket would help our fast bowlers significantly . . . I know the WACA Ground wicket pretty well and often it is better to bowl on it on the second day. Also I had a feeling that the absence of Zaheer Abbas from their batting line-up (with broken ribs from a Jeff Thomson delivery in the game against Queensland) would throw their batting into some confusion. It meant that they had two inexperienced players in Rizwan-uz-Zaman and Mansoor Akhtar in their first three. So I wasn't *too* concerned about our position as we went out to have a crack at the Pakistanis—but I had no idea things would go as they did. I started it going with the fifth ball of the first over, having Mudassar Nazar caught at the wicket, then two balls later Terry Alderman had the unfortunate young Rizwan leg before off the first ball he'd received in Test cricket.

That was the signal for one of the most sensational batting collapses in Test cricket. By lunch on that second day, after about an hour's batting, Pakistan were a remarkable 7 for 25. It was like taking candy from kids. I suppose we bowled fairly well, but to be sure the Pakistani batting wasn't all that special. After lunch Sarfraz Nawaz led a one-man fightback. He just batted sensibly and made 26. The next highest score was 6 and the innings was all over with Pakistan scoring a record low 62. At one stage it looked as though Alderman and I would have the distinction of being the only two bowlers required to dismiss the side. However, when I was bouncing along with just 9 overs bowled in one spell before lunch and one after *and* figures of 5 for 18, Greg Chappell took me off and Thommo bowled two overs before the innings ended.

Australia batted much better in the second innings and exposed shortcomings in the tourists' attack. Bruce Laird and Graeme Wood gave us another solid start and once again Laird went close to making his first Test century, falling just 15 runs short. But the innings of the game came from Kim Hughes, who made a very good, well-disciplined century. All our other batsmen, with the exception of Chappell, were in the runs and we declared at 8 for 424, leaving Pakistan the target of 543 runs to win in just under two days. That was asking them to break all records—and after their first two batsmen had gone with the score just 27 we were always going to win.

However, Miandad came out full of purpose at number four and was moving along quite well about three o'clock on the fourth day when he and I locked horns. I was bowling from the northern end, when Miandad played one away through the on-side and took off for a single. He could see there was going to be an easy one in it and had slowed to a walk about two-thirds of the way down the wicket. I had stopped in my follow-through and also had noticed there wasn't going to be much of a continuation of the action and so turned to go back to my mark. I had just made the turn when I felt a sharp blow in my side ribcage area. I recoiled and realised that it had been Miandad striking me with what I presumed had been his bat.

He then continued on down to the crease at the bowler's end. I followed him down the wicket and just by the stumps tapped him on the pad with my boot as if to say, 'What do you think you're doing? You can't get away with that.' It was not, as described in the media, a 'vicious kick', it was no more than a tap with my boot. That doesn't mean to say that I should have done what I did. I should not have retaliated in any way. The incident was unfortunate and I'm certainly not proud to have been a part of it. However, I am upset that the fellow who actually caused the whole thing has escaped untarnished and unpunished.

I was also disappointed that the Press and media generally jumped right on me for what happened, rather than assessing the thing first and then reaching a conclusion. When it was all boiled down, and the inquiry I attended had viewed the whole incident in its entirety from all angles, it was realised that what I had said was correct. Miandad had slowed to a walk and, even though the depth of vision of the television film indicated we were right on top of each other, he was in fact a couple of feet from me. And he did in fact lunge at me with his bat and smack me very hard with it. Anyway, I think I received due punishment in losing two one-day international games. The incident is now best forgotten and let's hope nothing like that ever happens again in any form of cricket.

Miandad went on to make a good 79, but it was nowhere near enough. Bruce Yardley, wheeling down his off-spinners, cleaned out the middle-order and tail to end up with career-best figures of 6 for 84 and we won by 286 runs. It was a nice, comfortable feeling to go one-up in the series—and it felt even better when we were two-up after the second Test at Brisbane. The Pakistanis rang a couple of changes in their batting line-up, with Zaheer available and Mohsin Khan arriving as a replacement from Pakistan. This stiffened things a little, but still there was a lack of discipline about their batting and we had them out for 291 in the first innings.

Wood and Laird gave us a century opening partnership and this paved the way for a grand double century by Chappell, his fourth double 'ton' in Tests and his nineteenth Test century. It had been a doubly good knock because Greg hadn't been in the best form leading up to this game. And he had to battle on in hot and oppressive conditions. Thanks to Chappell's score, we were able to declare at 9 for 512 and press on for victory by 10 wickets. I picked up 5 in the first and 4 in the second for a total of 15 from the 2 Tests and I was very happy with my form at that stage of the season.

When we went to Melbourne for the third Test I was under great pressure ... by the law of averages it was estimated that I would break the world record in this game by taking the 5 wickets that were required. But that wasn't to be, not by a long straw. As it turned out I failed to take even 1 wicket in the only innings the Pakistanis needed to defeat Australia. As soon as I knew that the tourists had won the toss and decided to bat I knew I'd be hard pressed to take too many wickets. By far the best time to bowl on the Melbourne Cricket Ground wicket as it had been playing for a couple of seasons was late in the piece, when the ball was keeping low and survival was very difficult, never mind run-making.

Pakistan did bat very well, with Mudassar and Zaheer each making scores in the nineties and all of their batsmen getting a good start. It was a strange fact that in three Tests there was not one Pakistani century. Miandad finally declared their innings closed at 8 for 500 late on the second day and Yardley went off to bathe his spinning finger—he'd bowled no less than 66 overs in the innings and had bettered his career best figures once more with a return of 7 for 187. He certainly was improving with each outing with his new style of off-spin deliveries. And to think that he began his first-class career as an opening bowler for WA ... perhaps there's hope for me yet!

Once again Laird and Wood served up a good start for Australia, Wood going on to be the cornerstone of our innings with a century, his sixth in Tests. Each of our batsmen, with the exception of Allan Border, got a start but failed to go on with it and all of a sudden we faced the prospect of having to follow-on. That became a reality when Imran whipped in with 3 wickets for no runs in the space of 10 deliveries to end the innings with our score just 8 runs short of avoiding the follow-on. For once our openers failed to give us a good start and we went on a steady downhill slide—Chappell going for a duck, Border being run out for a second time in the match and Kim Hughes being dismissed in freak circumstances.

Hughes pushed forward to a delivery from spinner Iqbal Qasim, then decided to pull his bat away and let the ball go through outside off stump. However, the ball just took the bottom of his bat, falling from there on to the right boot of keeper Wasim Bari and bouncing clean from there into the hands of Majid Khan at slip. Almost as remarkable as the nature of the dismissal was the sharpness of umpire Robin Bailhache's vision in picking up what happened from twenty-two yards and being able to give Hughes out. Despite a gritty half-century by Bruce Laird, we managed just 125 as the MCG wicket fell to bits and the ball kept lower and lower. So we lost by an innings and 82 runs and the Pakistanis pulled back a lot of lost prestige.

Having picked up a two-one result against Pakistan, we had just a couple of weeks to gather ourselves for the main business of the season: the confrontation with the world champions, the West Indies. As if that wasn't a big enough task to comprehend, without having to take into the first Test with me the spectre of that world record! We were playing at the MCG and I was all smiles when I learnt that Greg Chappell had won the toss and we were to bat. I gave myself a good chance of picking up 5 wickets bowling in the last innings of the match, which would at last put the record behind me. As it turned out, our decision to bat first looked like back-firing when Michael Holding and Andy Roberts had our first 4 batsmen back in the pavilion with just 26 runs on the board.

One of them was Greg Chappell, who was caught at the wicket off Holding from the first ball he faced. It was the second time in successive Tests against the West Indies that the Australian captain had suffered this fate, having fallen first ball to Andy Roberts in the third Test at Adelaide in 1979-80. And it was Greg's fourth duck in successive international innings—no doubt a nightmare for him, but really unbelievable for the rest of us. It wasn't so much that Greg was hopelessly out of form, it was just that any time he went near the ball he got out. Others played and missed, or edged safely, but Greg edged fine and was caught. He must have been in the depths of despair, though he was wearing it pretty well in the dressing-room. He usually is one to keep this sort of thing to himself.

Australia's moment of need summoned up a major performance

from Kim Hughes. He just put his head down and ground out one of the most characterful innings I have ever seen him play. There was never a moment when things were easy, when he and Australia looked like getting on top of the attack, but he kept on plugging away at the job. Hughes was 71 when the ninth wicket fell at 155, then it was Terry Alderman's turn to call up a big effort. He stayed with his Perth clubmate until he had made what must rank among the finest Test centuries ever played. Terry stayed there just long enough for the Hughes' 'ton' to be posted, then was dismissed for 10 and we were all out for 198 some 40 minutes before stumps.

That gave us the marvellous situation of being able to go out and bowl for about half an hour—and really give it everything. Nothing untoward happened in my first over, then all hell broke loose. Alderman had Faoud Bacchus caught in the slips and it was 1 for 3. Two runs later I had Desmond Haynes and it was 2 for 5. By this time the crowd in the outer at the MCG were screaming in their support, they were ecstatic at our comeback after a disappointing batting effort. Colin Croft had come in as nightwatchman at the fall of the first wicket and he walked in front of one to make the score 3 for 6. As I ran in to bowl to the great Viv Richards there was a total frenzy behind my back in the outer. Viv went for the big drive, took the inside edge and the ball cannoned into his stumps—4 for 10 and stumps!

It had been an incredible period of play, one I'll always remember, inspired almost solely by the 'voice' of the outer crowd. As I have already recounted early in the book, they really carried us along in grand style. The West Indies 4 for 10 . . . it was almost unbelievable. And I had 3 for 3, including 3 wickets for 1 run in the space of 12 deliveries. I had to pinch myself to make sure that I was awake and not dreaming it all. Clive Lloyd and Larry Gomes continued for the Windies the following morning and when the score was 4 for 24, Greg Chappell dropped Gomes at slip off my bowling. We got Lloyd with the score at 62, but then Gomes and Jeff Dujon, in his first Test match, stemmed the flow in an excellent partnership.

It wasn't until about halfway through the afternoon session that we drew new blood. I'd noticed that Dujon was a bit of a compulsive hooker, so we set two men behind square in the deeps and I dropped one in short. He hit it hard and high and I fancy that on most cricket grounds he would have been counting six. But there was Hughes, dashing around to take a well-judged catch. I had equalled Gibbs' record. Thirteen runs later, about five minutes before three o'clock,

184

Gomes was tempted to flick at one outside off stump, it took the outside edge of his bat and this time Greg Chappell held the catch. At last the record was mine! I bowed my head in relief, before raising it to share the moment with my team-mates, in particular Rod Marsh, who had teamed up with me in no fewer than 83 of those 310 dismissals.

I also spared a thought for the gang in the outer at the MCG, who had meant so much to me, and, of course, to Helen and the boys, Mum and Dad, 'Pop' Halifax and all the others who had given so much over all the years to help put me where I was—on top of the world.

But the game must go on. We pushed on against the odds of some stubborn tail-end resistance and some fickle Melbourne weather and, after a couple of stops for rain, the second day closed with the Windies 9 for 187. The following morning they went on to get their noses in front by 3 runs and I finished with 7 for 83 from 26.3 overs, ironically my best figures in a Test innings.

So then the game entered a new phase and we held the advantage by batting third with the Windies to bat last. Laird and Wood gave us another splendid start, Border batted soundly and, despite a lamentable performance by our final 7 batsmen (we lost 7 for 38), we were able to total 222. Holding had bowled magnificently again, taking 6 in this innings for match figures of 11 for 107. What a superb operator this fellow is. His long stride and a lightning-fast delivery make him a sight to behold. He is able to maintain great accuracy, too, which is a real asset at his speed. I knew he was struggling under the handicap of a knee injury on this tour and this made his performance all the better.

The wicket was showing signs of keeping very low as the game progressed and I was mildly confident that our lead of 219 would be enough. And it turned out that way. Once again Terry Alderman set things in motion, trapping Bacchus in front for a duck with the third ball of his first over. But who would have dreamt that two deliveries later he would bowl Viv Richards neck and crop for a duck also!

It was crazy stuff . . . Richards two and a duck and Chappell a duck and six, two champions humbled in the same game. But that's cricket. The Windies fought back gradually, but when Bruce Yardley bowled Gomes with his first ball, a beautiful drifter that straightened up, the game began to go our way.

Dujon again made a score in the 40s and showed that he has the ability to become a big runmaker for his country in the future . . . sound technique, aggressive attitude and a good eye. Haynes went soon after and we just chipped away at them to go on to victory. That was a big moment for the Australians, because we'd suffered so much stick from the West Indies in recent years that it was something special to be one-up after one in a three-Test series.

I finished with 3 wickets in the second innings for a total of 10 for the game—the seventh time I'd taken 10 or more in an innings and the fourth time on the MCG. And talking of the MCG, there were many words said about the quality of this wicket and there's no doubting it had deteriorated to the stage where it was of a standard unacceptable in Test cricket. Something had to be done and I was relieved when I learnt that it was planned to lay new wickets.

And so to Sydney for the second Test. Young Dirk Wellham lost his place in the side and in came John Dyson, who had been making one big score after another for New South Wales. He was picked to bat at the fall of the first wicket, largely to allow Greg Chappell to drop one down the order and hopefully pick up a bit of form. As it turned out, Dyson played a major role in saving the game for Australia with an enterprising second-innings century after a laborious 28 in the first innings, which drew much criticism. The West Indies made a couple of changes, too. They left out veteran fast bowler Andy Roberts, who I thought had bowled pretty well in Melbourne, and included Sylvester Clarke. Champion opening batsman Gordon Greenidge went into the line-up carrying a bad leg injury, at the expense of Bacchus.

Greenidge, badly inconvenienced by his injury, hobbled along with great courage to give his team a good start after Clive Lloyd had won the toss and decided to bat. In fact he made 66 and laid the foundations for a big West Indies innings of 384. However, once again the pillar of strength in the Windies batting was the quiet, but extremely efficient, Larry Gomes. This little left-hander is the ideal foil for the cavalier strokeplayers all around him in the top half of the Windies' batting.

Viv Richards made 44, again batting like a man in too much of a hurry. It's true he played some scorching shots, but at no stage did the great player look like trying to settle down and build an innings. He finally fell into a trap set by Rod Marsh. I was just starting my run in when Rod called for one to be bounced high. I was able to land it right and Viv went after it, got the edge and was on his way. It was quite strange to see the champion batting the way he did

186

pretty well throughout the series. I thought he was getting himself into trouble technically by playing so far forward to the fast bowlers and then having to play across the line if the ball didn't come to him on or outside the off stump.

Once again Dujon made a score in the 40s and he was involved in an invaluable stand of 96 with Gomes. What a player he looked! In breaking this stand we also broke the back of the innings and, in fact, the final 6 wickets fell for just 59 runs. For some unaccountable reason we really struggled when it came our turn to bat. Perhaps it was the fact that Chappell failed again and that Kim Hughes was battling under the handicap of a badly bruised right hand, suffered in making his century the game before in Melbourne. It wasn't until late in the piece that Bruce Yardley was able to really liven things up with a swashbuckling 45, made in 57 minutes from just 32 deliveries. Allan Border battled along with an unbeaten half-century, but when our innings ended we trailed by 117, Holding adding 5 wickets to his 11 from the first Test.

Half-centuries from Desmond Haynes and Lloyd plus *another* score in the 40s from Dujon and 43 from Gomes enabled the Windies to score 255 for a lead of 372. And it would have been a whole lot more if it hadn't been for Yardley's spinning finger. At lunch on that fourth day his figures were 1 for 62 from 20 overs . . . before the following session of play was out he'd taken 6 more wickets to wrap up the innings and finish with his career best figures of 7 for 98 in a splendid piece of spin bowling. Added to his 3 for 87 in the first innings, that meant Yardley had posted his first 10-wicket match. It seemed he simply had the West Indies batsmen mesmerised.

Dyson opened in the second innings in place of Graeme Wood (who had injured a hand fielding) and was dropped before scoring and then again at 22 before he and Bruce Laird saw Australia through to stumps without loss. We began the final day needing 319 for victory and an interesting chase was promised. However, as the morning progressed it became obvious that we weren't able to stay with the run rate required. Laird was first to go with the score at 104 and then, unbelievably, Chappell edged the first ball he faced to the wicketkeeper and had suffered his third first-baller in three successive Tests against the Windies. It was a truly sad sight to see him walking forlornly from the ground. After that blow Australia just pushed along to draw the match at 4 for 200, aided by bad light in the end.

Inspired bowling on the first day by Holding and Roberts (who had been reinstated) put the West Indies well on the way to victory in the third Test at Adelaide. The tourists had won the toss and sent Australia in to bat on a wicket that had a good grass covering and certainly helped the quicks early in the piece. In fact, we had slumped to 4 for 17 at one stage, before Chappell rose from the ashes to play a great captain's knock of 61 and, along with Border, pull our innings out of the fire. Still we were dismissed for just 238, Holding taking 5 again and Roberts 4.

Once again Gomes was the fly in the ointment when the tourists batted. He came in with the score 2 for 72 and was still there on 124 when the innings ended at 389. In what was almost certainly his last Test in Australia, Clive Lloyd scored a fine half-century in this innings and again in the second innings to end the series on a high note. I watched almost the entirety of this innings from the Australian dressing-room, having strained my groin early on. I sat there with Chappell, who had a broken finger suffered while batting, and Hughes, who had a broken bone in his foot, and we made a pretty morbid trio as the game slipped away from Australia. Without Greg and myself, the attack laboured on a wicket that had flattened out to be a perfect batting strip. Hell, it was frustrating!

Yardley soldiered on against the odds to pick up 5 more wickets and Thommo had his best haul of the summer with 4 for 112. Actually he'd bowled very well indeed all season, but without an ounce of luck. He'd been as fast as I'd ever seen him bowl—perhaps too fast for the catches to stick! With Chappell and Hughes so badly inconvenienced, we couldn't have hoped to make much of an impression going into the second innings with a deficit of 151. However, after losing our second wicket at 35, we fought back magnificently. Laird and Border took the score on to 201, Laird making 78, then Border went on to make his ninth Test century and pass the 3000-run mark in Tests. He was finally dismissed for 126 and at stumps on that fourth day we were in with a fair chance of saving the game.

We were just 4 wickets down, with Hughes battling his injury (superbly) to be 72 and Marsh on 22, and leading by 190. The stage was set for a great final day. However, our innings fell apart, the final 6 wickets going for just 45 more runs, wilting before magnificent bowling by Joel Garner. This gave the West Indies the target of scoring 236 in about 3 hours 15 minutes plus 20 overs. Thommo drew blood with the score at 7, but after that it was just a one-day cricket task for their batsmen and their years of experience in this style of play really showed as they timed it to a nicety, winning in the eighteenth of the final 20 overs. Being 2 bowlers light Australia just couldn't maintain pressure . . . and a string of dropped catches in the closing stages didn't help the cause, either.

So the series had ended one-all, though I fancy we might have drawn or won that third Test had Greg and I been able to contribute with the ball. I actually went out on the field late in the second innings to try to do my bit with the ball, but I was unable to get over a regulation medium-pace and we soon realised it was pointless me carrying on. The injuries to Chappell and Hughes gave Rod Marsh a chance to enjoy an extended experience of on-the-field captaincy of a Test team. I think he thoroughly enjoyed it and it certainly looked to me as though he did a marvellous job out there. What a shame Rod hasn't been given the opportunities he has so richly deserved in this regard.

Perhaps the highlight of the summer, from an Australian point of view, had been the performance of Yardley in taking no fewer than 38 wickets in the 6 Tests—not a bad performance when it's related to his 44 wickets from 6 previous Test outings! 'Roo' took 18 in just 4 innings against Pakistan and 20 from 6 innings against the Windies and ended with the wonderful average of 22.23 runs per wicket. Four times in that magical summer he took 5 or more wickets in an innings and on one occasion he took 10 wickets in a match. It was no wonder that at the end of the Tests he was named the international cricketer of the year and won a lovely motor car. 'Roo' hasn't always had it easy with his cricket, but he has stuck at it with admirable optimism and determination and he thoroughly deserved the success he no doubt enjoyed.

As for myself, I was obviously delighted to have gone into the final Test of the summer with 31 wickets under my belt. However, that painful injury in Adelaide took some of the icing off the cake for me. It cost me the chance to take more wickets and it badly let the team down in its efforts to win or save the game and so clinch the series against the West Indies. But, above all, it left me wondering about my ability to go on with the job down in New Zealand—or even to come back strongly for any future Test series. For an ageing fast bowler, who stretches so much in his delivery stride, it was a major blow to suffer a groin injury and I was particularly worried when I packed my bags to go home after the Adelaide Test.

18. To New Zealand, 1982

I have left Australia on two Test tours against my innermost better judgment. The first was the 1980 jaunt to Pakistan, where I just *knew* that I would be on a hiding to nothing as far as the quality of the wickets was concerned. I went along because I felt honour-bound to do so, following the withdrawal of other leading fast bowlers, only to find out that my fears were well founded. Sadly, the same thing happened when I went to New Zealand in 1982.

After returning to Perth from the Adelaide Test against the West Indies I had some ten days to gather myself before the team left for NZ. I went about the business of having treatment, resting and then jogging and trying to get fit for the trip, but I had the underlying doubt throughout as to whether or not I should go. The doctors passed me as fit enough to tour, but still I was deeply concerned about whether my groin could stand up to any real pressure. When we reached NZ I felt all right jogging around, but it was a different matter when I tried to bowl. The stretch at the delivery stride caused a tremendous pulling and tightening through the whole of the left thigh area.

Still, I lived in the hope that I could get by if I didn't do too much bowling early and if I didn't over-stretch. If I eased my way through the bracket of one-day games which opened the tour, then perhaps I'd be able to last out the three Tests. Unfortunately, this wasn't to be the case. I made it through to the first Test at Wellington, then, as I put real pressure on myself, I caused another major injury . . . I threw a disc out of place in my spine. The doctors and physiotherapists I saw all agreed that the new trouble had been caused by the fact that I was heavily favouring my groin when I bowled.

In doing so I had radically changed my action—I wasn't getting my left leg up at the delivery stride. I was splaying it out a bit and falling away, and this was throwing extra strain on my back. Something had to go. This meant another week or so of resting and treatment, and then a few more days of trying to get fit in time for the second Test at Auckland. Through that period my back troubles left me and my groin seemed to be on the mend. Still, when it came to the Test I tried awfully hard not to favour the left leg and consequently still suffered, even though I was taking tablets to ease the pain.

I came through that game quite satisfactorily and went to Christchurch for the final Test three days later feeling warmly confident of bowling well. And everything was going along quite nicely—at one stage I had figures of 3 for 13—but then all of a sudden it happened. I landed on my back foot, about to deliver, when my right knee just collapsed on me. This had happened once before, during a one-day game at the Melbourne Cricket Ground two months earlier, but it had seemed to come good again as I walked back to bowl the next ball. I had seen a doctor about it and he had said I'd definitely have to have an operation on the knee at the end of the season. That knee collapse at Christchurch was about the last nail in the coffin for me ... I'd gone to NZ with a groin injury, had suffered a back injury and then my knee had given away.

One way or another, it wasn't a very happy tour personally. But all of my problems aside, I think it was an extremely successful tour, especially for cricket in NZ. We soon found that cricket is riding high in that country, something which I hadn't noticed in my previous tours in 1970, 1977 and 1979 (with World Series Cricket). People in the streets were all talking cricket and cricketers there were probably as well-recognised and talked about as the All Blacks rugby side, which is quite something. This new following for the game was reflected in the record crowds at the one-day games and the generally good support for the Tests.

It can be put down to two or three factors, the first and most important being the emergence of NZ in recent years as a very good international side. Secondly, there has been the influence of television and especially the coverage of the Kiwis' tour of Australia in 1980-81. No doubt, too, the champion local fast bowler Richard Hadlee has attracted a certain cult following and helped to bring the spotlight on the game in his country. He's a very, very good player. I've seen his bowling improve over the years to the point where he's a bowler who'd fit into any side in the world.

Though it seems strange to say it, the 'underarm incident' certainly played an important part in heightening interest in cricket in NZ. It was an act which apparently shocked the nation and got people thinking about the game, giving them something they felt strongly about and could relate to. We were left in no doubt about that early in the tour. Those big crowds at the first couple of one-day games were dead-set against the Aussies. However, Greg Chappell, the perpetrator of the underarm act, had done much to defuse the issue on his arrival by stating publicly that the incident was a 'thing of the past . . . we're here now to play cricket, so let's forget it'. I must say that the local journalists did their bit in letting the matter rest and it soon died a natural death. The ironic twist came at the end of the tour when Greg was named as 'sportsman of the series'.

Apart from the threat of controversy, this was never going to be an easy tour for Australia, coming, as it did, on the end of eighteen months' virtual non-stop cricket and particularly at the close of a tough series against the West Indies in Australia. To add to our problems, we encountered some truly miserable weather in the early stages. There was no play day after day and the best we could hope for was a run in the rain or some indoor practice—far from a satisfactory build-up for a fast bowler. Indoor nets are just all right as an alternative for batsmen, but close to useless for fast bowlers. We all struggled desperately to find rhythm and form going into the first Test and bowled accordingly at the start.

The first Test suffered because of the weather. It ended in a drawn game which could easily have gone Australia's way, given enough play for a result to have been achieved. Jeff Thomson really hit his straps and on the fast track at Wellington I'm sure he could have been responsible for NZ being knocked over twice. Having come out of that game with a moral advantage, I felt we went into the second Test at Auckland perhaps not quite as desperate as we should have been. We relaxed just a little and allowed NZ to slip under our guard and win that one.

If there's one thing I don't like to do, it's to criticise umpires, but I do believe something must be said about the standard of the umpiring in this game and, indeed, throughout the tour. In Auckland there were some very bad umpiring decisions and I know that the NZ officials were totally embarrassed by it all. So, too, was the NZ captain Geoff Howarth and, as for Greg Chappell and the Aussies, we were very upset and frustrated. Also I don't like to make excuses after losing a Test match, but there's no doubt whatsoever that Australia got the worst end of the umpiring and that had a big bearing on the outcome of the match.

From that umpiring fiasco came more talk of the need to form an international panel of umpires for Test cricket and I would wholeheartedly support such a move. Certainly, the wheels were set in motion by Howarth and Chappell in their discussions during the final two Tests. Their thoughts on the subject were transmitted to our team manager Alan Crompton, who is an Australian Cricket Board representative, and to the chairman of the NZ Board, Bob Vance. Such an international panel could be sponsored for travel, accommodation and expenses. Initially most on the panel would be English umpires, but it would be a great incentive for umpires all round the world to work to improve their standards.

The Australian team was jolted back to reality by that loss in the second Test and went into the third at Christchurch with great determination. We remembered in a hurry that Test matches are Test matches and you don't win them by simply going through the motions. They are won through gritty, hard, determined, gutsy cricket— and the team produced that and more in a magnificent victory. Much credit must go to the attack who, without myself for most of the time, responded superbly when NZ were forced to follow-on and bowled their side to victory.

However, the game was won well and truly before then by some fantastic batting in extremely difficult conditions. The ball was seaming about a lot and conditions considerably favoured the NZ bowlers, making survival a struggle and comfortable strokeplay almost an impossibility—unless, of course, your name was Greg Chappell. He played a truly phenomenal innings of 176, an innings which I rate as one of the best I've ever seen. I make that assessment purely and simply from the difficulty of the situation when he went in and the way that he gradually got to the stage where he was completely in command, virtually deciding where he was going to put the ball.

At one stage I watched him on the television monitor in the dressing-room and he was picking up the ball just short of a length and flicking it high in the air to whatever part of the field he wanted. Sometimes it went for six and sometimes in between the fieldsmen for four . . . I just cried out, 'Eat you heart out, Viv Richards!' There's just no way Viv, great player that he is, could have picked and placed the ball as perfectly as Greg did on that occasion. The period when he went from his century to his dismissal produced one of the most fantastic displays of controlled aggressive batting that I've ever seen. Greg's innings was more than a solid performance when a team badly needed one . . . much more than that, it was in itself a demoralising influence on an opposing side.

It was on one of the nights during this Test, I can't remember

193

which one, that I had a few quiet drinks with Bruce Laird and he told me some home truths about a traumatic personal experience. Bruce had given great service to Australia during the twin series against the West Indies and England during 1979-80 and had looked set for a long stay in the Australian side. Previously he'd quit his job as an insurance officer to become a full-time professional cricketer and with the improved pay for cricketers since World Series Cricket was doing very well. The future looked rosy for Bruce—until, that is, he couldn't find form at the start of the 1980-81 season.

As a result he was overlooked for the opening Tests of the new twin series, against New Zealand and India. He battled on and ran into form with two big scores for Western Australia against India and looked set to return to the Test team when he snapped an Achilles tendon while batting in a club game. That put Bruce out of action for the best part of that season and being out of action meant being out of the money. After a great effort he got back into the WA side towards the end of the season, but was overlooked by the Australian selectors for the tour of England.

Through all of this Bruce found himself having to face up to the fact that he was unemployed. He'd put all his eggs in the one basket and they'd gone bad on him. He told me how he'd tramped around from place to place in the conventional way looking for a job, but had been told by one employer after another that they wouldn't consider taking him on because he was a cricketer and was likely to be away too much. Finally, desperate for any work at all he'd gone to the local 'dole office' and filled in all the forms. He'd picked up some temporary work knocking on doors for the electoral office, but he spoke of the degrading experience of filling in that form and grovelling about for work.

Bruce subsequently got a job as a new car salesman and has done very well in his new career, but his story touched a resonant chord within me. In the field of professional cricket, everything's fine *until* something goes wrong. I go back to the old argument that our cricketers should have fallen in behind the senior players who tried so hard to get a national players' association off the ground. Such a body could give players support in these circumstances and perhaps assist them in finding work, perhaps in coaching or at indoor facilities. Without such back-up the individual has to think very carefully about his own future.

That was a sobering thought coming at the end of a tour and during a game which Australia went on to win well, giving the team

194

some renewed credibility before its return to Australia. Reflecting upon the tour, I couldn't help feeling that it was high time Australia made a full tour of NZ with five Tests. Bearing in mind that their domestic season lasts only a month or so, a full tour would mean an extended summer with more gate money, more television rights and a far greater attraction to sponsors.

But on the subject of overseas tours, a few of us got our heads together in NZ and nutted out what we thought would be an improved format for the in-between games during Test tours all over the world. Among the players the universal complaint is that games against County sides or States or provinces tend to be meaningless, with little or nothing hingeing on the result. The suggestion we came up with centred around two-day games, rather than meandering contests over three or four days. The games would offer each team one day to bat and receive a maximum of 100 overs—plenty of batting for the batsmen and enough bowling for the bowlers—with a winner at the end of the second day. We reckon that format would be better for the players, their sponsors and the public.

•

19. The Last Word

I'm afraid to say that for the final few days of our stay in New Zealand all I did was look forward to getting on the plane and going home. That knee injury culminated a personally disappointing and frustrating period of six weeks or so. I'd limped through four Test matches, one against the West Indies and three against NZ, and I hadn't enjoyed it one little bit. And, as I have said, it had all come at the end of a long period of concentrated international cricket. When I finally got on that plane and headed back to Perth my main need was a period of rest and recuperation.

As I sit down to write this closing chapter I am faced with the rather daunting prospect of surgery on my right knee, that much-needed rest and then a rigorous build up for another tilt at Test cricket. As I see it all at this moment, I'm not particularly thrilled at the thought of all the back-breaking work that lies ahead if I'm to go into a series against England in 1982-83 with the sort of preparation I'll need to be competitive at that level. However, I'm sure when I reach the time when I've got to saddle up and get out on the road again I'll have a much fresher outlook and will probably become quite excited at the prospect of taking on the 'old foe' once more.

I've played a lot of Tests over a lot of years, but there's no question that the biggest thrill and challenge for an Australian is to play in an Ashes series. There's just no Test cricket like Test cricket against England. That thought even now offers me inspiration to stir my limbs and get back to peak fitness and meet the challenge of being a part of helping Australia to regain the Ashes. My desire in that regard is heightened by the inner knowledge that the coming summer is quite likely to be my final in cricket.

I look forward to that contest even more so, because I treasure a long relationship with two other players in Greg Chappell and Rod Marsh. We all began our Test careers against England in Australia in 1970-71 and it would be somehow fitting if our partnership broke up against England in Australia. I'm sure Rod will play on for sometime, but I've got my doubts about Greg's future and my own. Greg could go on for some time, but cricket certainly isn't his life these days and psychologically he is close to the end of it all. Our nostalgic trip through next summer would have a dream ending if we were to be part of an Ashes-winning combination.

After that, who knows what lies ahead? What does a fast bowler do at the end of the cricketing road? I've thought a bit about that, but I don't have a ready answer. Not that it worries me for one minute, because I feel sure that one way or another I'll be able to get an employment situation to suit me. However, beyond the horizons of a mundane office job I have been nurturing a pipe-dream for some time: a nice piece of country property with a herd of beef cattle, a few Angora goats and a piggery. I know just the area in the big tree country some 300 kilometres south of Perth, where the scenery is breathtakingly beautiful.

That may not be everybody's cup of tea and I'll admit it may not even suit my own family if we ever do give it a try, but it does appeal to me as a terrific way of bringing up our children. I'm sure I could make a living as a farmer and I like the attitude to life you find among the people in that area of Western Australia. You don't hear of too many coronary cases among country people—they take life very steadily. It may be no more than a dream at present, but I've often joked with my old mate Marshy about the fact that when it does happen I'll need a couple of farm hands. There'd be free board and lodgings and a small wage in return for hard labour ... who knows, we might even get up a game for the local cricket team!

DENNIS LILLEE
STATISTICS TO APRIL 1982

Prepared by Jack Cameron

TEST BY TEST

Test	Date	Opponent	Ground	Test	Score	C	Balls	Mdns	Wkts	Runs
1	29.1.71	England	Adel.	6	10	1	224		5	84
							56			40
2	12.2.71		Sydney	7	6		104	5	1	32
					0	1	112		2	43
			3-0-10-16			2	496	5	8	199
3	8.6.72	England	Manch.	1	1+		174	14	2	40
					0+		180	8	6	66
4	22.6.72		Lord's	2	2+		168	3	2	90
							126	6	2	50
5	13.7.72		Nott.	3	0		174	15	4	35
							150	10	2	40
6	27.7.72		Leeds	4	0		157	10	2	39
					7		30	2	1	7
7	10.8.72		Oval	5	0+		146	7	5	58
							194	8	5	123
			7-4-7-10			0	1499	83	31	548
8	22.12.72	Pakistan	Adel.	1	14		163	7	4	49
							120	3	1	53
9	29.12.72		Melb.	2	2	1	134	1	1	90
							88	1	2	59
10	6.1.73		Sydney	3	2		80	2	1	34
					0+		184	5	3	68
			4-1-14-18			1	769	19	12	353
11	16.2.73	W.I.	King.	1			156	4	0	112
							36	1	0	20
						0	192	5	0	132

Continued next page

Test	Date	Opponent	Ground	Test	Score	C	Balls	Mdns	Wkts	Runs
12	29.11.74	England	Bris.	1	15		184	6	2	73
							96	2	2	25
13	13.12.74		Perth	2	11		128	4	2	48
							176	5	2	59
14	26.12.74		Melb.	3	2 +		160	2	2	70
					14		136	3	2	55
15	4.1.75		Sydney	4	8		153	2	2	66
							168	5	2	65
16	25.1.75		Adel.	5	26	2	101	2	4	49
							112	3	4	69
17	8.2.75		Melb.	6	12		48	2	1	17
					0 +					
			8-2-26-88			2	1462	36	25	596
18	10.7.75	England	Birm.	1	3		90	8	5	15
							120	8	2	45
19	30.7.75		Lord's	2	73 +		120	4	4	84
							198	10	1	80
20	14.8.75		Leeds	3	11		168	12	1	53
							120	5	2	48
21	28.8.75		Oval	4	28 +		114	7	2	44
							312	18	4	91
			4-2-73 + -115			0	1242	72	21	460
22	28.11.75	W.I.	Bris.	1	1		88	0	3	84
							128	3	3	72
23	12.12.75		Perth	2	12 +		160	0	2	123
					4					
24	26.12.75		Melb.	3	25		112	2	4	56
						1	120	1	3	70
25	23.1.76		Adel.	5	16 +		80	0	2	68
							112	0	2	64
26	31.1.76		Melb.	6	19 +		91	0	5	63
							144	1	3	112
			6-3-25-77			1	1035	7	27	712

Continued next page

Test	Date	Opponent	Ground	Test	Score	C	Balls	Mdns	Wkts	Runs
27	24.12.76	Pakistan	Adel.	1	0		152	1	1	104
						1	383	10	5	163
28	1.1.77		Melb.	2	—		184	4	6	82
					6		112	1	4	53
29	14.1.77		Syd.	3	14		179	0	3	114
					27		32	0	2	24
			4-0-27-47			1	1042	16	21	540
30	18.2.77	N.Z.	Christ.	1	19		250	6	2	119
							144	1	2	70
31	25.2.77		Auck.	2	23+	1	139	4	5	51
						1	127	2	6	72
			2-1-23+-42			2	660	13	15	312
32	12.3.77	England	Melb.	1	10+		107	2	6	26
					25		276	7	5	139
			2-1-25-35			0	383	9	11	165
33	1.12.79	W.I.	Bris.	1	0		175	8	4	104
							12	0	0	3
34	15.12.79	England	Perth	1	18		168	11	4	73
					19		138	5	2	74
35	29.12.79	W.I.	Melb.	2	12		216	7	3	96
					0		18	0	0	9
36	4.1.80	England	Syd.	2	5		81	4	4	40
							147	6	2	63
37	26.1.80	W.I.	Adel.	3	16	2	144	3	5	78
					0		156	6	0	75
38	1.2.80	England	Melb.	3	8		199	9	6	60
							198	6	5	78
		W.I.	5-0-16-28			2	721	24	12	365
		England	4-0-19-50			0	931	41	23	388
39	27.2.80	Pakistan	Kar.	1	12+	1	168	4	0	76
					5		66	2	0	22
40	7.3.80		Faisal.	2	0		126	4	0	91
41	18.3.80		Lahore	3	1+		252	9	3	114
			4-2-12+-18			1	612	19	3	303

Continued next page

Test	Date	Opponent	Ground	Test	Score	C	Balls	Mdns	Wkts	Runs
42	28.8.80	England	Lord's	1			90	4	4	43
							84	5	1	53
						0	174	9	5	96
43	28.11.80	N.Z.	Bris.	1	24		108	7	2	36
							90	1	6	53
44	12.12.80		Perth	2	8		138	5	5	63
							91	7	2	14
45	26.12.80		Melb.	3	27		126	4	0	49
					8		78	3	1	30
			4-0-27-67			0	631	27	16	245
46	2.1.81	India	Syd.	1	5		123	3	4	86
						1	108	2	3	79
47	23.1.81		Adel.	2	2		204	10	4	80
					10+		114	7	2	38
48	7.2.81		Melb.	3	19		150	6	4	65
					4		193	5	4	104
			5-1-19-40			1	892	33	21	452
49	18.6.81	England	Nott.	1	12		78	3	3	34
							100	2	5	46
50	3.7.81		Lord's	2	40+		214	7	0	102
							160	8	3	82
51	16.7.81		Leeds	3	3+		113	7	4	49
					17	1	150	6	3	94
52	30.7.81		Birm.	4	18		108	4	2	61
					3		156	9	2	51
53	13.8.81		Manch.	5	13		145	8	4	55
					28		276	13	2	137
54	27.8.81		Oval	6	11		190	4	7	89
					8+		180	10	4	70
			10-3-40+-153				1870	81	39	870
55	13.11.81	Pakistan	Perth	1	16		54	3	5	18
					4+		120	3	1	78
56	27.11.81		Brisb.	2	14		120	3	5	81
							114	4	4	51
57	11.12.81		Melb.	3	1	1	219	9	0	104
					4					
			5-1-16-39			1	627	22	15	332

Continued next page

Test	Date	Opponent	Ground	Test	Score	C	Balls	Mdns	Wkts	Runs
58	26.12.81	W.I.	Melb.	1	1		159	3	7	83
					0	1	163	8	3	44
59	2.1.82		Syd.	2	4		234	6	4	119
							120	6	2	50
60	29.1.82		Adel.	3	2		29	3	0	4
					1	1	24	0	0	17
			5-0-4-8			2	729	26	16	317
61	26.2.82	N.Z.	Well.	1			90	5	0	32
62	12.3.82		Auck.	2	9	1	234	7	3	106
					5	1	78	5	1	32
63	19.3.82		Christ.	3	7		72	6	3	13
			3-0-9-21			2	474	23	7	183

CAREER FIGURES

Season	Opponent	Inns.	N.O.	H.S.	Agg.	C	Balls	Mdns	Wkts	Runs
1970-71	England	3	0	10	16	2	496	5	8	199
1972	England	7	4	7	10	0	1499	83	31	548
1972-73	Pakistan	4	1	14	18	1	769	19	12	353
1973	W.I.					0	192	5	0	132
1974-75	England	8	2	26	88	2	1462	36	25	596
1975	England	4	2	73 +	115	0	1242	72	21	460
1975-76	W.I.	6	3	25	77	1	1035	7	27	712
1976-77	Pakistan	4	0	27	47	1	1042	16	21	540
1977	N.Z.	2	1	23 +	42	2	660	13	15	312
1977	England	2	1	25	35	0	383	9	11	165
		40	14	73 +	448	9	8780	265	171	4017
1979-80	W.I.	5	0	16	28	2	721	24	12	365
	England	4	0	19	50	0	931	41	23	388
1980	Pakistan	4	2	12 +	18	1	612	19	3	303
	England					0	174	9	5	96
1980-81	N.Z.	4	0	27	67	0	631	27	16	245
	India	5	1	19	40	1	892	33	21	452
1981	England	10	3	40 +	153	1	1870	81	39	870
1981-82	Pakistan	5	1	16	39	1	627	22	15	332
1981-82	W.I.	5		4	8	2	729	26	16	317
1982	N.Z.	3		9	21	2	474	23	7	183
		85	21	73 +	872	19	16441	570	328	7568

COUNTRY BY COUNTRY

Opponent	Inns.	N.O.	H.S.	Agg.	C	Balls	Mdns	Wkts	Runs
England	3	0	10	16	2	496	5	8	199
	7	4	7	10	0	1499	83	31	548
	8	2	26	88	2	1462	36	25	596
	4	2	73+	115	0	1242	72	21	460
	2	1	25	35	0	383	9	11	165
	4	0	19	50	0	931	41	23	388
					0	174	9	5	96
	10	3	40+	153	1	1870	81	39	870
	38	12	73+	467	5	8057	336	163	3322
Pakistan	4	1	14	18	1	769	19	12	353
	4	0	27	47	1	1042	16	21	540
	4	2	12+	18	0	612	19	3	303
	5	1	16	39	1	627	22	15	332
	17	4	27	122	3	3050	76	51	1528
W.I.					0	192	5	0	132
	6	3	25	77	1	1035	7	27	712
	5	0	16	28	2	721	24	12	365
	5	0	4	8	2	729	36	16	317
	16	3	25	113	5	2677	62	55	1526
N.Z.	2	1	23+	42	2	660	13	15	312
	4	0	27	67	0	631	27	16	245
	3	0	9	21	2	474	23	7	183
	9	1	27	130	4	1765	63	38	740
India	5	1	19	40	1	892	33	21	452

BOWLING—STYLE OF DISMISSAL

```
                        1st Inns    2nd Inns     Match       Series
S   T   O       G   T W M C B L  W M C B L  W M C B L  W M C B L
e   e   p       r   e i a a o b  i a a o b  i a a o b  i a a o b
a   s   p       o   s c r t w w  c r t w w  c r t w w  c r t w w
s   t   o       u   t k s c l    k s c l    k s c l    k s c l
o       n       n     e h h e    e h h e    e h h e    e h h e
n       e       d     t e d      t e d      t e d      t e d
        n                s s        s s        s s        s s
        t

1970-  1 England Adel.  6 5 0 3 2 0  0 0 0 0 0  5 0 3 2 0
71     2         Syd.   7 1 1 0 0 0  2 0 1 0 1  3 1 1 0 1  8 1 4 2 1
```

Continued next page

Season	Test	Opponent	Ground	1st Inns						2nd Inns					Match					Series				
				T	W	M	C	B	L	W	M	C	B	L	W	M	C	B	L	W	M	C	B	L
1972	3	England	Manch.	1	2	1	0	0	1	6	3	2	0	1	8	4	2	0	2					
	4		Lord's	2	2	0	0	1	1	2	1	0	1	0	4	1	0	2	1					
	5		Nott.	3	4	1	0	1	2	2	0	0	1	1	6	1	0	2	3					
	6		Leeds	4	2	1	0	0	1	1	0	0	0	1	3	1	0	0	2					
	7		Oval	5	5	2	1	1	1	5	1	0	3	1	10	3	1	4	2	31	10	3	8	10
1972-73	8	Pakistan	Adel.	1	4	2	2	0	0	1	0	1	0	0	5	2	3	0	0					
	9		Melb.	2	1	0	0	0	1	2	1	1	0	0	3	1	1	0	1					
	10		Syd.	3	1	0	1	0	0	3	1	1	1	0	4	1	2	1	0	12	4	6	1	1
1973	11	W.I.	King.	1	0					0					0					0				
1974-75	12	England	Bris.	1	2	1	0	1	0	2	0	2	0	0	4	1	2	1	0					
	13		Perth	2	2	0	2	0	0	2	0	2	0	0	4	0	4	0	0					
	14		Melb.	3	2	0	2	0	0	2	0	2	0	0	4	0	4	0	0					
	15		Syd.	4	2	0	2	0	0	2	1	0	1	0	4	1	2	1	0					
	16		Adel.	5	4	2	1	1	0	4	1	2	0	1	8	3	3	1	1					
	17		Melb.	6	1	0	0	0	1						1	0	0	0	1	25	5	15	3	2
1975	18	England	Birm.	1	5	0	1	2	2	2	0	2	0	0	7	0	3	2	2					
	19		Lord's	2	4	1	0	0	3	1	0	1	0	0	5	1	1	0	3					
	20		Leeds	3	1	0	1	0	0	2	0	2	0	0	3	0	3	0	0					
	21		Oval	4	2	1	0	1	0	4	2	0	2	0	6	3	0	3	0	21	4	7	5	5
1975-76	22	W.I.	Bris.	1	3	0	2	0	1	3	0	1	1	1	6	0	3	1	2					
	23		Perth	2	2	1	1	0	0						2	1	1	0	0					
	24		Melb.	3	4	1	2	1	0	3	3	0	0	0	7	4	2	1	0					
	25		Adel.	5	2	0	1	0	1	2	0	0	1	1	4	0	1	1	2					
	26		Melb.	6	5	3	1	1	0	3	1	2	0	0	8	4	3	1	0	27	9	10	4	4
1976-77	27	Pakistan	Adel.	1	1	1	0	0	0	5	1	2	0	2	6	2	2	0	2					
	28		Melb.	2	6	2	1	1	2	4	1	1	1	1	10	3	2	2	3					
	29		Syd.	3	3	0	3	0	0	2	1	1	0	0	5	1	4	0	0	21	6	8	2	5
1977	30	N.Z.	Christ.	1	2	1	0	1	0	2	1	0	1	0	4	2	0	2	0					
	31		Auck.	2	5	2	3	0	0	6	1	3	1	1	11	3	6	1	1	15	5	6	3	1
1977	32	England	Melb.	1	6	3	2	0	1	5	1	1	1	2	11	4	3	1	3	11	4	3	1	3
1979-80	33	W.I.	Bris.	1	4	3	0	0	1	1	0	0	0	0	4	3	0	0	1					
	35		Melb.	2	3	0	1	1	1						3	0	1	1	1					
	37		Adel.	3	5	1	1	1	2						5	1	1	1	2	12	4	2	2	4

Continued next page

Season	Test no.	Opponent	Ground	1st Inns						2nd Inns					Match					Series				
				T	W	M	C	B	L	W	M	C	B	L	W	M	C	B	L	W	M	C	B	L
1979-	34	England	Perth	1	4	2	1	0	1	2	1	0	1	0	6	3	1	1	1					
80	36		Syd.	2	4	1	2	1	0	2	0	1	1	0	6	1	3	2	0					
	38		Melb.	3	6	1	2	2	1	5	2	1	2	0	11	3	3	4	1	23	7	7	7	2
1980	39	Pakistan	Karachi	1	0	0	0	0	0	0	0	0	0	0	0	0	0	0	0					
	40		Faisal.	2	0	0	0	0	0						0	0	0	0	0					
	41		Lahore	3	3	1	2	0	0						3	1	2	0	0	3	1	2	0	0
1980	42	England	Lord's	1	4	1	1	2	0	1	0	0	0	1	5	1	1	2	1	5	1	1	2	1
1980-	43	N.Z.	Bris.	1	2	0	2	0	0	6	0	6	0	0	8	0	8	0	0					
81	44		Perth	2	5	1	3	0	1	2	2	0	0	0	7	3	3	0	1					
	45		Melb.	3	0	0	0	0	0	1	0	0	1	0	1	0	0	1	0	16	3	11	1	1
1980-	46	India	Syd.	1	4	2	2	0	0	3	0	2	0	1	7	2	4	0	1					
81	47		Adel.	2	4	2	1	0	1	2	2	0	0	0	6	4	1	0	1					
	48		Melb.	3	4	2	2	0	0	4	0	1	2	1	8	2	3	2	1	21	8	8	2	3
1981	49	England	Nott.	1	3	0	3	0	0	5	0	4	0	1	8	0	7	0	1					
	50		Lord's	2	0	0	0	0	0	3	1	1	1	0	3	1	1	1	0					
	51		Leeds	3	4	2	1	0	1	3	0	3	0	0	7	2	4	0	1					
	52		Birm.	4	2	0	2	0	0	2	1	0	0	1	4	1	2	0	1					
	53		Manch.	5	4	0	3	0	1	2	0	2	0	0	6	0	5	0	1					
	54		Oval	6	7	1	3	2	1	4	1	2	0	1	11	2	5	2	2	39	6	24	3	6
1981-	55	Pakistan	Perth	1	5	3	2	0	0	1	0	1	0	0	6	3	3	0	0					
82	56		Brisb.	2	5	1	2	2	0	4	1	1	1	1	9	2	3	3	1					
	57		Melb.	3	0															15	5	6	3	1
1981-	58	W.I.	Melb.	1	7	1	4	1	1	3	0	0	0	3	10	1	4	1	4					
82	59		Syd.	2	4	2	1	0	1	2	0	1	0	1	6	2	2	0	2	16	3	6	1	6
	60		Adel.	3	0					0					0									
1982	61	N.Z.	Well.	1	0					0					0									
	62		Auck.	2	3		2	1		1	1				4	1	2	1		7	3	2	2	
	63		Christ.	3	3	2	0	1	0	0	0	0	0	0	3	2	0	1	0					

TEST VICTIMS

Innings	Wkts	Catches		Bowled	LBW
		Marsh	Others		
1st	190	56	75	28	31
2nd	138	33	56	24	25
	328	89	131	52	56

TEST VICTIMS—
NUMBER OF TIMES DISMISSED

England (163)

12: A. Knott.
8: D. Amiss, J. Edrich, G. Gooch, D. Gower.
7: I. Botham, G. Boycott, M. Brearley, K. Fletcher, R. Taylor.
6: A. Greig, R. Illingworth.
5: M. Gatting, B. Luckhurst, J. Snow, D. Underwood, R. Willis.
4: P. Lever, P. Parfitt, M. J. K. Smith.
3: B. d'Oliveira, C. Old, D. Randall, P. Willey.
2: C. Cowdrey, M. Denness, W. Larkins, D. Lloyd, D. Steele, R. Woolmer.
1: G. Arnold, W. Athey, G. Dilley, J. Emburey, N. Gifford, J. Hampshire, G. Roope, C. Tavare, F. Titmus, B. Wood.

West Indies (55)

9: V. Richards.
6: Deryck Murray, A. Roberts.
5: G. Greenidge, J. Garner.
4: M. Holding.
3: A. Kallicharran, C. Lloyd, D. Haynes.
2: R. Fredericks, L. Rowe.
1: L. Gibbs, Inshan Ali, B. Julien, C. King, C. Croft, L. Gomes, J. Dujon.

Pakistan (51)

6: Mushtaq Mohammad, Majid Khan, Zaheer Abbas.
4: Wasim Bari, Mudassar Nazar, Wasim Raja.
3: Sadiq Mohammad, Iqbal Qasim, Javed Miandad.
2: Intikhab Alam, Salim Altaf, Imran Khan.
1: Asif Iqbal, Asif Masood, Nasim-ul-Ghani, Saeed Ahmed, Sarfraz Nawaz, Mohsin Khan.

New Zealand (38)

4: P. McEwan.
3: G. Howarth, W. Lees, J. Wright.
2: M. Burgess, L. Cairns, B. Congdon, B. Edgar, H. Howarth, P. Petherick, J. Morrison, M. Crowe.
1: J. Bracewell, E. Chatfield, G. Edwards, R. Hadlee, J. Coney, J. Parker, I. Smith, G. Troup, G. Turner.

India (21)

3: Chethan Chauhan, Sandeep Patil, Dilip Vengsarkar, Yashpal Sharma.
2: Sunil Gavaskar, Syed Kirmani.
1: Roger Binny, Kapil Dev, Dilip Doshi, Karsan Ghavri, Gundappa Viswanath.

TEST MATCHES—GROUNDS

	Tests	Wickets	Totals—Tests	Wickets
Australia				
Melbourne	13	77		
Adelaide	8	39		
Sydney	7	35		
Brisbane	5	31		
Perth	5	25	38	207
England				
Lord's	4	17		
The Oval	3	27		
Leeds	3	13		
Old Trafford	2	14		
Edgbaston	2	11		
Trent Bridge	2	14	16	96
Pakistan				
Karachi	1	0		
Faisalabad	1	0		
Lahore	1	3	3	3
New Zealand				
Auckland	2	15		
Christchurch	2	7		
Wellington	1	0	5	22
West Indies				
Kingston	1	0	1	0
			Totals— 63	328

SUMMARY OF WICKETS TAKEN IN TESTS

Country	Batsmen											Total
	1	2	3	4	5	6	7	8	9	10	11	
England	19	23	16	21	13	14	15	17	10	11	4	163
West Indies	7	5	6	4	5	4	6	6	5	4	3	55
Pakistan	9	4	7	7	5	5	3	3	3	4	1	51
New Zealand	2	6	6	4	1	5	4	2	2	4	2	38
India	2	3	2	1	3	3	1	3	1	1	1	21
	39	41	37	37	27	31	29	31	21	24	11	328

SUMMARY OF ALL ONE-DAY GAMES

	Inns	N.O.	H.S.	Agg.	Ball	Mdns	Wkts	Runs
For W.A.	16	2	32	104	1243	21	44	612
For Australia to 1977	7	2	16+	51	826	21	17	508
For Australia 1979-80 to 1982	28	6	42 n.o.	210	2395	62	76	1331
	51	10	42 n.o.	365	4464	104	137	2451

ONE-DAY GAMES
FOR W.A.

Season	Competition	Opponent	Ground	Score	Balls	Mdns	Wkts	Runs
1969-70	V & G	Vic.	Melb.	9	64	1	2	30
1970-71	V & G (semi)	Tas.	Launc.	5	64	2	2	29
	V & G (final)	Qld	Melb.	3	24			9
1971-72		World XI	Perth	0	64	1	2	25
1972-73	Coca-Cola	S.A.	Perth	1	64	1	2	27
1974-75	Gillette	S.A.	Perth	—	64	1	3	22
	Gillette (semi)	Qld	Perth	—	64	1	1	14
	Gillette (final)	N.Z.	Melb.	1	48		2	27
1975-76	Gillette	Vic.	Perth	9	64		3	33
	Gillette (final)	Qld	Bris.	32	64	1	3	41
1976-77	Gillette	S.A.	Adel.	26+	64	1	2	28
	Gillette (semi)	Qld	Perth	0	59	1	4	21
	Gillette (final)	Vic.	Melb.	5	56		2	30
1979-80	McD's	S.A.	Adel.	0+	60		4	30
	McD's	Vic.	Perth	—	60	1	2	34
	McD's (semi)	N.S.W.	Syd.	8	60	1	3	43
	McD's (con. fin.)	Tas.	Syd.	—	60	1	2	43
1980-81	McD's	S.A.	Perth	—	60	2		26
	McD's	Vic.	Perth	4	60	3	3	28
	McD's (final)	Qld	Bris.	0	60		1	37
1981-82	McD's	Qld	Bris.	1	60	3	1	35
		16-2-32-104			1243	21	44	612

Season	Competition	Opponent	Ground	Score	Balls	Mdns	Wkts	Runs
1972		Sussex	Hove	–	36	1	1	15
	Prudential	England	Manch.	–	66	2		49
	Prudential	England	Lord's	–	66		2	56
	Prudential	England	Birm.	13	66	2	3	25
1973		Tobago	Tobago	9				
1975		E. Can.	Toronto	3	96	5	1	49
		Toronto	Toronto	–	54	3		17
	Prudential	Pakistan	Leeds	–	72	2	5	34
	Prudential	Sri Lanka	Oval	–	60			42
	Prudential	W.I.	Oval	3	60		1	66
	Prudential (semi)	England	Leeds	–	54	3	1	26
	Prudential (final)	W.I.	Lord's	16+	72	1	1	55
		M'sex	Lord's	5+	42	1	1	17
1975-76		W.I.	Adel.	–	64	1	1	44
1977		N.Z.	Christ.	2	18			13
		7-2-16+-51			826	21	17	508
1979-80	B & H	W.I.	Syd.	–	36	2	2	10
	B & H	England	Melb.	13+	60	1	2	36
	B & H	W.I.	Melb.	19	60	1	1	48
	B & H	England	Syd.	14	60		4	56
	B & H	W.I.	Syd.	12+	53		4	28
	B & H	England	Syd.	2+	60			47
	B & H	England	Syd.	0	60	6	4	12
	B & H	W.I.	Syd.	0	60	3	3	17
1980		Worcs.	Worcs.	–	24	1	1	8
	Prudential	England	Oval	0	66	1	4	35
	Prudential	England	Birm.	21	66		1	43
1980-81	B & H	N.Z.	Adel.	3	60	2	3	40
	B & H	N.Z.	Syd.	–	42		1	26
	B & H	India	Melb.	5	42	1	2	22
	B & H	N.Z.	Melb.	–	60	3	3	19
	B & H	India	Syd.	–	60	1	2	29
	B & H	India	Syd.	–	30	2	1	3
	B & H	India	Melb.	–	60	1	1	29

Continued next page

FOR AUSTRALIA—*Continued*

Season	Competition	Opponent	Ground	Score	Balls	Mdns	Wkts	Runs
	B & H	India	Syd.	4+	60	1	4	32
	B & H	N.Z.	Syd.		60	2		27
	B & H	N.Z.	Syd.	0	18	1		6
	B & H	N.Z.	Syd.	7	60		2	47
	B & H	N.Z.	Melb.		48		2	25
	B & H	N.Z.	Melb.		60	1	1	34
	B & H	N.Z.	Syd.		60	2	3	27
1981	Prudential	England	Lord's		66	3	2	23
	Prudential	England	Birm.	8	65	2	3	36
	Prudential	England	Leeds	0+	42			37
1981-82	B & H	Pak.	Adel.	7	60			23
	B & H	Pak.	Syd.		48	1		38
	B & H	W.I.	Perth	42+	36	1	1	36
	B & H	Pak.	Melb.	8	60	1	1	37
	B & H	W.I.	Melb.	1	60			34
	B & H	Pak.	Syd.		45	1	2	23
	B & H	W.I.	Bris.	11	54	2	1	32
	B & H	W.I.	Syd.	6	60		2	47
	B & H	W.I.	Melb.	11	60	3	1	35
	B & H	W.I.	Melb.	0	60		1	53
	B & H	W.I.	Syd.	1	60	4	2	18
	B & H	W.I.	Syd.	4	60	4	1	30
1982	B & H	N.Z.	Auck.	1	60		1	56
	B & H	N.Z.	Dun.		60	3	3	24
	B & H	N.Z.	Well.		60	3	3	14
	Cen. Dis.	N. Plym.	10		54	2	1	29
	28-6-42+-210				2395	62	76	1331

WORLD SERIES CRICKET SUPERTESTS
Batting—Bowling

Season	S/Test	Opponent	Ground	Score	Ct	Overs	Balls	Mdns	Wkts	Runs
1977-78	1	W.I.	Melb.	37		16	96	4	2	77
				5	2	20	120	1	2	100
	2	W.I.	Sydney	1		17	102	1	1	75
				27		5	30	0	0	32
	3	W.I.	Adel.	1		11	66	0	2	48
				9+		14.3	87	0	3	61

Continued next page

Season	S/Test	Opponent	Ground	Score	Ct	Overs	Balls	Mdns	Wkts	Runs
	4	World	Perth	1		27	162	1	4	149
				8						
	5	World	Melb.			27.1	163	2	2	141
				8+		15	90	1	5	82
		W.I.	6-1-37-80		2	83.3	501	6	10	393
		World	3-1-8+-17		0	69.1	415	4	11	372
1978-79	6	World	Sydney	2		32.4	196	13	4	51
				0		38	228	16	1	68
	7	W.I.	Melb.	10+		42	252	16	3	91
				20+		12	72	6	0	13
	8	W.I.	Sydney	2		15	90	4	2	33
						14	84	3	7	23
	9	World	Sydney	8		18.5	113	6	5	51
				9+		17	102	4	1	57
		World	4-1-9+-19		0	106.3	639	39	11	227
		W.I.	3-2-20+-32		0	83	498	29	12	160
1979	10	W.I.	King.	1		18.2	110	3	4	68
				12	1	25	150	3	4	100
	11		Bridge.	6		13	78	2	3	56
				8+		14	84	3	1	53
	12		P. of Sp.	30	1	22	132	4	1	76
				12		31	186	5	3	77
	13		George.	3	2	24	144	4	1	98
	14		Antig.	6		33.2	200	2	6	125
		W.I.	8-1-30-78		3	180.4	1084	26	23	653

+ denotes not out

CAREER

Season	Opponent	Inns	N.O.	H.S.	Agg.	Ct	Balls	Mdns	Wkts	Runs
1977-78	W.I.	6	1	37	80	2	501	6	10	393
1977-78	World	3	1	8+	17	0	415	4	11	372
1978-79	W.I.	3	2	20+	32	0	498	29	12	160
1978-79	World	4	1	9+	19	0	639	39	11	227
1979	W.I.	8	1	30	78	4	1084	26	23	653
		24	6	37	226	6	3137	104	67	1805

COUNTRY

Opponent	Inns	N.O.	H.S.	Agg.	Ct	Balls	Mdns	Wkts	Runs
W.I.	6	1	37	80	2	501	6	10	393
	3	2	20+	32	0	498	29	12	160
	8	1	30	78	4	1084	26	23	653
	17	4	37	190	6	2083	61	45	1206
World	3	1	8	17	0	415	4	11	372
	4	1	9+	19	0	639	39	11	227
	7	2	9+	36	0	1054	43	22	599

+ denotes not out

BOWLING—STYLE OF DISMISSAL

Column legend (read vertically): Season · Supertest · Opponent · Ground · Wickets · Marsh · Catches · Bowled · Lbw

Season	No.	Opponent	Ground	1st Inns					2nd Inns					Match					Series				
				W	M	C	B	L	W	M	C	B	L	W	M	C	B	L	W	M	C	B	L
1977-78	1	W.I.	Melb.	2	0	1	0	1	2	1	0	1	0	4	1	1	1	1					
	2	W.I.	Sydney	1	0	0	0	1	0	0	0	0	0	1	0	0	0	1					
	3	W.I.	Adel.	2	1	0	0	1	3	0	2	1	0	5	1	2	1	1					
	4	World	Perth	4	0	4	0	0						4	0	4	0	0					
	5	World	Melb.	2	2	0	0	0	5	1	4	0	0	7	3	4	0	0	21	5	11	2	3
1978-79	6	World	Melb.	4	0	1	2	1	1	0	1	0	0	5	0	2	2	1					
	7	W.I.	Melb.	3	2	0	1	0	0	0	0	0	0	3	2	0	1	0					
	8	W.I.	Sydney	2	1	0	1	0	7	0	4	2	1	9	1	4	3	1					
	9	World	Sydney	5	1	0	1	3	1	0	1	0	0	6	1	1	1	3	23	4	7	7	5
1979	10	W.I.	King.	4	1	2	1*	0	4	2	2	0	0	8	3	4	1*	0					
	11		Bridge.	3	1	1	1	0	1	1	0	0	0	4	2	1	1	0					
	12		P. of Sp.	1	0	0	1	0	3	0	2	1	0	4	0	2	2	0					
	13		George.	1	1	0	0	0						1	1	0	0	0					
	14		Antig.	6	3	0	2	1						6	3	0	2	1	23	9	7	6*	1
				40	13	9	10*	8	27	5	16	5	1	67	18	25	15*	9					

* denotes hit wicket

VICTIMS

West Indies		World	
Greenidge	8	Greig	3
V. Richards	7	Asif Iqbal	2
Lloyd	5	Barlow	2
Austin	5	Imran Khan	2
King	4	Majid Khan	2
Allen	3	Knott	1
Fredericks	3	Le Roux	1
Haynes	3	Procter	1
Deryck Murray	3	B. Richards	1
Daniel	2	Underwood	1
Holding	2		
Rowe	2		
Croft	1		
Garner	1		
Holford	1		
Roberts	1		
	51		16

FULL CAREER ANALYSIS

Games played		Batting					Bowling				
		Inns	N.O.	H.S.	Agg.	Ave.	Balls	Mdns	Wkts	Runs	Ave.
63	Tests	85	21	73+	872	13.63	16441	570	328	7568	23.07
93	First class	106	34	54+	1125	15.63	18106	456	380	8488	22.34
4	Rest of World	5	1	11	19	4.75	940	20	24	482	20.08
160	Total first class	196	56	73+	2016	14.40	35487	1046	732	16538	22.59
80	One-day	51	10	42+	365	8.90	4464	104	137	2451	17.89
14	Supertests	24	6	37	226	12.55	3817	104	67	1805	26.94
254	Total all games	271	72	73+	2607	13.10	43768	1254	936	20794	22.22

+ denotes not out

SEASON BY SEASON—BATTING

Season	Internat. opponent	Shield-Internationals				Tests				All first-class games			
		Inns	N.O.	H.S.	Agg.	Inns	N.O.	H.S.	Agg.	Inns	N.O.	H.S.	Agg.
1969-70		9	3	26	64					9	3	26	64
1970	N.Z.	4	3	26+	66					4	3	26+	66
1970-71	England	13	5	32	143	3		10	16	16	5	32	159
1971-72	World	3	1	4	7					3	1	4	7
1972	England	6	3	11+	20	7	4	7	10	13	7	11+	30
1972-73	Pakistan	7	1	14+	33	4	1	14	18	11	2	14+	51
1973	W.I.	6	1	36	59					6	1	36	59
1974-75	England	12	3	46	159	8	2	26	88	20	5	46	247
1975	England	5	2	30+	39	4	2	73+	115	9	4	73+	154
1975-76	W.I.	10	1	36	134	6	3	25	77	16	4	36	211
1976-77	Pakistan	6	2	23	79	4		27	47	10	2	27	126
1977	N.Z.	3		5	12	2	1	23+	42	5	1	23+	54
1977	England	1	1	1+	1	2	1	25	35	3	2	25	36
1979-80	W.I.	3		1	1	5		16	28				
	England					4		19	50	12		19	79
1980	Pakistan					4	2	12+	18	4	2	12+	18
1980	England	4	1	33	81					4	1	33	81
1980-81	N.Z.	11	4	31+	144	4		27	67				
	India					5	1	19	40	20	5	31+	251
1981	England	1	1	5+	5	10	3	40+	153	11	4	40+	158
1981-82	Pakistan	2	2	54+	78	5	1	16	39	12	3	54+	125
	W.I.					5		4	8				
1982	N.Z.					3		9	21	3		9	21
		106	34	54+	1125	85	21	73+	872	191	55	73+	1997

+ denotes not out

BOWLING

Season	Internat. opponent	Shield-Internationals				Tests				All first-class games			
		BAlls	Mdns	Wkts	Runs	Balls	Mdns	Wkts	Runs	Balls	Mdns	Wkts	Runs
1969-70		1578	17	32	705					1578	17	32	705
1970	N.Z.	743	19	18	296					743	19	18	296
1970-71	England	2002	39	23	897	496	5	8	199	2498	44	31	1096
1971-72	World XI	918	15	24	450					918	15	24	450
1972	England	1242	36	22	649	1499	83	31	548	2741	119	53	1197
1972-73	Pakistan	1658	38	44	778	769	19	12	353	2427	57	56	1131
1973	W.I.	216	9	5	106	192	5		132	408	14	5	238
1974-75	England	2094	32	37	963	1462	36	25	596	3556	68	62	1559
1975	England	828	35	20	426	1242	72	21	460	2070	107	41	886
1975-76	W.I.	1462	22	35	778	1035	7	27	712	2497	29	62	1490
1976-77	Pakistan	1250	28	34	594	1042	16	21	540	2292	44	55	1134

Continued next page

BOWLING—*Continued*

Season	Internat. opponent	Shield-Internationals Balls	Mdns	Wkts	Runs	Tests Balls	Mdns	Wkts	Runs	All first-class games Balls	Mdns	Wkts	Runs
1977	N.Z.	320	11	8	80	660	13	15	312	980	24	23	392
1977	England	157	6	4	69	383	9	11	165	540	15	15	234
1979-80	W.I.	561	18	13	309	721	24	12	365	1282	42	25	674
	England					931	41	23	388	931	41	23	388
1980	Pakistan					612	19	3	303	612	19	3	303
1980	England	494	16	15	295	174	9	5	96	668	25	20	391
1980-81	N.Z.	1743	76	32	765	631	27	16	245	2374	103	48	1010
	India					892	33	21	452	892	33	21	452
1981	England	396	21	8	158	1870	81	39	870	2266	102	47	1028
1981-82	Pakistan	444	18	6	170	627	22	15	332	1800	66	37	819
	W.I.					729	26	16	317				
1982	N.Z.					464	23	7	183	474	23	7	183
		18106	456	380	8488	16431	570	328	7568	34547	1026	708	16056

OUTSTANDING PERFORMANCES

Match total	1st Inns	2nd Inns	Tests Match	1st Inns	2nd Inns	Other first-class Match	
12				8-29	4-63	12-92	Aust. v Rest of World, Perth, 1971-72
				7-41	5-72	12-113	W.A. v S.A., Adel., 1975-76
11	5-51	6-72	11-123 v N.Z., Auck., 1977				
	6-26	5-139	11-165 v Eng., Melb., 1977				
	6-60	5-78	11-138 v Eng., Melb., 1979-80				
	7-89	4-70	11-159 v Eng., Oval, 1981				

Continued next page

OUTSTANDING PERFORMANCES—*Continued*

Match total	1st Inns	2nd Inns	Tests Match		1st Inns	2nd Inns	Other first-class Match	
10	5-58	5-123	10-181	v Eng., Oval, 1972	6-24	4-46	10-70	W.A. v Qld, Bris., 1971-72
	6-82	4-53	10-135	v Pak., Melb., 1976-77	3-65	7-67•	10-132	Aust. v M.C.C., Lord's, 1975
	7-83	3-44	10-127	v W.I., Melb., 1981-82	6-78	4-68	10-146	W.A. v Vic., Perth, 1976-77
					5-44	5-37	10-81	W.A. v S.A., Perth, 1976-77

In innings	Tests	Supertests	Other first-class
8			1
7	2	1	3
6	6	1	8
5	14	2	11

Index